Get the eBook FREE!

(PDF, ePub, Kindle, and liveBook all included)

We believe that once you buy a book from us, you should be able to read it in any format we have available. To get electronic versions of this book at no additional cost to you, purchase and then register this book at the Manning website.

Go to https://www.manning.com/freebook and follow the instructions to complete your pBook registration.

That's it!
Thanks from Manning!

Managing Machine Learning Projects

Managing Machine Learning Projects

FROM DESIGN TO DEPLOYMENT

SIMON THOMPSON

MANNING
SHELTER ISLAND

Manning Publications Co.
20 Baldwin Road
PO Box 761
Shelter Island, NY 11964

Development editor:	Doug Rudder
Review and production editor:	Aleksandar Dragosavljević
Copy Editor:	Katie Petito
Technical proofreader:	Vojta Tůma
Typesetter:	Tamara Švelić Sabljić
Cover Designer:	Marija Tudor

ISBN: 9781633439023
Printed in the United States of America

brief contents

v

contents

preface

I can't pin down a moment or weave a convincing anecdote that explains how I came to realize that writing a book about how to manage a machine-learning project would be a good thing to do. The gist of it is that sometime in 2019 I realized that I was talking to a lot of people who had started an ML project and were in trouble with it, and usually I knew why.

There wasn't one common malady or even a single theme, rather failures seemed to come from lots of different directions. Disparate as the failings of these projects were, there was a common cause at work here. The folks leading these projects were talented, clever, articulate, and skilled, but they were inexperienced.

I was very lucky in the timing of my career. I got into ML when it was on the edge of applications. In the late 1990's, ML was out there in the wild, and we could do real things with our three-layer perceptron's and decision trees. It was much harder to deliver, algorithms needed to be coded by hand, data was vanishing rare, and everything ran sooooo slowly. Most of all, ML skills were as rare as the projects that needed them and applied ML was seen as R&D. For me this meant that I had the opportunity to develop and work on project after project. Most of them failed—but the ones that did come off really, really, really came off.

The rare wins kept me in work and kept my career going. In turn, this paid the mortgage and filled the freezer. With hindsight, I can say now that it was the failures that were the most valuable. I had the luxury of failure and learning, which isn't often afforded to people today. I also got the opportunity to join communities of people going through the same thing, and we would all get really drunk and tell each other sad (and funny) stories of catastrophe. A bunch of practices and behaviors became common knowledge in the clique of AI researchers working in big western companies in those days. I sat on the fringes and had the luck of being able to pick this all up and then use it.

Having had the luck of getting enough experience to steer an ML project or ten to success, it would be dumb not to share it. ML and AI are technologies that can be used for good, hopefully helping to confront climate change, pandemics, and economic woes. Maybe by sharing knowledge about how to manage ML projects I can help someone else do a couple of projects that make the world a better place!

Two events really prompted the push that took the book from an idea into the real world. First, Andy Rossiter, who was my boss at the time, told me that my team needed to have a methodology to tell customers how we would tackle their problems. I realized that I couldn't really point at one, so I'd have to write one. That probably wouldn't have gone all that far if it wasn't for the second event—the CoVID-19 pandemic—that meant that I stopped spending hours travelling about and started to have some time to commit to writing something.

So, here it is. Thank you for buying it. I hope you find it useful and most of all I hope you will share any ideas or thoughts you have for how it should be improved so that I can do better next time.

acknowledgments

Anyone who's written a book knows it's an unreasonably hard thing to do. I've needed a lot of help. Doug Rudder, my editor, and the team at Manning exceeded expectations and helped me transform a huge random mess of a manuscript into something I hope is much more useful to readers..

I don't think that anyone who hasn't worked with Manning can really know just how much value they add. This book could be a lot better if someone else wrote it, but without the work that everyone at Manning put in, it would be immeasurably worse.

Manning arranged an extensive reviewing process that provided me with anonymized feedback, of course, I don't know who did which review, but every review was immense: Andrei Paleyes, Chris Fry, Darrin Bishop, Florian Roscheck, Igor Vieira, João Dinis Ferreira, Kay Engelhardt, Khai Win, Kumar Abhishek, Lakshminarayanan AS, Laurens Meulman, Maria Ana, Marvin Schwarze, Mattia Di Gangi, Maxim Volgin, Ricardo Di Pasquale, Richard Dze, Richard Vaughan, Sanket Naik, Sriram Macharla, Vatsal Desai, Vojta Tůma, William Jamir Silva. The amount of work, attention to detail and honest, direct input that you provided was just amazing.

Thank you, if and when we meet up collar me for a beer or beverage of your choice. I owe you one for sure.

I have been very fortunate to have some amazing mentors in my career, and one of the most important things I think that anyone can do is to find some people who will help you as you develop your skills and abilities.

Professor Max Bramer gave me an amazing start in machine learning when he took me on as a PhD student, I had four brilliant years of exploring everything that ML could offer in the mid-1990s, and that changed my life.

Paul O'Brien took a similar risk when he recruited me at BT Labs, Paul is my professional role-model, the manager and mentor I aspire to be. Literally, whenever I have a problem at work I think "what would Paul do".

The other thing that everyone needs is colleagues who will indulge your ideas and peculiar thinking, point out where you are wrong, and share their own thoughts. For this I would like to particularly thank Rob Claxton who spent hundreds of hours talking to me on any and every topic to do with Data Science, AI and ML. There were many other people at BT, The Turing Institute, and MIT who were prepared to let me test their patience and gave me time I didn't deserve, but the conversations I've had with Rob over the last twenty odd years were (and are) intellectually formative for me.

When I was writing this book, I was generally bad-tempered, preoccupied, and generally insufferable. My wife, Buffy, and my daughter, Arwen, put up with this nonsense sometimes, but mostly told me to stop it. Which was what I needed.

Buffy and Arwen, I love you very much.

Thank you everyone.

about this book

This book sets out to provide a step-by-step prescriptive guide to implementing a machine learning project. It is built from a large body of work that has emerged since the 1990's which addresses the challeges that ML developers face.

The approaches documented in this book are not original, although some are unpublished because I've tried to codify best practice as well as academic publication. I've tried to provide references where I can, but I am sure I have missed some. In any case, please take it as read that where there are no references there is no claim of invention or novelty – it's just I can't find an attribution, apologies if I have slighted you.

There are lots of technical books on AI and ML so this book doesn't seek to fill that gap. If you do not have a good grasp of these topics, then the following list of texts are good places to start before attempting to apply this methodology:

- *Artificial Intelligence: A Modern Approach* by Stuart Russell and Peter Norvig, Pearson, 2016. This textbook is used as the backbone of most undergraduate AI courses and provides an overview of the key concerns of AI as a topic. This is a great place to start.

- *Hands on Machine Learning with Scikit-Learn, Keras, and TensorFlow*, Aurelien Geron, O'Reilly, 2019. This book focuses on practical applications of a selection of ML techniques but covers most of the ground that a practitioner will need for an overview of the field. This book is good for readers who are from a software background and are less interested in the mathematical aspects of ML.

- *Probabilistic Machine Learning: An Introduction*, Kevin Patrick Murphy, MIT Press, 2021. This book provides a comprehensive modern treatment of the core aspects of AI and machine learning. It's suitable for readers who want to understand the underpinnings and mechanics of the techniques and who have a mathematical bent.

The books listed provide expositions on the techniques and problems that AI has developed and tried to resolve respectively. In contrast, this book brings together the tools and approaches that are required to deliver an AI project, and gives a perspective on how to handle commercial challenges and delivery in a commercial environment.

How this book is organized: A roadmap

In each chapter, apart from this one, the content is presented in a structured manner with the goal of achieving accuracy and conciseness.

- Chapter 1 provides a description of the core concepts and motivations that have been in my mind when writing the book and hopefully will allow the reader to get a picture of what the book is trying to communicate and how it can help.
- Chapter 2 outlines the steps for establishing a common understanding of the project among the client, oneself, and the organization, whether the organization is separate from the client's or within a *different* department. *You will learn how to organize the process, collaborate with the client to establish requirements, gain insight into the client's data, and determine the necessary tools.*
- Chapter 3 covers the process of creating a project hypothesis that can be understood by your team and stakeholders this includes the process of creating estimates that will allow the project to be appropriately funded and resourced and also the work that needs to be done in order to get the project formally agreed and running. *You will learn what needs to be understood to start the project, who needs to understand it and who needs to agree.*
- Chapter 4 introduces the work that is required for sprint 0. This sprint contains the activities that get the work on the project underway and onboards the team into the project. *In chapter 4 you will learn about what is required to enable a team to start work and become productive on an ML project.*
- Chapter 5 covers the first part of sprint 1. This work requires that a technical team is in place and has access to the systems and information that's needed to make progress. *In this chapter the focus is on getting the data that the team will need to create a machine learning model into an environment that can be used to support modelling.*
- Chapter 6 completes the work of sprint 1 utilizing the data pipelines to gain an understanding of the clients data and to construct the first prototype models. *You will learn what kinds of data exploration are required and the steps that are needed to set the foundation for the team to successfully start building models.*

- Chapter 7 starts the work on sprint 2, focusing on the process of building useful models using a structured and systematic process and identifying the models that will be taken forward for detailed evaluation and selection for integration into the production system. *In Chapter 7 you will learn what structures and process a modelling team should adopt.*

- Chapter 8 completes sprint 2 with instructions for structured testing and selection of models in both online and offline environments and includes a discussion of the traps and pitfalls that are often encountered when evaluating models. *You will learn what to look out for when ML models are evaluated and compared and how you the process of doing these comparisons should be managed.*

- Chapter 9 delves into the implementation of Sprint 3, detailing the process of integrating the chosen models into the production system and deploying them for use. It also highlights the important considerations that must be made for providing user-friendly interfaces. *Here you will learn what is takes to move models from interesting experiments to being part of a running system in an organization.*

- Finally in chapter 10 the implications & required practices of managing a machine learning system in production are described. *The objective of chapter 10 is to show what kind of processes and structures need to be set up and run in order to sustain an ML project as an engine for value.*

LiveBook discussion forum

Purchase of *Managing Machine Learning Projects* includes free access to liveBook, Manning's online reading platform. Using liveBook's exclusive discussion features, you can attach comments to the book globally or to specific sections or paragraphs. It's a snap to make notes for yourself, ask and answer technical questions, and receive help from the author and other users. To access the forum, go to https://livebook.manning.com/book/managing-machine-learning-projects/discussion. You can also learn more about Manning's forums and the rules of conduct at https://livebook.manning.com/discussion.

Manning's commitment to our readers is to provide a venue where a meaningful dialogue between individual readers and between readers and the author can take place. It is not a commitment to any specific amount of participation on the part of the author, whose contribution to the forum remains voluntary (and unpaid). We suggest you try asking the author some challenging questions lest his interest stray! The forum and the archives of previous discussions will be accessible from the publisher's website as long as the book is in print.

about the author

Simon Thompson has spent 25 years developing AI systems, usually but not always using machine learning. He led the AI research program at BT Labs in the UK, helped pioneer Big Data technology in the company, and managed an applied research practice for nearly a decade. His teams delivered projects that used Bayesian machine learning, deep networks, and good old-fashioned decision trees and association rule mining to provide insight on telecoms networks, customer service, and business processes at a big corporation. Simon left BT in 2019 and now works in consultancy. At the moment, he and his team are busily delivering machine learning projects as a consultant to banks, insurance companies, and in manufacturing using cloud AI platforms, large language models, and vector databases. Simon is a family man and loves his garden and dogs. You can follow him @AISimonThompson on Twitter or look him up on LinkedIn.

about the cover illustration

The figure on the cover of *Managing Machine Learning Projects,* titled "Le March-and De Coco," or "Hot chocolate vendor," is taken from a book by Louis Cur-mer published in 1841. Each illustration is finely drawn and colored by hand.

In those days, it was easy to identify where people lived and what their trade or station in life was just by their dress. Manning celebrates the inventiveness and initiative of the computer business with book covers based on the rich diversity of regional culture centuries ago, brought back to life by pictures from collections such as this one.

Introduction: Delivering machine learning projects is hard; let's do it better

1

This chapter covers

- Describing the structure and objectives of this book
- Defining what machine learning is
- Explaining why machine learning is important
- Exploring why machine learning projects are different
- Listing other approaches to machine learning development

This book describes an end-to-end process for delivering a machine learning (ML) project to solve a business problem that's big enough and difficult enough to need a team. The rapid surge of interest in ML and the sudden change in ML's capability with the development of practical deep neural networks documented by LeCun et al. [1] and other advanced methods such as MCMC algorithms discussed by Carpenter et al. [2] means that there are a lot of new opportunities for ML projects. So, a lot of people are going to be managing these projects, and this is a guidebook for them.

Why is a guidebook needed specifically for ML projects? It's claimed by Gartner that 85% of ML projects fail [3], although tracking down the precise origin and evidence for this claim is more work than this author is willing to put in! Even so, it's clear from scholarly studies that there are "challenges to these steps of the machine-learning development workflow" and "practitioners face issues at each stage of the development process". For example, see the work by Paleyes and co-authors [4]. As the difficulties of developing and deploying ML systems are becoming clearer, there are increasing concerns that ML is being applied unethically and harmfully [5]. Fundamentally, ML projects have a different development process (model building from data) from normal software projects, have different needs in terms of organization and infrastructure, and deliver outputs (ML models) that have to be handled differently from normal programs.

One driving idea behind the book is that doing ML projects is a bit like going on a roller coaster ride. The brightly painted roller coaster is what everyone focuses on, but riding it only takes three minutes. To ride it, you have to get everyone in the car, drive for an hour, park, walk to the ticket office, get tickets, and queue for the ride. The point is that to have fun, you have to prepare. After the ride, what then? Well, then you get to the real point of the ride. You get to sit with your kids and eat ice cream and talk about how good it was and what you are going to do next and why. If the before and after parts of the process aren't good, then the fun part (the ML in the ML project) doesn't happen.

This book focuses on the preparation required to use ML, the work necessary to use the results, and the safeguards to prevent ML from going astray. After all, if you fall off the roller coaster, then it would have been better if you had stayed in bed that morning.

This book is largely nontechnical; it aims to help people understand what needs to be done and what the problems are, but it does not provide much detail on delivery. In some parts of the book, there are technical examples and explanations. These are there to provide guidance when it wasn't possible to avoid being a bit technical. However, these examples can be safely skipped by nontechnical readers without missing out on the main themes and concepts in the text.

It helps to have some idea of what SQL is and some basic math skills, but even if you don't know or don't care about these things, the book should still be largely accessible to you. On the other hand, it's expected that most readers will have a deep knowledge of ML and data science and are reading this because they are interested in the softer skills and project practices that can help them apply their AI magic.

In the next section, we describe the basic concepts of ML and how they can be applied to set the scene for those new to the arena. Any readers who are already familiar with ML concepts and technology are free to skip forward to section 1.4, where the rest of the book is introduced or beyond to start on the meat of the book. For other readers, section 1.2 introduces some basic terminology and then after that, in section 1.3 the significance of ML and issues and challenges with ML that motivate a special approach to ML projects are described. *In section 1.4*, we'll outline other approaches that have been tried for developing software and ML systems. Finally, the roadmap for the rest of the book is presented as well as the case study that illustrates how to use the tools and approaches advocated.

So, onward to learning about ML and the need for a special approach to ML projects, or off to chapter 2 and the start of the project!

1.1 What is machine learning?

Machine learning (ML) is a set of algorithms that we can use to create (learn) models from data. The model can be expressed in lots of ways, e.g., a set of if/then/else statements, a decision tree, or a set of parameters or weights for a neural network. The ML algorithm generates a model from the data that is fed into it:

MACHINE LEARNING + DATA = MODEL

Models are approximations. You might imagine a model that associates having four legs and being hairy with a dog. Of course, that's far too general a description to be useful. Much more information is required to create a model that captures the difference between dogs and cats or the commonalities between Great Danes and Chihuahuas. In this case, the model is combined with partial data about the entity (e.g., leg count, hair, size, etc.) and an inference about the missing bit of data (the type or entity), which the ML algorithm can extract:

MODEL + (partial) DATA = INFERENCE

When humans build models manually, they choose the association rules or the network parameters, so the amount of experimentation that they can do is limited. The advantage of an ML approach is that the machine can check a large number of parameters or associations. Machines can search over millions or billions of different settings and links quickly and cheaply. The human's advantage (for instance, a statistician or an epidemiologist) is that they know what they are doing. Often, this ability to apply common sense and a wider knowledge of the world means the models chosen and created by humans are superior to the models learned by machines. It also means that humans can build models without needing to access large amounts of data. Recently, though, ML has gained importance because using the huge computing power that's now available to process abundant supplies of data is much, much cheaper and easier than devising the models by hand.

Figure 1.1 shows a schematic of the sort of system that ML developers are building. On the left of the figure, data enters the system, it's processed and transformed, and fed to ML algorithms, which creates models. These are integrated into applications and human-driven processes. On the right of the figure, the inferences created from the models affect human users.

Before data is consumed by the models, it needs to be processed. This normally means that it must be cleaned and assembled into examples that can be passed into the models. Once that's done, the models can consume it. Sometimes we can use a single model, but as figure 1.1 illustrates, it's also common for a set of models to be produced and chained together to create the inferences that we require, and these models need to be managed and governed by a support team of operators. Occasionally, the models' output is reviewed by a supervising human who makes decisions about how they will affect their ultimate consumers. In other scenarios, the model results are mediated by another system and then consumed by users more directly.

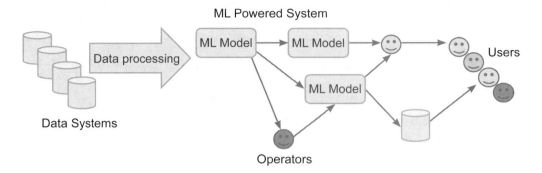

Figure 1.1 The kind of system that ML projects attempt to deliver

ML algorithms can learn models from data sets that are too complex to be dealt with by humans, and they can be integrated into systems that are extremely useful (e.g., systems that power many aspects of modern life such as internet searches, data networks, and movie recommenders). Everyone seems to agree that ML can be an important technology to revolutionize our economy and our society. Yet, ML can be hard to apply, and there are many issues that can trip up a team working on an ML project. To shed some more light on specific problems that can cause issues for an ML team, the next section explores the promises and pitfalls of ML in more detail.

1.2   Why is ML important?

What's so exciting and promising about ML? In the last few years, there have been transformative results in ML R&D, which have led to the development of machines that can:

- Write text that is hard or impossible to distinguish from human efforts such at the output of large language models like GPT-3 [6].
- Demonstrate revolutionary performance in deriving the shape of proteins as with Alphafold-2 [7].
- Outplay all humans at all board games as per the work from DeepMind on AlphaZero [8].

Also, ML has created models that can create novel and relevant images when given text prompts as seen with the DALL-E model [9]. These advances are seen by many as signposts, indicating the potential of ML technology, and there is a widespread expectation that more seismic innovations are just round the corner. At the same time, many commentators have noted that there are still gaps between the promise and hype of ML and the reality of what the models can do, Gary Marcus being a prominent example [10].

Importantly, the way that the models work and the mistakes they make can create deep ethical problems [11][5].

It's worth noting that ML isn't just the preserve of a few technology gurus in Silicon Valley and the great universities of the world. You can download off-the-shelf models and libraries for free and then easily use them. This allows programmers (increasingly, nonprogrammers as well) to build ML components into their projects. Now there are ML-powered tools that identify safety risks in factories, select new music that suits a consumer's taste, or check email grammar. These all make small but tangible and valuable contributions to many people's lives and happiness. It's likely that every few minutes of the day ML makes some sort of difference to our lives.

Technologists find this all to be amazing, but unsurprisingly, there are some problems that have arisen as the technology is applied in the real world. Models can be used to do things that they are not suited to, such as deciding if people are likely criminals based on the way they look and determining how long criminals should stay in prisons. This kind of application is so problematic that entire books are devoted to explaining in detail all of its aspects [11]. It's safe to say that using an algorithm to determine the course of a person's life is not a good idea.

It's easy to find stories of ML producing disappointing results when real applications were tried. A good example is to look at the huge effort that the ML community put into producing tools for treating COVID-19. One study [12] looked at 232 models that were developed but found that just two were of sufficient quality to warrant further testing. Similar stories can be found about systems that were intended to interpret medical images or diagnose cancers. Even Elon Musk is reported to have said that building a self-driving car has turned out to be much harder than he thought [13].

What then are the drivers of ML project complexity and challenge? As for software projects, ML projects have to understand and accommodate the challenges of working in a domain, whether that's a business selling bikes, oncology, or epidemiology. In addition to these problems, an application's domain ML project is complicated because it handles and manipulates complex data resources, sophisticated models, and the code to orchestrate them. When it comes to complexity and challenge, it's good to keep these points in mind:

- ML systems are dependent on data, in particular, on the structure and quality of the data assets that they use to create the models employed in the resulting system. Modern data assets are huge and wildly complex. Practices and processes for understanding and handling data assets that are complex, noisy, large scale, and riddled with personal and confidential data are required by teams that are going to deliver. The data needs to be understood and handled at the system level and at the statistical or value levels. We need to engineer it and understand what it means.

- ML projects create and use models. The properties of the models that are created need to be measured and understood by the team, and this understanding must inform the design process of the system into which the models are embedded.

We need to make the models, but also, we need to evaluate them (technically and in a business context), and we need to manage their lifecycle.

- ML systems should be developed to align with scientific, stakeholder, and societal requirements as recommended by Wixom and co-authors [14]. Both business and broad ethical considerations must be woven into the process of developing an ML system.

Figure 1.2 shows how these three concerns can be represented as a Venn diagram. This diagram is helpful because we can use it to map out the work and responsibilities in an ML project.

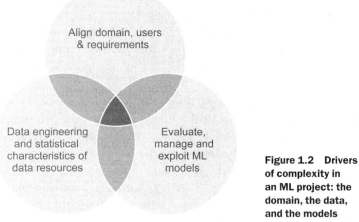

Figure 1.2   Drivers of complexity in an ML project: the domain, the data, and the models

The challenges that an ML project brings are one thing, but in addition to addressing these, there are tasks that should be done to ensure that we deliver a timely, efficient, and high-quality outcome. In this book, four needs are identified:

- *Identify risk and opportunity in the project as quickly and as practically possible.* The ability to understand project risk in a ML delivery requires work and time.
- *Enable the team to react and adapt to problems fast.* Teams need to cope with unexpected problems and need to be able to change course as user requirements become clearer during the project. Being able to pivot to deal with unexpected model performance problems is critical.
- *Tie the customer into the process.* Building engagement and sponsorship, and eliciting feedback and information makes a project useful and effective for any business.
- *Deliver everything that is required to run and maintain the system.* The teams building ML systems think that they are delivering a system, but they also must provide everything needed to understand, use, run, and maintain the system. In particular, appropriate documentation and record-keeping is required if the system is

going to impact the lives and happiness of human beings, and of course, appropriate documentation is required by the teams that will have to run and maintain the code and models when your team has moved on.

In summary, ML projects have turned out to be hard to handle, and ML models are approximate, hard to interpret, and hard to develop. They don't give the right answers most of the time, and they are robust and appropriate for some applications but not others. There is more uncertainty and risk in an ML project than in normal software development. Also, ML systems are heavily dependent on large-scale data resources. Data is collected by people with agendas, whether they know that or not, and so it's riddled with bias. The way that humans interact with ML systems can create loops and spirals of behavior that the original designers find surprising. Handling large data resources reliably and efficiently is problematic and can be challenging for teams used to running software projects.

To tackle these issues, we require a different and tailored approach to using ML. Failing to approach ML projects in the right way risks failure or worse and creates something that visits harm on others. Not only is this an impossible position for a professional person to get into, but there are tough new laws with penalties, especially in China [15] and the European Union (EU) [16] for people who do so.

Following the processes described in this book doesn't guarantee that your project will succeed (and it won't prevent you from constructing a system that's harmful). Hopefully, the steps that are laid out in the book will help, as will an understanding of how each of these steps should be strung together with the other and used to deliver the end product. In the next two sections, how we arrived at the structure of the work outlined in the book is explained, including references to how other people have structured similar projects.

1.3 Other machine learning methodologies

People have created software systems for more than 50 years, and for a great chunk of that time, they've built ML systems as well. It's therefore worth checking what other people have done. For many years, software development was planned and organized around predictions of the complexity and work required to deliver a project. We call this approach *waterfall*. Essentially the idea is that the required information was gathered, and this was transformed into a design. The design was then changed into a work program for the programmers, and next, the programmers wrote the code and submitted it to testing. Finally, the system was accepted by the users—the waterfall.

As software systems became more complex and less limited by the fundamentals of the hardware that it ran on (because that hardware got a lot faster), the value of the waterfall approach dried up. The ultimate users of waterfall-developed systems found that the software was irrelevant to their real needs because they were disconnected from the process that produced it. There were other problems too, including the inability of project managers to correctly estimate complexity and cost because they were too distanced from the implementation activity itself.

The significant costs of following the prescriptions of structured waterfall methodologies, coupled with a lack of evidence that these practices delivered clear value, led to the widespread disillusionment with "big requirements upfront" approaches. In turn, this led to a reevaluation of the waterfall approach as a more iterative methodology with "uphill feedback" at each stage (Royce 1970) and the development of and exploration of new approaches: Spiral (Boehm 1986), based on plan-do-study-act cycles developed to support decision making under pressure, and V models. The most widely adopted and popular of these approaches is known as agile development (Beck et al 2001).

Agile emphasizes the early delivery of working software, collaboration with customers ("individuals and interactions" instead of "processes"), and the acceptance of change. Change and discovery during the project is held to be better managed by this approach because the customer rapidly has something useful rather than a raft of features and components that can't be used without further development.

A further evolution of agile thinking is the idea of DevOps (Ebert 2016), which is an attempt to build a bridge between developers (dev) and the support teams that operate the software (ops). The insight driving DevOps is that the operations team is a group of experts, more in touch with software than any other part of an organization. A major barrier to using this software is the cost of the mismatch between the dev teams' understanding of the production environment and reality. This cost is borne by both the dev team (trying to achieve its goal of delivering software) and the ops team (trying to achieve its aim of faultless business continuity).

Figure 1.3 illustrates the key activities in a DevOps project, which supports rapid and adaptive software development. A DevOps team develops automation around the processes of developing and delivering software. This allows them to focus on the development itself as the project matures. Information flow into the project activities is promoted by reducing the cost and risk of changing the software later in its development cycle. Typically, this is when (late in the project) users and stakeholders realize what it's actually going to do and how it's going to create value. Having flexibility at this point has a disproportionate impact on the quality of the delivered software.

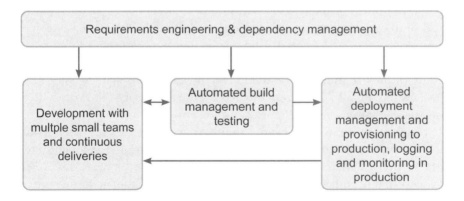

Figure 1.3   A generic DevOps production and delivery process (modeled after Ebert, 2016; redrawn and amended by the author)

Some attempts at providing specific guidance for ML and AI systems development were made in the past. For example, KADS (born, 1990) was a pan-European effort to develop a common engineering methodology in the late 1980s and early 1990s. We used knowledge engineering at that time to create rule-based reasoning systems to make decisions in complex domains. This kind of system turned out to be less practical than it was hoped to be, and because ML systems are different, it makes KADS more or less obsolete.

A more relevant effort was CRISP-DM, which was a data mining methodology developed from 1997 to approximately 2007. Data mining used early ML technology, where patterns are extracted from data to create insights about what is going on. In a 2007 poll, CRISP-DM was cited as the methodology most used by data-mining practitioners (Piatentsk-Shapiro 2007).

In recent years, many in the ML community have adopted approaches inspired by agile and DevOps under the banner of MLOps. Additionally, work such as that described in *Machine Learning as the High Interest Credit Card of Technical Debt* (Sculley et al 2014), articulated some of the problems with ML system development. The ML community has responded by developing approaches that draw on the DevOps style of system development but aimed specifically at ML projects. One example is outlined in an online booklet, *Machine Learning System Design* (MLSD) (Huyen 2020) which provides information for people who want to become ML engineers. MLSD provides a structure and information on the tasks that are required to create a production ML system. The booklet explains the different perspectives and considerations that we should apply when developing a production system by contrasting the needs of research implementations. An overview of design considerations (performance requirements and compute requirements) is also included. The main part of the booklet describes four phases (figure 1.4):

- Project setup is the process of figuring out as much detail as possible about the problem at hand. The methods of doing this are couched as a discussion in a technical interview, and the source of information is seen as the interviewer. Goals, user experience, performance constraints, evaluation, personalization, and project constraints (people, compute power, and infrastructure) are identified as significant elements to be considered.

- The data pipeline element considers privacy and bias, storage, preprocessing, and availability.

- Modelling is considered in terms of model selection, training, debugging, hyperparameter tuning and scaling (in the sense of covering a large amount of training data).

- Serving is framed in terms of the evaluation of the model and the assumptions that we need to understand when running the model in the field.

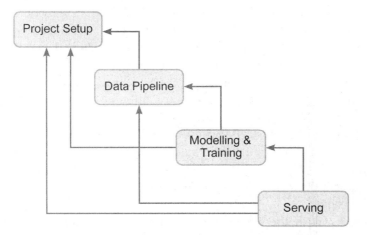

Figure 1.4   ML project flow as described in Huyen and Hopper (2020). Figure redrawn and adapted by the author. Arrows represent dependency relations rather than workflow.

Another attempt to describe this kind of methodology is given in the book, *Machine Learning Engineering* (MLE) (Burkov 2020), which provides a comprehensive review of ML engineering best practices and design patterns.

MLSD and MLE share significant commonalities, both represent the modeling process as being iterative and requiring re-entry into other parts of the development lifecycle. Both books [18, 19] can be seen as MLOps; they are agile and adaptive and emphasize automation in the form of pipeline development. In addition, these approaches take advantage of a range of tools that support the objective of automation. Version control is used for code, models, and features; automated pipelines are used to move and transform data and to test and deploy models.

Recently there has been work on approaches that emphasize the role of documentation, especially with respect to the lineage and provenance of data and models. One example, the publication of Model Cards/Model Reports, was developed for some models published by Google and Hugging Face. An evolution of this was the development process advocated by the TeleManagement Forum (TM Forum), which provides for the maintenance of a chain of custody to assure that models are understood and controlled [20]. These practices emphasize the need to document the models produced, enabling them to be chosen and used appropriately and easily in the future.

1.4   *Understanding this book*

As described in section 1.3, DevOps (iterative development supported by automation), strong documentation, and careful ethical evaluation and process control are important and are widely adopted approaches to ML development. As such, they feature heavily in this book. In addition to seeing how we can use these tools to create models with ML, the book addresses:

- Commissioning and running projects, including estimating project cost and duration.
- Working with and organizing a team to deliver the project.
- Dealing with the data assets that underpin the project, constructing data pipelines, dealing with diverse data gathered for varied purposes, and setting up and running exploratory data analysis.
- Evaluating ML models and making decisions about which ones to use (if you are thinking "the best ones," then prepare for a surprise).
- Moving ML models from development and testing to production.
- Using ML models in applications.

The book uses the conventions of an agile development project [17] to explain the structure of the work. Each chunk of work (figure 1.5) is described as a *sprint*, and the list of tasks in each chapter is called a *backlog*. The backlog list is followed by information detailing the structure and approach of each subtask with additional explanations to help the engineer undertaking the work.

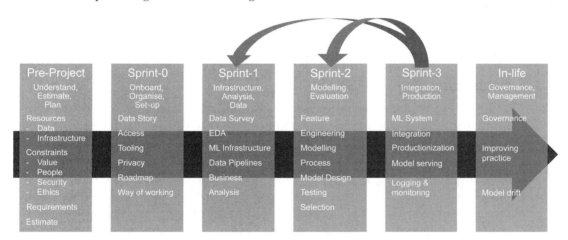

Figure 1.5 The structure of the project described in this book; from creating and developing the project through to managing the final models in production.

At the end of each of the sprints, a checklist is provided to enable teams to work together to ensure that all tasks are completed. The checklist flags the documentation requirements for the tasks in a particular project phase, ensuring that a growing portfolio of documentation detailing the progress that the team makes is assembled. These documents are valuable assets, providing a way for information to be shared and reused. Additionally, the documentation supports the maintenance and governance of the system in production.

Interspersed through the book, there's a case study (The Bike Shop) with a narrative that's intended to illustrate the process and the application of the techniques and tasks described. Some chapters (chapter 2, chapter 5, and chapter 7) don't refer to the case study because they are the start of a sprint, and the relevant narrative appears in the next chapter instead.

Most of the project steps are intended to be viewed as iterative and adaptive, and as can be seen from figure 1.5, it's expected that some of the steps in the project may produce findings that require work to be redone. In particular, the process of EDA, modeling, evaluation, and integration described in chapters 5-8 are, in practice, iterative. It's assumed that there will be false starts and repetitions due to discovery and adaption. For example, the modeling process may lead to the discovery of data features that weren't exposed by the EDA process. This means that more or different data is required.

Integration may expose an unexpected model property, which requires a restart and repeat of modeling. The ordering and detail of the tasks in the EDA phase and in the modeling and evaluation phases are designed to minimize this and to expose issues as early as possible. It's also designed to enable the project leader (you) and your team to communicate what's happening to your stakeholders, reassuring them that you made the best possible efforts to avoid an unexpected dead end and reset of the project.

The objective of using this book allows you to determine what needs to be done at each step of a significant ML project and gives you some support in doing it. Hopefully, it will also provide you with a guide to how much time you'll need, a way of justifying the activities and expenses to project sponsors, and a method for discerning how to accommodate the necessary adaptation and iteration.

1.5   *Case study: The Bike Shop*

To bring this book to life, we include discussions around an example based on real-world data and real-world project experience. Anonymized and reimagined, it's described next.

A chain of bike stores (The Bike Shop) manages its sales and inventory data using disparate systems. Sales is managed by a software as a service (SaaS) system, whereas the inventory is managed by an off-the-shelf inventory system, which is run using a server cluster managed by The Bike Store's IT team. By moving the data from these two systems into a single cloud database, The Bike Store management team hopes to generate insight and create a business case to justify this, based simply on co-hosting the data and providing a dashboard interface that allows business users to consume it. However, they have the idea that applying ML to their business will yield a large benefit, but they have little idea of exactly how that is to be achieved.

At the end of each chapter, the story of how you as the project lead for The Bike Shop's ML initiative, manage the ML system is narrated from your perspective. This includes:

- Building the proposal and estimating the costs.
- Structuring and setting up the team.
- Accessing the systems and data to figure out what's in the data.
- Determining what ML can do with the data.

- Understanding how the users will use the outcome.
- Choosing the models to use and setting up to build the models.
- Building the models and integrating them into a production system.

In the next chapter, this journey begins.

Summary

- The explosion of data and computing in the last 10 years proves that machine learning (ML) has become an important technology.
- There have been problems in terms of both successfully delivering ML projects and the negative impacts that these can have when they are delivered.
- ML projects are different because they depend on complex data, require the team to produce and manage models created from the data, and need to be carefully aligned with the needs of the users and stakeholders.
- A successful ML project drives out risk from requirements and data, captures nonfunctional and functional requirements, and develops capabilities for handling and evaluating models.
- The ML project needs to be aligned with the needs of society and stakeholders throughout its lifecycle to avoid undesirable outcomes.
- We can borrow ideas from agile software and the DevOps community to help us develop the projects.

Pre-project: From opportunity to requirements

This chapter covers

- Understanding the project type and the stakeholders' expectations of scale and structure
- Setting up a pre-sales/pre-project process
- Understanding requirements for model performance
- Understanding data assets
- Understanding the project's general requirements
- Coming to grips with the tools and infrastructure to deliver successfully

Project success and failure are defined by the pre-project/presales activity that surrounds it. The challenge is to move from knowing that there's an opportunity to get paid for an ML project to a job that you can use to pay your mortgage. The purpose of this chapter is to lay out the activities and actions that need to happen to understand if an ML project is possible and if it's useful. Then, we need to determine what effort is required to get it done and by whom.

It's tempting to gold plate these activities because we can do all of them in deep, deep detail. Unfortunately, we live in a competitive world and, sometimes, it's difficult for organizations to invest time or money in projects before they are agreed.

Realistically, we need to understand that the organizational commitment that's needed to support deep dives into customer data or access to high-performance servers won't exist until the ink dries on the contracts. At that point, it becomes everyone's job to make the project happen. Before that, it's all just theory. So, the work that we do before funding is secured and time can be allocated is just a shadow of what happens later.

A strong focus on this process reduces the risk that you and the team are taking on. Failure to understand the project's business requirements puts your team at risk, misdirecting their efforts, and in all likelihood, you'll bid too low to provide the resources that are required for delivery. Failure to understand the available data resources means that it's impossible to determine how to approach the project with ML or to judge the prospects for success. Furthermore, failure to understand security, privacy, or ethical considerations means exposing you, your team, and your organization to embarrassment and liabilities. Looking at all of these facets of the project now allows you to make some timely and effective decisions that could make life a lot better later.

In some ways, these issues arise for any project. Some specific risks for ML projects, however, must be addressed:

- It's often easy to develop ML models, but developing models that have the right properties to solve a particular business problem is much harder.
- Poor quality or inaccessible data introduces considerable friction, and until the data is obtained, project progress typically stalls.
- Data sourcing and usage constraints may mean that it's unethical or illegal to use the results of the project. For example, if the origin of personal data is unknown, using it may violate consumers privacy, and the owners of the data may not consent to its use.
- It's hard to predict the performance of ML algorithms in learning models a priori. Despite the team's best efforts, results may be disappointing.
- Misunderstanding or not anticipating the IT architecture, which deploys the ML system in production, can mean that the results of the project will be unusable.

Work to mitigate these issues is described later in this chapter and in chapter 3. As promised in chapter 1, the following pre-project backlog provides a list of tasks that are required to deliver pre-project activity. After that, we describe the work required to set up this activity and then discuss what's needed to understand the requirements that the client outlines. Subsequent sections tackle understanding the data resources, security and privacy, ethics, and the IT architecture.

2.1 Pre-project backlog

Table 2.1 provides a summary of the activities required to create the outcome for a successful pre-project. We can use this list as a pre-sale (PS) backlog. Each item can be a ticket in a system like Jira or GitLab, which then allows us to track progress, which prevents forgotten tasks. Using a ticketing system to track progress comes in handy because it will be easy to determine when a meeting should be run and to see who was responsible for each task and what they did.

Table 2.1   Pre-sale backlog for pre-projects

Ticket No.	Item
PS1	Set up a project backlog/task board and use it.
PS2	Create a document repository and make it available to the project team.
PS3	Establish a risk register to determine what's the unknown diligence and estimate what's required to mitigate that.
PS4	Create an organizational model to support your knowledge of the customer and the customer's challenges.
	Undertake an organizational analysis by mapping project stakeholders to the organizational chart and the impact to specific business units (if affected) and to business priorities (increased revenue, decreased costs, growth of market, etc.).
PS5	Understand the system architecture and nonfunctional constraints.
PS6	Get a data sample and document what is known about the data resources: statistical, nonfunctional (scale, speed, history, etc.), and system properties (where it is, what infrastructure it lives on, what it does).
PS7	Check and document security and privacy requirementsace and include as project assumptions.
PS8	Check and document corporate social responsibility and ethical requirements, then challenge, provide feedback, and include as project assumptions.
	Create PDIA and AIA documents.
PS9	Develop a high-level delivery architecture. The architecture should cover dev, test, and production components (sometimes also pre-production/staging) and should be able to support the customer's nonfunctional requirements such as availability, resilience, security, and throughput.
	Qualify this architecture with the appropriate stakeholders for feedback, if possible.
	Document key aspects of the architecture as assumptions for the project.
PS10	Understand the business problem: use a consensus to build a project hypothesis, validated by the customer and the delivery team.
	Ensure that this clearly communicated and documented in any contractual agreement.
PS11	Undertake project diligence. Will the stakeholders be available? Is the data available and manageable? What team members are available and what skills do they have?
PS12	Create an estimate of the work for a model project, delivering on the required project hypothesis, taking into account the available team and the scale of the work that is needed.
	Ensure that all project risks are accounted for in your estimate.
PS13	Create a plan for team design and resourcing and share it with the customer.
PS14	Run a review meeting and go through a checklist to ensure that the presales process is properly completed.

We cover tickets PS1 through PS9 in this chapter, which deals with identifying and documenting the requirements for the project. We cover tickets PS10 to PS14 in chapter 3, which uses those requirements to create estimates and proposals. This secures the funding and gets the project ready to go. The first thing to undertake is PS1.

> **Project management infrastructure tickets: PS1**
>
> - Set up a project backlog/task board and use it.

We can implement this ticket using Jira, GitLab, GitHub, Microsoft ADO, or many other options. As soon as you have done that, you can sign off on PS1! Congratulations, you've started the pre-project work. PS2 and PS3 are up next. By setting up a project management infrastructure (building on the ticketing system), you make it easier to progress with everything else.

2.2 *Project management infrastructure*

PS2 and PS3 are the tickets that set up the project management infrastructure, bringing it into use. As such, they're a good place to start. As a reminder, they're listed here.

> **Project management infrastructure tickets: PS2**
>
> - Create a project document repository, and make it available to the project team.

> **Project management infrastructure tickets: PS3**
>
> - Establish a risk register to determine what's the unknown diligence and estimate what's required to mitigate that.

The first step, as per PS2, in completing the pre-sales process is to create a shared project document repository, where we can keep the documentation covering the presales activity. We might use the repository for the whole project, although customer data retention and management requirements may mean that we migrate it to another, customer-owned, and standardized repository. Even so, the information gathered at this step will be useful through the end of the delivery and probably beyond, and being organized about documentation from now on is crucial.

One thing to remember is that your organization likely has a document retention policy; this may require deleting the documentation after a particular period or at the end of the project. Alternatively, it may mean that the documentation is archived so that it can be found later. Although it is important to check retention policies, the information gathered is likely to be your organization's property. If pre-sales fail, and there is no project proper, then these documents are still useful if the customer returns with another project in the future.

Importantly, in all cases, the documentation you develop and capture now supports the evolution of your team and your working practice. By doing this, you are capturing value from day one, and you are also helping yourself in the future. It's common to think, "Oh, I came across a problem like that before and then we decided…" If, in the future, you can remember that and pull out the documents, you'll find that you've got a real advantage.

The other thing to do on day one is to set up a *risk register*. Determining what might go wrong and what's unknown is a key step in creating a project that is manageable. This is a way to prevent important issues from being forgotten, and it's a way to establish the difference that the work on the project is making. As you move an identified risk from live to retired, problems are solved, and they are solved by you and the team.

We can handle risk items by turning them into questions to be explored. If the project's objectives are substantially defined in terms of questions that need to be answered, it's substantially less risky. This approach exposes uncertainty that we need to deal with before establishing business value. Exposing questions in this way also informs customers of the value of the exploration that needs to be done.

Setting up a project risk register sounds like a complex and fancy thing, but it's actually simple. A risk register is a document identified and versioned in your repository (of course!). It records all the project's risks and actions. If the actions are successful, the risk register also records that we mitigated the risks and discharged them from the register.

In the project proper, the identification and management of risks is part of the project's heartbeat (more about this soon) and managed in a weekly meeting with the key project stakeholders. All parties accept the entry of new risks into the register and agree that they are dealt with or not.

In the pre-sales process, risks are managed closely by the presales team. At this stage, risks are also the concern of the project team because assessing and controlling the project's risks defines the estimates that the team provides. This also underpins the client's decision on whether to adopt the team's proposal.

2.3   *Project requirements*

Having set up a working project infrastructure with the ticketing system, document repository, and the risk register, the real work starts. PS4 and PS5 call for developing the project's requirements.

Requirements ticket: PS4
- Create an organizational model to support your knowledge of the customer and the customers challenges.
- Undertake an organizational analysis by mapping:
  - Project stakeholders to the organizational chart.
  - The impact to specific business units (if affected) and to business priorities (increased revenue, decreased costs, growth of market, etc.).

Requirements ticket: PS5

- Understand the system architecture and nonfunctional constraints.

Get to know your customer. Figure out what they need in order to call this project a success by the time their budget is spent. This knowledge enables you to sign off on the spirit of the project as well as the letter of the contract, and it makes negotiating and managing change much easier and less fraught.

2.3.1 Funding model

The first challenge is to understand the funding model for the project. There are three types of projects: fixed-price, time-and-materials, and mission-driven. Fixed-price and time-and-materials projects deliver a specific outcome, which is often defined upfront. Mission-driven projects are more exploratory and are aimed at improving the performance of an area of a business or for a smaller business (or bigger project), transforming it overall. The type of project we deliver impacts the way that we should manage it and the approach that we should take.

With a fixed-price, fixed-time project, we should deliver the defined result at a specific time, so the delivery organization bears the risk of delivery. It's important to note that there are two ways that risk materializes when the project goes wrong:

- The team experiences "crunch" and overworks to deliver the goods.
- The project's costs escalate, commercially damaging the business that delivers it.

Usually, both these things happen. Verheyen [12] discusses the challenge of dealing with fixed-price contracts using agile approaches. He concludes that fixed-price contracts are so problematic as to be simply immoral!

Despite their pathologies, fixed-price, results-oriented contracts are a business reality that many teams deal with every day. This is because these contracts provide a well-understood mechanism for customers authorizing payment for the service. In fact, this type of arrangement is so simple that even where formal contracts don't exist, working with a fixed-resource, fixed-time structure can provide clarity and buy-ins from stakeholders.

The greatest virtue of working with fixed-price, fixed-time (and, approximately, fixed-outcome) structures is transparency. The team knows what they are signing up for, and the customer knows (as much as a customer can know) what they are going to get. The trade-off is that the risk of fixed-price projects is largely shifted onto the delivery team. The team can end up being pushed to make up for mis-estimated or mis-priced projects by working overtime. As a team leader, you need to guard against this with the investigation and preparation you do before the project starts.

Projects on a time-and-material basis work based on the customer paying when the team finishes the project, or the customer runs out of money. Time-and-materials projects have their own pathologies. For example, it's easy to set unrealistic expectations, and the project team and other technical stakeholders may be unaware of the real expectations and goals of the project until a late state. This, in turn, ends up precipitating a situation where the pressure on the budget holders spills over to the team, which finds impossible targets and demands or a project that fails. However, it's generally agreed that the time-and-materials project risk is more shifted toward the client stakeholders.

Contrasted to fixed-price or time-and-materials, a mission-driven project can sometimes seem like a dream. The team has a high-level mission and an agenda of ideas and hunches that are supported by their stakeholders. These are the things that the team goes after to get a result.

In the best case, as the team goes deeper and deeper into the project, they see more and more opportunities; in the worst case, they see more and more problems. Team members can become energized and engaged because of the importance and value of the work. They can come to see themselves as having agency and importance through saving the business and so forth. On the other hand, folks can get switched off by the never-ending story of false starts and disappointing outcomes. Sometimes the achievements of the team are understood and acknowledged, but sometimes the achievements are subsumed into other business initiatives.

If the project you are investigating looks likely to be funded on a time-and-materials basis, or if it's a more open and mission-driven project, then this chapter and the next may be less relevant to you and your team. Using a structured, pre-project process, however, helps for all three types of projects:

- For fixed-price, it gives your organization evidence for making a bid (or not) at a particular level.
- For time-and-materials, it limits the dangers of crunch and stakeholder frustration.
- For mission-driven, it focuses the team, helping both the team and the organization to manage and structure how they intend to go after the strategic opportunities they want to grasp.

2.3.2 *Business requirements*

Having established the funding model for the project and made the decision to do a structured pre-project investigation, the next step is to look at the customer's business objectives. We often view requirement's analysis as part of the "big design upfront" approach to software developmentXE "software development:approaches:big requirements upfront" . But for an ML project, there are some issues that must be understood to determine if the project is practical. As an illustration, no matter how agile the team is, they will not be able to make a large general model run as fast as might be desired for a lot of users on an old slow processor, nor will the effort to optimize it be cheap. We need to understand three general types of requirements for this analysis:

- *Functional requirements:* What will the system do and for whom? What is the model's function that will drive the delivered system? What classification, recommendation, or labeling tasks are the models built from the customer's data expected to do? How well must the models perform in terms of accuracy, robustness to strange events and data, and reliability in the face of change?
- *Nonfunctional requirements:* How quickly must the models execute or run? What throughput is required? What latency must the models react within? How much will executing the models cost in terms of money and carbon footprints?
- *System requirements:* Where is the model to live? How will it be maintained? What systems must it integrate with? How will the results of the model be consumed and what work is required to make it consumable? What resilience or business continuity measures are required?

It isn't realistic to tackle these requirements in order. Instead, we need a process of clarification and reflection, a deepening of understanding. Next, we can pin down the specifics in terms of the requirements and the implications of providing it in a particular way. Then, how do we start?

The obvious first step is to listen to what the client or sponsor says about what they want. This may be articulated at a high level, or it may be that the client lacks the technical background to describe their requirement in a way that's technically achievable. Alternatively, you might get a detailed and coherent specification straightaway. Having listened carefully to the client's understanding, we need to go deeper, asking why, who, and what.

BUSINESS REQUIREMENTS: WHY?

It's important that you ask why the customer has these needs and objectives. If you can understand this, then it becomes possible for you to do several things:

- Fit the customers' requirements to technically realizable solutions.
- Refine the customers' requirements to provide more value.
- Develop several alternate routes to value, which you can explore during the project.

Imagine a customer who wants to create a smart building: the articulated objective is to develop models that use the sensor data gathered throughout the building to control the heating and air conditioning more efficiently. Why? The answers could be:

- To reduce costs.
- To improve the environment within the building for its users.
- To reduce carbon consumption.
- To reduce the use of particular chemicals in the air conditioning.
- To improve the image of the company.
- Because we've been told to do it.

All of these are valid reasons for the objective; all imply potential alternative solutions. The next question to ask is who?

BUSINESS REQUIREMENTS: WHO?

One simple thing to do is to obtain an organizational chart from the customer: what is the organization that you are delivering to and where does the customer fit in? Figure 2.1 shows an example that identifies the departments and responsibilities that are important to The Bike Shop customer. The people who are initiating the project are in IT, but the end users are in the manufacturing, marketing, and ops sections of the retail department. The project touch points are indicated with the dots in the figure. It's interesting to see where the project is going to rub up against the customer's organization and where it's not.

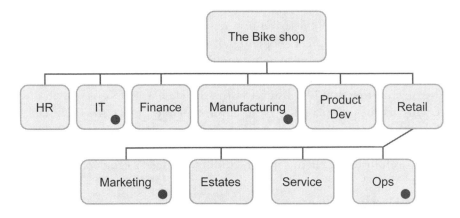

Figure 2.1   The Bike Shop organizational chart. Dots represent stakeholders and users, the touchpoints for the project.

Locating and decorating an org chart with the names and roles of the contacts and users is a good start, but we can build a deeper understanding using more formal tactics. The concept of building an organizational model comes from the CommonKADS knowledge methodology [6]. The authors propose developing a model of your customer iteratively, focusing on the issues that brought you into the engagement:

- *Problems and opportunities:* A short list of the perceived problems and opportunities that the customer uses to justify the engagement with you.
- *Organizational context:* The attributes of the organization that put the problems into perspective, including mission or vision of the organization, external factors effecting the organization (competition, regulation, economy), strategy of the organization, the value chain it sits in (who does it buy from, who does it sell to, what are the ultimate customers and producers of the goods and services that the organization deals in).
- *Solutions:* Ideas about the solutions that you might offer.

In the KADS world, it's suggested that we can obtain this knowledge from the stakeholders in the organization. It's important to note that KADS uses an outmoded hierarchy in their stakeholder map. In a modern organization, the stakeholders might be:

- *Budget holders:* The "shot callers" that you'll bring value to. They might be your customer but also the folks from finance or procurement who have to agree that the money allocated to the customer is spent properly or that the organization's procurement policy and standard is complied with.
- *Business experts:* —Those who understand the domain and how your system connects it to their business.
- *End users:* The people who are going to use your system and will be impacted by it.
- *Security signoff:* The person who evaluates your system so that it is compliant with the organization's security standards.
- *System signoff:* The person who agrees that you've designed and implemented the system compliantly.
- *Data admin:* The person who gives you access to the data resources you will need.
- *Data protection signoff:* The person who confirms that you've handled the data compliantly.
- *QA signoff:* The person who verifies that you've achieved a working, quality system.

Many of these people can veto the outcome: whether this project is going to be a success or a failure. The challenge is to identify them and to then figure out what it is they are going to demand from you and the team. Determine who they are, what they want, and how to talk to them.

This is an intimidating list. Realistically, you will have to prioritize who it is that you are going to approach. Working with the stakeholders in your organization (not the customer), make sure that you are licensed to engage with the people whom you have identified. The engagement managers and account development executives that are running the opportunity in a consultancy will not thank you for derailing a bid by approaching someone you are not allowed to talk with for commercial reasons.

If this is an internal project, politics must be considered as funding is competed for, so approaching the wrong stakeholder at this point could lead to the project being vetoed before it has a chance to begin. Once you do have a qualified list of contacts, there are additional questions that you'll need to get answers to:

- *Organizational context:* What is the unit's mission? What are the sources of business pressure (regulation, competition, supply, disruption, etc.)? How do the customers make their money and justify their place in the organization?
- *Problems and opportunities:* Why does the person that you are engaging with need a solution? Could they be more productive? Are they wasting time on repetitive tasks? Are they unable to make good decisions because they lack information? Are they overwhelmed with options? Do things move too fast?

The answers to these questions define the needs and opportunities for the functional part of the project. Of course, if there is one obvious and clear functional need (for example, a system to do *x*), then all is well because that's the functional requirement. It's likely, though, that things may be a bit more obscure, and you will get a range of needs and ideas. That's OK. By understanding the constraints on what can be done, you will be able to synthesize, qualify, and select from the laundry list that you've created with this task. This leads to the next clarifying question: what?

BUSINESS REQUIREMENTS: WHAT?

The first place to start the process of figuring out the *whats* of the system is to get a handle on the system or IT architecture in the client organization. Then, begin to get a handle on the nonfunctional requirements in terms of scale and speed.

Unfortunately, it's not possible to get a nice chart to represent a large organization's IT setup or architecture (the first step). It's common for companies to have hundreds or thousands of applications (or even tens of thousands in some cases). The essential task is to understand the organization's general policy and facilities that are currently in place and to comprehend the legacy assets that might impact the project. The key questions are:

- What kind of data systems are in use: Hadoop? Presto? Oracle? SAP? Is there a single vendor policy ("we are a Microsoft shop") or is there a user/application first policy ("any database so long as it works")?
- What processing systems are available: SPARK? Kubernetes? OpenShift?
- Is there something missing? Is there any vital infrastructure that you think should be available for use but isn't there? Will that be an issue, and what impact will it have on the project and the possibilities for a viable solution?
- Is the organization on the cloud? Which cloud? What are the policies about using relevant components in that cloud? (Often, organizations choose not to use some components for cost and security reasons.)
- Are there legacy components that you have to interact with? For example, is some part of the relevant architecture on premise, whereas the cool, new stuff is in the cloud?

Then, you need to understand the scale of the business challenge. That way, you can determine if the infrastructure that's available will be up to the task at hand:

- How many customers are there?
- How much do they spend?
- How many transactions a day does the organization run?
- How many parties are involved in a typical transaction?
- What are the key trading hours for the organization?

It's a certainty that more questions will come into focus as you investigate. To get the answers, you will need to create a picture of the operating environment and the landscape where the system to be created will function in.

This knowledge and the understanding of the functional needs of the system underpin the creation of the project hypothesis. What is the solution that is going to be the goal of the project by the customer and the team? It'll also be enormously helpful in framing user stories and pinning down more specific requirements as the project evolves. But for now, the model you are working up tells you and your organization if this is something real to do with ML and if that something is feasible.

Because you are working on an ML project rather than on an app development, there are more specific questions that you need to get in to. These are investigated in the next few sections, starting with the big one in section 2.4: what kind of data are you working with?

2.4   *Data*

People doing ML projects need to understand the data. By getting information about the data early, it's possible to gain insight into the scale and depth of the challenges that the team will face and what they can really do. There's understanding the characteristics of the data in statistical terms, but also the data engineering that's required to set the implementation up, and what the limitations or potentials of that are. PS6 requires that you get an insight into the data that you are going to use in this project.

Data discovery tickets: PS6

- Get a data sample and document what is known about the data resources:
  - Statistical properties of the data
  - Nonfunctional properties (scale, speed, history, etc.)
  - System properties (where it is, what infrastructure it lives on, what it does)

Your client may have a clear idea of the data that you can use to train an ML model, but it's valuable to delve further into their knowledge of what is available. This allows you to develop ideas about what kind of ML solution might be possible. There are four benefits of doing this:

- By asking open-ended questions about the available data in the client's systems, you can uncover data sources that might not have seemed relevant to the client and put those resources to good use.
- You can explore and validate the data sets that are known to the client and that are recommended to you, even if only in a narrow and simple way at this stage.
- You can get some idea of the deficiencies of the data that the customer has, which informs you of the need to find data from an open source or from commercial sources to supplement the data if needed.

- You can get information about the work that will be required to use the data, in terms of improving the quality and cleaning it, and whether you'll need to employ methods that squeeze more out of limited data sets.

The first thing is to get a sample of the data you will be working with. Getting the full data set would be ideal, but at this stage, this may be unrealistic for several reasons: the technical difficulty of extracting a large data set may be great and require funding that may be unavailable at this stage. Additionally, the full data set may contain trade secrets and other intellectual property that cannot be released until a contractual relationship is established. (Typically, the security requirements for access to corporate data stores can't be negotiated in a putative project.) Finally, the work required to handle and manage the data may be substantial and unaffordable at the moment. However, getting a representative sample should be feasible and is extremely important. Even the process of obtaining the sample itself may reveal important issues with the customer's understanding of the data and data infrastructure.

If the full data set is available and the project scale and risk provide commercial justification to pay for this (you are still in pre-project, so this is on your coin at this point), then you may want to drag the whole or parts of the data investigation and EDA (exploratory data analysis) exercises from later in this book forward to the pre-project stage. The more depth that you can afford to get now, the fewer risks you face later. Realistically, though, it's much more likely that at this point all that will be available will be a sample.

Questions to ask about statistical properties and things to look for in the data sample include the following:

- Is it really representative? Are there some data points from across the time period that the data was accumulated? Are there data points from all the source systems? Are there some data points from the extremes of the data ranges?
- What is the range of values in the entities in the sample? Is it sparse with few or dissimilar items? Is it dense with a lot of repeating values?
- How was the data collected? Was it part of a survey? Was it from an experiment? Was it exhaust from a business process? Was it picked up at regular intervals or at an event?
- Does the data remind you of other data that you have previously used? Is this data that is suitable for processing by a well-known ML algorithm without extensive transformation? For example, if it's image data, then is it 256 x 256 pixels with 8 colors or is it gigapixel images with 2.4M colors? What well-known data set is it like?

Some nonfunctional questions to ask include:

- What is the scale of the available data? If the source data is large, then the sample provided may be unrepresentative of most of the data, even if it is sampled in a sensible way from the source. (Often, sample data is not systematically sampled.)

- How many different data assets or tables were brought together to create the sample? How long did that take and what was the cost and time spent on the queries? Was this data that could be picked up easily from the corporate information architecture or was it prized out by heroic, patient, and ingenious means? Did any of it come from third parties or exotic sources?
- How fast does the data change? How often is it updated? How much arrives and how quickly?
- What is the schema of the data assets used to create the sample set? Sometimes samples are provided as large, flat tables that are joins from underlying databases. Understanding what the source schema is can show where there are problems and where effort will be needed in the ETL process to use this asset.

Systems questions include:

- What platforms host the data? Does your team have the skills required to access and manipulate the data on these platforms? If not, how is it expected that the data will be made available to the team?
- Has anything significant happened to the data sets in their life cycles? For example, has there been a data migration or a data quality improvement campaign?
- Which business unit or stakeholder owns the source tables and the derived data? What organization owns the system that implements and manages the data tables? This knowledge leads an investigation into the IT systems' context that the team will operate in and the required security and privacy regime. This will be significant in the development of the ethical approach to the project.
- What was the process used to prepare the sample? Although the process used can be guessed at from the answers to the previous questions, it's always worth trying to get some documentation about this process, especially to understand if there are any manual steps like "then we picked through the items to discard the ones that don't fit." In the first phases of the project, the team may want to reproduce the sample provided to test their understanding of the resources. Is there sufficient information to do this?

Unfortunately, sometimes customers will be unable or unwilling to disclose real data during the pre-project process. This can be because of contractual concerns or simply because their infrastructure requires work before the data can be extracted. Many customers simply have no idea of how to get at the data that's required.

The people that you talk to probably won't know the answers to all your questions, and there won't be time to get them. The solution: put these items on the risk register. If you are working on a contract, make sure that they are written into the statement of work as assumptions. These are big risk items; essentially, you are flying blind on the ML part of the project unless you have a good idea of the data that you'll use.

If this is the case, then an alternative approach is to push for a short project to understand the ML readiness of the organization. This should provide the contractual cover to support the extraction and inspection of the data, including provisions on privacy, data retention, and use and undertakings on security and data handling. This work gives the team a strong understanding of the data to have some confidence in predicting the kinds of results that they should get in the modelling phase of the project.

Despite the challenge of getting access to data resources, it is essential that every effort is made to both understand and document the data model that the team will be working with and to apprehend the real characteristics of the data. Attempting to dimension and structure an ML project without sufficient knowledge of the data is risky. If these tasks are not well bottomed out, it is important to introduce significant contingency items into your project estimate, both in terms of clock time and funding. This ensures that your team isn't desperately coding around huge data problems late at night for weeks on end. Bear in mind, if no one knows "what's in there," then that's a strong indicator that there are real problems waiting to be found.

2.5   *Security and privacy*

ML projects are tightly coupled to data resources, often sensitive and important data resources that many business processes depend on or that contain details that are both protected in law and private to individuals. This leads us to PS7 in our pre-sale backlog.

> **Security and privacy tickets: PS7**
>
> - Check and document security and privacy requirements and include both as project assumptions.

Any insecure project can create vulnerabilities for an organization, so it is natural that an ML project needs to meet the security requirements of the organization(s) that it is working with. To achieve this, it's necessary to engage with the security infrastructure of the target organizations as quickly as possible. In the pre-sales phase of the project, we want to gather the information that's required to assess and factor in the impact of security constraints and requirements.

A different organization often handles the sign-off for the security aspects of a system. Sometimes the security organization is completely decoupled from IT with a CSO reporting directly to the CEO. In the best case, there is a single security stakeholder who's engaged in the client organization that we can identify. More often, several security stakeholders will need to be involved in the project.

Figure 2.2 shows an example of a security organization that we may have to engage in an ML project. Data sets can be required from several lines of business, including the line of business that has engaged the team for the project. Additional data may be required from group operations (for example, pricing and costing information). A cross-cutting concern is IT security for the development infrastructure and activity, and also for access to the required production platforms needed for deploying the system.

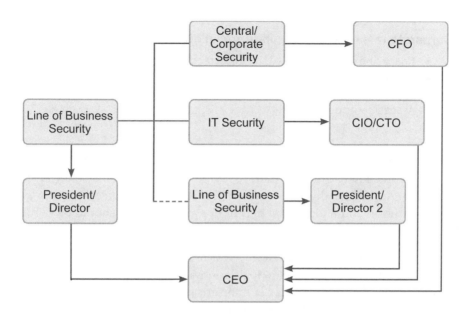

Figure 2.2   An example of a security organization within a large company. Each market-facing unit owns the security relevant to that line of business. A group of marketing units also has a security function, which reports to the CFO, and an IT security unit that reports to the CIO or CTO.

For each of the core data sets, relevant organizations, and IT platforms, it's necessary to establish the relevant security stakeholders. Also, we need to understand the data privacy issues and requirements (at the top level initially), and the processes and requirements that need to be negotiated.

Equally important is to establish (preferably with the security stakeholders) what problems are likely to be exposed during the security processes. Often, security personnel will say that the requirements are straightforward and unlikely to be a problem. If they are unwilling to say that it's a sign that a significant hitch may be in the prospect. Determining what would need to be done to deal with that problem may be impossible at this stage but entering it in the project risk register is vital. Either the resolution becomes a contractual assumption that provides the team with cover and scope for flexibility, or it becomes a financial problem that needs to be considered carefully when assessing whether this project is viable and how much it may cost. . !

2.6   *Corporate responsibility, regulation, and ethical considerations*

As for security, many readers reach this part of the book and say, "This should be the first thing that's considered," and they are somewhat correct. It's hard to think about CSR (corporate social responsibility) and ethics before you understand the project. Once the project hypothesis is clear, it's time to think critically and ethnically about what you are doing. This is the task in PS8.

> ## Corporate responsibility, regulatory, and ethical consideration tickets: PS8
>
> - Check and document CSR and ethical requirements.
> - Challenge and provide feedback and include as project assumptions.
> - Create PDIA (Privacy & Data Impact Assessment) and AIA (Algorithmic Impact Assessment) documents.

Ethics are important in an ML project. Laws and legalities, such as the European General Data Protection Regulation (GDPR), impose a limitation on what you should consider doing. At present, there isn't much specific legislation on ML systems per se, and there's confusion about algorithm definitions and how they should be regulated. It is likely that this picture will change.

> **NOTE** Being cognizant of the relevant laws is important. Bear in mind, a failure by a team to understand and follow legislation because of ignorance is just as bad as a deliberate attempt to flout or circumvent the rules. Take every opportunity to familiarize yourself with the regulations and laws that might apply to your project and team.

It's also important to be aware of any laws that apply to the domain that you are working in, as well as generic data and ML laws that are in force in the relevant jurisdictions. For example, you need to know the relevant legislation for patient safety and testing in medicine, for risk and process in finance, and for health and safety in industry. It is necessary to investigate and clarify what if any domain-specific legislation applies to the system under consideration.

Just sticking to the laws relevant to the project isn't going to be a strong enough approach to create a good outcome for the client, your organization, and your team. The ICO (Information Commissioner's Office) in the UK has developed a framework for the audit of AI and ML systems [8]. This guidance stresses that these systems must be accountable for data protection, and this must be demonstrable. The system (in the ICO's view) must:

- Allow the customer to be responsible for compliance.
- Allow the risks of the system to be assessed and mitigated.
- Allow the documentation and demonstration of how the system is compliant, justifying the choices that have been made.

The ICO also notes that "due to the complexity and mutual dependency of the various kinds of processing typically involved in AI supply chains, you need to take care to understand and identify controller/processor relationships," and that "demonstrating how you have addressed these complexities is an important element of accountability."

In addition to implementation concerns, the ethical implications of the proposed system's impact must be part of the requirements analysis. The impacts are very real and far-reaching. A number of monographs [9] and a wider literature of conferences [3] and journals [11] address the concerns that have emerged about the impact of AI, ML, and algorithmic decisions. These impacts are especially significant to marginalized and disempowered groups within our society.

Furthermore, efforts are underway to capture and manage databases of so-called AI incidents [2]. At the time of writing, the database records 1,225 incidents. Some examples include the impact of fine-grained work-scheduling systems that do not take into account common sense or the needs of employees outside the workplace. Other examples are content moderation and content generation problems on social media (for example, by AI bots and multiple accounts of fatal accidents involving industrial robots).

Although the discussions in the literature are wide-ranging and informative, they are driven from an academic and philosophical standpoint. This means that there is an additional challenge facing teams working in a commercial organization: a requirement to both create systems that deliver business value and have ethical integrity.

The business cases that support the development of computer systems often involve ethically questionable trade-offs. In the first wave of office automation, many desk-bound jobs were lost because it was possible to cost effectively implement and install computer systems that did the work of hundreds or thousands of claims processors, invoice adjusters, or expense managers. These systems made fewer mistakes and could be reprogrammed to reflect changes in business policy faster than retraining the previous workforce. (This is sometimes claimed, although the long history of failed system upgrades in this context makes some people a bit doubtful.) Were these systems unethical? From the perspective of millions of people who lost their jobs, they appeared so, and indeed, strikes and protests were organized about these projects [10].

The consensus, however, is that technological innovation is inevitable and that organizations or economic sectors that fail to innovate and implement these systems will become obsolete, destroyed by competition. Additionally, at the time that these innovations were being developed, there were compelling needs to grow the global economy. This was the era of widespread childhood hunger and famine. With hindsight, it seems true that the change in the economy delivered improvements in the conditions of billions of people, but the growth in inequality in all societies points to the partial application of new technology as a tool that favored the ruling classes and socially dominant groups in society. The experience of the late 20th century and the third industrial revolution that transformed the economy changed the perception that innovation is anything but a choice. Sometimes, for some people, it's a bad one.

These lessons and the negative impact of social networking applications on society offer a reminder to ML practitioners: business cases that look positive overall must be carefully weighed and balanced with the perspectives of all those impacted. We need to review a proposed project with the overall hypothesis, user stories, and system outline from the perspective of those impacted and, where possible, with their direct input. We also need to perform a personal data impact assessment and review the system with respect to the accountability and governance requirements of the application. A state-of-the-art implementation with respect to the ethical considerations relevant to AI systems is emerging, and at the time of writing, subject to considerable debate. For example, see writing in *Wired* [13], and the extensive debate around the article on the dangers of large language models written by Bender et al [4].

It's hard to avoid personal and subjective biases when evaluating a system's impact and implications. Although every engineer has a duty to attempt to avoid harming others via the solutions that they build, there is a distribution of both experience and capability among engineers. It may be that you and your team are empathic, insightful, and have the range of perspectives required to understand the long-term consequences of the solutions that you advance. It may also be that you have the same tendency to blind spots and biases as some humans, so you overlook this.

Given human fallibility, it makes sense to take advantage of the structured tools that introduce process into the evaluation. One example is the Algorithmic Impact Assessment (AIA) tool developed by the Canadian government [5]. This tool provides a questionnaire that determines the likely harm or extent of harm for projects that introduce algorithmic reasoning into business domains. The tool is limited in the application domain, lacking specialist questions with respect to medicine, construction, and manufacturing, for example. It, however, provides an indication of the shape and future use of tools for this purpose.

Another example for the application of algorithmic impact assessment tools is from The Ada Lovelace Institute [1]. Their guidance is helpful in suggesting how we can use these tools effectively to support the choices that AI and ML practitioners must make. Some available models allow a pragmatic approach to delivering a safe and ethical AI system. For example, work on safety in ML systems by Hendrycks et al [7] advocates a layered model of safeguards. Figure 2.3 shows the concept of building a set of layers of checks and guards that catch more of the mistakes that a system might cause.

The layers in figure 2.3 are:

- *External safety or deployment hazards:* Using a systematic approach to development means that you can pin down causes of failure. You can gradually identify problems and sort those out.

  The risk register provides one mechanism for doing this; others include running explicit evaluations and reviewing with users. Eventually, though, the system is released into the wild, so it's important to specify a post development system, which should be safe to run as well.

- *Monitoring:* Using system inspections, its behavior is made known to the users and its owners. The system's behavior should be surfaced and recorded, and there should be a procedure for alerts and notifications to bring the issues to the users' and stakeholders' attention.

- *Robustness:* Characterizing and testing how the system performs or acts in certain circumstances can be used (and should be understood) as part of the process of acceptance to service.

- *Alignment:* Thinking about who is in control of the system and the mechanisms for implementing and reporting on that, so it can be meaningfully steered and controlled by the appropriate humans.

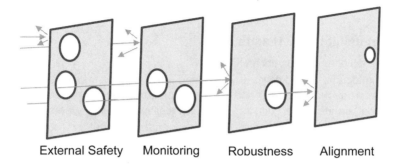

External Safety   Monitoring   Robustness   Alignment

Figure 2.3   A layered model of ML safety (adapted from Hendrycks et al [7])

Crucially you must consider and document who will be harmed if the system functions as intended, and who will be harmed if it doesn't function as intended. For example (functions/fails):

- *Generative art:* May put artists out of a job or may create harmful images.
- *Generative text:* May put journalists out of job or may flood the internet with nonsense.
- *Facial recognition:* May allow dissidents to be identified and arrested or may mean that innocent parties are identified as criminals.

By thinking about these pairs, it's possible to start to determine the harmful impacts your system could have and this allows decisions to be made about whether it's a good idea to continue to develop it, or alternatively, what mitigations you will need to develop in order to field it safely.

We've covered a lot of material in this section. In summary:

- Review the project hypothesis, user stories, and system outline to determine the list of stakeholders impacted by the implementation and by the use of data derived from them or their communities for training the models in the system.
- Review the system from the perspective of stakeholders, and where possible, with their direct input to determine the impact of the system on everyone.
- Undertake a systematic assessment of the proposed system using an Algorithmic Impact Assessment tool.
- Communicate the outcomes of the assessment to project stakeholders.

2.7   *Development architecture and process*

As well as the system produced for the users, the team needs to produce or onboard on to systems that allow for the creation and delivery of the model. PS9 captures the requirement to understand the work required in getting this done.

Development architecture tickets: PS9

- Develop a high-level delivery architecture.
- The architecture should cover dev, test, and production components (sometimes also pre-production/staging) and should be able to support the customers non-functional requirements such as availability, resilience, security, and throughput.
- Qualify this architecture with the appropriate stakeholders for feedback, if possible.
- Document key aspects of the architecture as assumptions for the project.

In operational domains, we typically need to set up three or four layers of environment and then configure and use these to get something in front of a real user. These layers are the development environment where the team works, the test environment, where we check the system for effectiveness and quality, and the production environment, where it actually runs. In some cases, there may also be a pre-production environment, which is provided because of regulatory or data protection concerns. In this environment, we can further screen a tested system for its behavior in the face of sensitive data. These layers are colloquially called dev, test, prod, and pre-prod (or QA). Figure 2.4 illustrates how these layers are arranged, the flow between them, and the version control systems used to manage code and other artifacts.

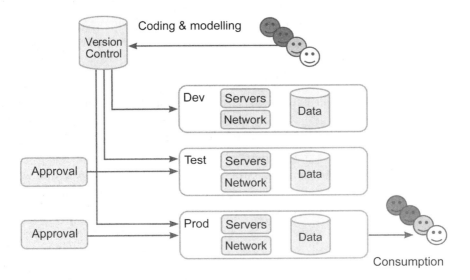

Figure 2.4   Environments for delivery; sometimes a pre-prod or staging layer that completely replicates production is also required.

Figure 2.4 shows these three environments:

- *Development (dev):* Where your team works to create the solution. The dev environment may include specialist tools such as compilers and GPUs or TPUs for model training, or alternatively, large parallel compute systems or many core machines for model search and evaluation.

  Read on for a short discussion about why it might be important to push for these machines in dev. Many dev environments do not contain live or sensitive data, and the ML dev environment often needs to contain this type of data. This requirement needs to be clear and managed effectively.

- *Test:* Where we conduct model evaluation and where we test required components for production. This environment typically replicates the production system with high fidelity, apart from the system databases that usually contain data snapshots or mockups, which preserve confidentiality and allow for testing.

- *Production (prod):* Where we deliver results to customers. The prod environment should be understood from the interaction with the organization during requirements analysis.

To figure out the system aspects that are required for the team to deliver models, you need to understand dev and test. Also, it's important to understand the flow between these and into the production environment. As well as understanding what the standard processes are in the client organization, you'll need to drill into the issues that are particular to ML systems.

2.7.1 Development environment

The dev layer of the architecture is where your team works, and it provides the support that they need to deliver quickly and effectively. Because of this, you need to establish what's available for use by your team. Fortunately, reference material that outlines some of the mechanisms that an MLOps team will use to deliver projects is available (Treviel 2021).

The MLOps environment includes the set of components required by the team if they are to rapidly iterate and release new models and solutions. These tools also allow them to control and govern the evolution of the models and to work in a systematic way as a team.

The team will either use a customer's MLOps setup or one that needs to be constructed. If there is an MLOps infrastructure in place, then it's important to verify that it's fit for your purposes. Alternatively, you need to determine what can be done (if anything) to bring it up to the standard that meets the team's needs. Questions to ask and answer when there is no MLOps at the customer include the following:

- Can required source code control systems accommodate the artifacts produced by the project? If not, are exceptions possible and agreed on?
- Is the data available in dev?

- Are there suitable servers for modeling work (GPUs, multicore systems) and enough memory?
- How does the dev system get to the test environment (with particular attention to the paths from nonstandard environments)?
- What testing is required to move from test to prod?
- What are the timelines for ordering or getting access to the infrastructure for all three delivery layers?
- Who approves the orders and expenditure on the infrastructure?
- Do any of the data systems require special access arrangements? Sometimes we can only access databases on the customer's premise or from a safe-listed laptop that's secured to prevent screenshots from being shared or other data-exporting tricks or workarounds from being used.

To determine if you have access to a fit for purpose working environment for the ML team Consider the issues below:

- Is there somewhere to host a model repository and feature store?
- Where can we host a tool to move files and artefacts between environments? For example, where can we run a Jenkins server?
- Where can we run data pipeline tools? For example, where can we host an Airflow server to run update and reformatting tasks?
- What effort is required to get these systems in place and who will undertake this?

If you are assured that there is an MLOps system in place, obtain a technical description and get it validated, if possible, by a hands-on data scientist. Ideally, this would be someone who is a member of the Modelling team for the project.

2.7.2 *Production architecture*

What's available in the development architecture informs and enables how you go about building models and developing them into a system. The production (prod) architecture, the IT kit that's in day-to-day use in the client, dictates the structure of the system that you are going to build.

When you've determined the properties and requirements for the models, a lot of work is required to create a detailed system architecture that can be implemented. At this stage, what's required is a high-level solution that could potentially be delivered as developed. To break that requirement up:

- We need to define the solution at a high level, meaning that we identify the components that will be responsible for the different functions in the system. The way that those components are used and how they interact is not defined in detail at this point.
- We can potentially deliver the solution, meaning that the components are available in the client's architecture, and the team and the client know how they can be commissioned and used.

The point of creating this design is that it demonstrates that there is a reasonable way to deliver the system. If there is a problem in creating this kind of high-level design because some of the components that are required are missing or the team doesn't have enough experience to use them, then this task has done its job. The fact that there is a gap that must be filled needs to be exposed now because it will be too late to fix it later in the project.

Returning to the smart building example, what are the system components that are required to provide a solution? The data from the sensors in the building need to flow into a database, and an execution environment needs to run a model to determine the control signals for the building. The signals need to invoke actions from the building's actuators, and information about the events and decisions in the system's life need to be presented to its users and owners to understand what's happening. The requirements (at a high level) are for:

- A messaging system that manages the flow of information from the sensors to the actuators.
- A database that holds the history of the sensor information and actuator instructions.
- An execution environment.
- A dashboard system.
- An authentication system (to manage user accounts).

The system architects for the building owners know what's currently in use. For example, they may have a pre-existing database and an authentication system that's used to manage all employees and access and entry to the building. In this example, the resulting architecture would be:

- MySQL for the database
- Tableau for the dashboard
- Active Directory for authentication

In this architecture, the messaging system is new. Then the questions that need to be asked are would the introduction of a messaging system like Apache Kafka be acceptable? What needs to be done to get Apache Kafka accepted and deployed to production? This work must be done by someone, but who is expected to do it, and when will it get done?

Summary

- A structured process to develop a project is necessary if you are going to successfully manage risk.
- It's important to understand how to manage the project and to comprehend the required project management infrastructure.
- ML projects have particular features that need to be captured as requirements.
- Particular attention needs to be paid to the data assets that will underpin the project, as well as getting a picture of what data is available.
- It's important to understand how the data will be accessed and what capability is available to manipulate and prepare it for use by ML.
- We need to understand specific requirements about the security and privacy of the data asset; this can introduce higher costs into the project.
- A well-understood and fit-for-purpose development infrastructure is needed, and the IT architecture that the project is going to be delivered into needs to be clear.
- Specific consideration to the corporate responsibility and ethical aspects of the project should be built in from the beginning.

Pre-project: From requirements to proposal

This chapter covers

- Creating a project hypothesis
- Generating an estimate for effort and time
- Doing the paperwork to get the project underway
- Completing your pre-sales checklist

In chapter 2, we covered the first half of the pre-project work. First, you set up the tools and infrastructure required to do the necessary work. Then, you undertook some tasks to gather the requirements for the project, emphasizing on the ML-specific issues that are the focus of the project. In particular, you looked at the data set for the project and found out how hard or easy it will be for the team to get it. You also documented the data-specific issues of security and privacy and understand what the key ethical and social concerns are for this project.

These requirements now need to be synthesized into a statement of what is going to happen, what the problems are with that intent, and how much it's going to cost. Once this is in hand, your organization and the client's business can make a rational decision about whether to plunge forward with the project. This is the work that we will cover in this chapter.

3.1 *Build a project hypothesis*

The project hypothesis states the purpose of the project and the major challenges to overcome. Continuing from the pre-sales backlog in chapter 2, let's look at ticket PS10. This is the work that needs to be done to understand the problem that is at the core of the project.

Project hypothesis ticket: PS10

- Understand the business problem: use a consensus to build a project hypothesis, validated with the customer and the delivery teams. Ensure that this is clearly communicated and documented in any contractual agreement.

One feature of an ML project is that the ML part is rarely articulated clearly by the business, and where it is articulated clearly, it is often unrealistic or unlikely to create much value. It's hard to imagine how an ML system solves a problem if you don't know how the specific ML algorithms work. For now, in our project, we want to:

- Document the challenges and benefits articulated by the shareholders.
- Reflect on the data, the system architecture, and the nonfunctional constraints.
- Document potential outcomes in light of what's known.
- Provide feedback to the stakeholders to build a consensus for the project.

It's easy to imagine the usefulness of a magic box that solves any problem. This leads to giant-sized gaps in our thinking that underpins ML project descriptions, sometimes as bald as an assertion that ML fixes whatever needs fixing. It also leads to the problem of getting stakeholders to buy into and understand any realistic project that you and your team come up with. Sometimes, reality just isn't as sexy as we'd like. Perhaps this will change in the future as ML becomes more mainstream, but the diversity and complexity of ML makes this reality a bit doubtful. Afterall, Microsoft Excel has been mainstream for 20 or more years, and yet, statisticians are still needed to design trials and experiments and to produce a meaningful analysis of the results.

You and your team need to identify and then articulate (compellingly) a concept that capitalizes on the available data to create value for the business; it also must have sufficient value to justify the investment. You can use the work that you've done so far to brief yourself, trusted collaborators, or potential team members on the problems and challenges of the project.

There are two classes of requirements that you need to capture:

- *Functional requirements:* The processes that the system needs to execute. A functional requirement describes a set of inputs and the required output. The process that transforms the input to an output is what the team will need to build. For example, Input = {user profile, budget, date} Output ={book recommendation_1, book_recommendation_2, . . . , book_recommendation_n}.

- *Nonfunctional requirements:* The constraints on how the functional requirements must behave. For example, the recommendation must cost less than $0.0001, the recommendation must be produced in less than 200ms.

The requirements analysis should produce a list of challenges and business opportunities. These are the things that could improve the client's business, but some of these may be unfeasible or impractical. So, the list needs to be validated in light of all the findings about the data, project setup, and security that you've made since you captured them.

If you do get to a list of viable concepts, then put some more detail into the description of those. Agile projects use systems stories (how the concept will be delivered) and user stories (who will use and be impacted by the project). At this stage, these activities are for validation: are there viable paths to implementation and are there mechanisms that will allow the solution to have an impact and a business effect? Later, if the project runs, you will have the funding and resources to dive deeper into this and flesh out these stories in detail. By writing the user stories now, you're hoping to:

- Identify and document key functionality and requirements.
- Identify items that could be part of the acceptance criteria for the project.
- Establish important problems and harms that must be avoided.
- Establish corner cases that would make the system irrelevant or unworkable.

You should develop user stories for as many relevant stakeholders as possible (business sponsors, employees/users, customers/affected persons) and cover three situations that reveal important requirements for the ML system: the first time the system is used or touches the stakeholder, normal use, and when the system stops being used. For your project, it is important to identify and describe the ML model that the user invokes in each of these stories. That's the model that will have to be built! Consider:

- What kind of model is it?
- What data is needed to create it?
- What data is needed to run it?

Additionally, each story must describe what the model will do for a particular stakeholder in this particular story. This should reveal at a high level the commonalities and differences among the needs of each stakeholder, the range of models that are required, and the set of requirements for each.

Project hypothesis ticket: PS11

- Undertake project diligence. Will the stakeholders be available? Is the data available and manageable? What team members are available and what skills do they have?

Once this is done, frame the concept in terms of a hypothesis (for example, we will test that we can use the data in Table XYZ to create a model that predicts customer churn) and an investigation (for example, we will investigate the mechanism by which that model can be used in the context of the business's operations). This framing moves the idea of the project from a concept that has to be constructed to a set of actions that need to be taken: test, create, model, investigate, use. Qualify the resulting concepts by checking for:

- *Technical feasibility:* How risky, new, and difficult is this project for your team? Obviously, if they have done something similar before and are familiar with the core technology, then the risk is lower.
  Often, however, some aspect of the project will be novel to the team. It's important to identify this, to understand how large a gap it represents, and to determine what mitigations are possible if it is substantial. Also, consider if the customer's infrastructure can cope with the (likely) nonfunctional demands of the solution.

- *A plausible business case:* It's unlikely that you will have sufficient access and insight to build a detailed case; the customer needs to develop this to get funding. However, understanding the scale of savings, revenue gains, improvement to quality of life, and so on, the mechanism that's enabled by the project gives you a powerful compass with which to steer the future outcome.

- *Commercial feasibility:* Is funding available to pay for all the work required to do the entire project? This is a distinct consideration versus the business case requirement. A project can offer amazing value for the money, but if the money to pay for it is not available, then the project won't happen.

Other things to consider when framing include:

- Which strategic business priorities of the customer are addressed by the concept (refer to your organizational model if you have that)?
- Can the project be delivered with the data resources that are described by the customer?
- Is there a way for the customers to use the outcomes effectively?

Figure 3.1 shows how these elements interact to create a functional project. As the figure shows, business priority and business case unlock sufficient funding. Normally, organizations have long lists of good business cases that aren't funded because they only use the monies for better and more strategically aligned projects. Often, just the case alone is not enough to agree on the project and get it running. If the money is there, you need to ensure that the technical means to execute the project are in place and the data resources will support it. Finally, although you have a perfectly viable and valuable system ready to go, the question now becomes can it be used? That is to say, can (or will) the folks who are supposed to make use of the outcome actually make use of it? Is the solution useful and feasible?

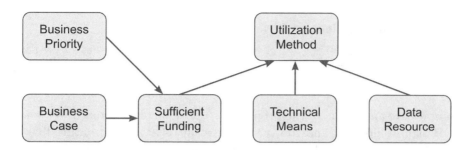

Figure 3.1 The project's drivers (Business Priority and Business Case), the supporting components (Sufficient Funding, Technical Means, and Data Resource), and enablers (Utilization Method).

If all the elements in figure 3.1 are in place, then you can write and communicate a workable project hypothesis. There is an element of iteration in this process, coupled with understanding, as you probe and clarify the project's value and the willingness of the customer to fund it. Hopefully, the structure you develop allows all the stakeholders to verify that there's a project worth doing.

Of course, you may find no workable concept for this project. Some part of figure 3.1 may prove to be elusive, but it's good that you see this now. In any case, looking at the project in this way means that you have used a structured and professional process to determine whether the risk of doing the project and the potential benefits of the project are appropriate to the funding that's required.

3.2   Create an estimate

It's great to have a clear project definition, but unless that definition can be turned into an estimate, it's about as useful as a teapot made of wax. Tickets PS12, PS13, and PS14 define tasks that help us move from definition to estimate.

Estimate-building ticket: PS12

- Create an estimate of the work for a model project, delivering on the required project hypothesis, taking into account the available team and the scale of the work that is needed.
- Ensure that all project risks are accounted for in your estimate.

Estimate-building ticket: PS13

- Create and socialize team design and resourcing.

Estimate-building ticket: PS14

- Run a review meeting and go through a checklist to ensure that the pre-sales process is properly completed.

You now have an outline of the project concept, some data about how a top-level system design would look, and you've systematically reviewed it to ensure that there are no known legal or ethical constraints. You've documented these things, and so the next task is to transform this outline into a project description that captures what will need to be done, by whom, and when to deliver. The fact is that your team will adapt to the realities of the project as it unfolds. What you are creating here is a credible envelop of resources and money to work with to get a viable result.

3.2.1   *Time and effort estimates*

All the prep and investigation so far hasn't produced an estimate. There are two actions to take in moving from the project structure that you've designed to an estimate of time and cost:

- Use the backlog lists for each chapter in this book to create a task list for your project as a starting point. You'll discover the job's content as the project evolves. You can freely add and delete tasks based on requirements, but if you are looking for a starting point, then this is it.
- If the people who are going to do the work build the estimate with you, they will own the plan from the start. Bring your team to the table to create the estimate. Challenge them to drill down to the work that needs to be done to deliver all the required tasks. Let them expose the time that needs to be spent on mechanical and administrative tasks, in addition to the high-profile technical work.

Although there is discovery to be done, we now have a grip on the nonfunctional and system side of the challenges we face. Share and clarify these with the people estimating the effort required for each task in the project. Building models that must meet extensive and demanding nonfunctional requirements, as well as performing functionally, is difficult. User interfaces that are going to serve thousands of users are much harder and more expensive than user interfaces that serve only a few users. Be clear about any experts that you will need to engage with about this process. Additionally:

- Ensure that you capture requirements for materials. For example, what are your needs for compute consumption? Will you need special hardware such as headsets, phones, sensors, or top-of-the-line laptops or displays (required by specialist developers)?
- Capture special requirements and costs for model training or data processing. It's easy for a team to assume that access to a powerful GPU will be inexpensive, but the discovery that they will need to consume hundreds of hours on a GPU,

which is very expensive, is problematic. Another easy-to-miss cost is importing and exporting data to and from cloud infrastructures, which are chargeable and expensive, but with ML projects, this may need to happen repeatedly and at scale.

As well as creating a task list or project backlog, which is subject to ongoing refinement as the project evolves, you need to estimate the scale of work for each of the backlog items. This can be done using *t-shirt sizing*. This is a simple way of getting an overall estimate for a portfolio of tasks. (It's called t-shirting because the tasks' efforts are allocated measures in terms of small, medium, large, and XL only, no more granularity than that.) Generally, those who do this can agree about these categories without too much debate, and an overall scale for the project soon emerges.

There are two ways to use t-shirt sizing. First, when the task sizes are agreed on, you can group the tasks in each size category and ask the team for an estimate in person days for each of the tasks in each category. For example, the team may look at all the tasks that they have nominated as small and agree that these will likely take one person, one day to deliver. Sometimes, this leads to some tasks being shuffled about, but that's OK. This allows you to take all the tasks in each category, then all the categories, and sum them up to give you an estimate of effort.

The second use for t-shirt sizing is to record how long the tasks that need to be done actually take, then use this information to determine how reliable the effort estimate is as the project unfolds. If the small tasks were thought to take a single day but start to consistently take more, then your estimate is wrong, and you need to do some urgent work to determine whether the project is in trouble.

Having developed an overview of the jobs to do in the project and the scale of the work required to do each of them, the next thing to consider is who will be doing all that work? Let's look at the answer to that question next.

3.2.2 Team design for ML projects

For an ML project, the required team dictates the largest part of the cost, with rare projects having a substantial cost, but in general, the team's time will be the largest part of the project's cost. This makes understanding the team design (who is going to deliver the work?) critical if you are going to accurately estimate how much the project will cost your organization or, if applicable, how much should be charged.

To do the actual resourcing work from the project roadmap, you need to be systematic and ensure that every task has an allocated resource that covers the scale of the anticipated challenge. It's difficult-to-impossible to do this accurately, but breaking the project into a set of tasks and estimating each one at a time makes it more tractable. A good practice is to do this in a group, perhaps bringing in the people who are working with you on the pre-project process or calling on the senior resources to work on the project itself. Essentially, you want to determine what kind of person will be able to deliver the task identified and the amount of time that they will require to do that. To understand who can be expected to deliver each task, it's good to know the types of people who may be available for the project.

In terms of specialist roles, there are four that have emerged from the intersections of the three drivers of complexity in an ML project (figure 3.2). In chapter 1, figure 1.2 makes the point that ML project complexity is driven by the need for specialists to overcome challenges from data, modelling, and domain alignment.

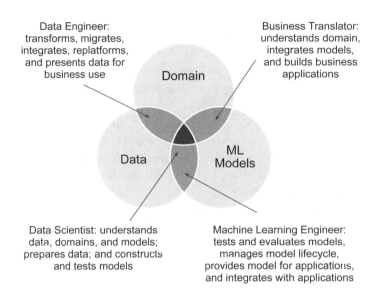

Figure 3.2   Team roles created by the three drivers of complexity in ML projects

Figure 3.2 also shows some of the roles that work across these areas of difficulty. The four roles are:

- *Business translators:* This is a trendy way of talking about business analysts and software engineers who have insights into ML systems and specialize in bridging the gap between the domain and the ML specialists.

  The idea of a business translator is compelling to IT leaders because it addresses some of the common complaints about ML specialists and teams being removed from reality. In some ways, in 2022, it's still unclear how a business translator contributes effectively to an ML project, especially as ML engineers and data scientists may have strong views themselves. However, someone who is interested in working closely with users and stakeholders to gather and develop insights for the team leader can be a lifesaver in a busy project.

  In some teams, this role is largely assumed by a client acting as the product owner (a description of this requirement follows). In other cases, the product owner's time is too valuable for detailed business investigations, and you will need to bring in a specialist for this role.

- *Data engineers:* These are specialists at getting, moving, mobilizing, and manipulating resources. They bring knowledge about platforms, tooling, programming languages, security, costs, and efficiency.

  Data engineers can enable your team to come to grips with awkward data resources. They may have some insight into the structures and properties of the data to be manipulated and some knowledge of the business uses of the data, due to working on previous projects in the organization, for instance. In many cases, however, they will be purely technical contributors, leaning on the business translators or product owner to understand what is in the data store.

- *Machine learning (ML) engineers:* These individuals work with the models that the project produces. They create and use the infrastructures that store, version, and manage the models, but they also undertake tasks such as setting up testing systems and running evaluations. Another important task for an ML engineer is to implement effective model-serving mechanisms to run a model over a scenario to produce a result. Being able to do this with resilience, low latency, high throughput, or low cost can be a real feat, so this is a great skill to have in any team.

  When models are embedded in an effective serving infrastructure, the ML engineers often work to integrate resulting subsystems with business applications to unlock value. This is where they overlap with and interact with the business translators.

- *Data scientists:* The people in the middle who specialize in creating models. They also understand the means to condition the data needed for valid modeling and test and evaluate models to determine their effectiveness.

You may also have people who aren't focused on ML projects available as resources. These folks can help the team as well:

- *Software engineers:* Programmers who have developed the specific skills required to work in teams to produce reliable and manageable software. Developers are generally more individualistic programmers who work more as solo problem-solvers and troubleshooters. Take care in enlisting these resources because some have a fuzzy grasp of what a software engineer or a developer is, so these terms are often used interchangeably.

- *DevOps engineers:* Specialists in setting up and administering software development infrastructures. Typically, they work in large projects where the development infrastructure is a big overhead. Sometimes ML engineers have DevOps engineering skills and backgrounds, so they may be able to cover these requirements. Bringing in a DevOps engineer can take up some of the ground that a ML engineer would cover.

- *Cloud engineers:* Specialists in setting up and managing cloud infrastructures such as private networks and IAM (Identity and Access Management) configurations. They are also often skilled in using cloud-managed service components such as data warehouses. You can often use these folks to support data scientists if a data engineering resource is unavailable.

- *Delivery managers:* People that can facilitate and support the management of a project by organizing and running meetings, talking with stakeholders, creating reports, and managing the flow of documentation.

- *UX engineers:* Specialists who develop user interfaces and interaction designs, usually by talking with the systems users and understanding the impact on them.

- *Test and QA engineers:* Specialists in creating and running the testing systems that will allow your system to get signed off and to enter production. In an ML project, there is extensive testing of the models to evaluate their performance (covered in detail in chapters 7 and 8). As well as the ML engineers and data scientists working on model testing, there may also be a need for the system to be tested from a user or platform perspective.

To be clear, the roles will often be shared by a number of team members or by a single team member. It's also fair to say that there are other takes on the skill matrix and distribution for each of the roles identified. For example, some organizations see data engineers as generalists working through the lifecycle of an ML project, sometimes supporting data scientists or ML engineers. This concept is not wrong or worse than the previous breakdown; it's just different and more appropriate for some organizations.

Another thing that determines the team members is who is available. It's rare for a project manager to find that they can put together the perfect team for the job. You must be ready and able to cut your cloth to suit your pocket. Here's some tips for handling this challenge:

- *Fit the big pieces first:* It's a cliché, but if you focus on the most important elements of the project and team first, then you can improvise around the more peripheral activities and roles.

- *Look for the right behaviors in preference to achievements:* Team members who share skills and insights and mentor colleagues are especially valuable. Also of high value are team members who can think critically and constructively and so contribute to the group's creative problem-solving.

- *Generalists are often more useful than specialists.* Especially in small teams, people with specialist skills who are also willing and able to work as generalists when there is a need are valuable resources. These are the fabled T-shaped people, as opposed to the I-shaped folks who have only a narrow and deep specialism.

  More generalist-leaning people can contribute across the whole of the project rather than dropping in for a couple of weeks and then leaving. Often, people working on a project from "soup to nuts" tend to be more motivational. The other advantage is that people who stick with the project know what's going on; there's much less effort in briefing people and so on.

  A team that works together to develop an in-depth understanding of the ins and outs of a particular challenge can end up delivering more quickly with a higher quality overall. The big caveat here is that if specialist skills are required for the project, expert contributors are not only useful they are essential. Typically, this is the case in larger and more complex projects. Luckily, these projects (and the organizations that sustain them) can afford to engage the specialists required.

- *Look for development opportunities for your team:* By helping people acquire skills and experience, you are ensuring future value. They'll want to work with you again, and when used, the more senior folks on the team will benefit from the mentoring experience as well. On the other hand, you can only carry so much of this before the team's productivity suffers.

Figure 3.3 shows how a team might evolve over a project as skill requirements change, new team members join, and folks who have made their contribution leave. For example, a short assignment for a cloud engineer in sprint 1 (figure 3.3) might be problematic. The engineer might resent being dropped into the project to clear up a few issues, or they might enjoy the quick assignment between longer-term jobs.

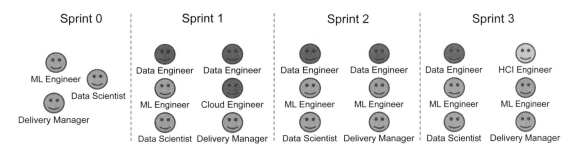

Figure 3.3 Team evolution over project sprints

In the figure, the HCI (Human-computer interaction) engineer, who can be called a UX engineer, is shown only in sprint 3. In this case, a two-week assignment might work well for that individual because it's an opportunity to really add value to a showcase project. On the other hand, this might be problematic if the HCI engineer lacks the project context to do what a proper job. These issues are sometimes hard to avoid. Really, all that you can do is to check in with the people concerned and try your best to make the assignments work for everyone.

When you have a good idea of the team structure, it is probably a good idea to set up some pre-project team orientation meetings. This allows the team to understand what will be expected of them individually and to figure out who they will be working with. Also, check that the resources will be available at the time that the task is required. Then aggregate the task and allocations to create an agile team for each of the sprints in the project.

A large core of the project team should remain stable throughout the duration of the project, but as discussed, some people may drop in and out to provide the required expertise and delivery muscle. To summarize, the process is:

1 Create a task list using the set of tasks outlined in the backlogs in the book and supplement and elaborate on them with the project team where you can.

2 Identify what roles and specialisms will be required to deliver each of the tasks.

3 Estimate the effort required for each task.

4 Aggregate the effort and determine how much commitment will be required per role.

5 Create a role-resourcing plan that most closely approximates the required effort.

6 Identify a potential team design that meets the role-resourcing plan.

7 Determine the overall cost from the commitment costs of the team required.

In addition to all of these considerations, it's important to understand that the client needs to support the project as well. They will have to provide knowledge and IT support, and you need to know who (from the customer) will act as the product owner. At this stage, it's often not possible to book people from the client into your project and reserve their time; nothing is agreed yet, but having some identified candidates is reassuring. Typically, you will need to identify:

- *A product owner:* The customer representative who can provide feedback and input that allows the team to focus effort and effectively react to issues and discoveries that aligns with the customer's needs.
- *A technical/admin troubleshooter:* The person who can help the team overcome any administrative roadblocks that they encounter. An internal representative typically knows better how to deal with issues inside their organization and will be in a better position to communicate with the customer's infrastructure and administration.

A final point on the team: people that you are expecting to bring into the team may have conflicts (holidays booked or other events) that prevent them from participating in the project. If someone you think might join your team but is about to retire or to move to another organization, then that resource option just isn't going to work!

Once a team is identified and the full task list is in hand, you can review the project roadmap that you have created and check for potential optimizations or problems. To optimize, run tasks in parallel and make sure that high-value resources are focused on high-value productive work. Problems that can be identified at this stage are typically things such as a task that needs to be completed before unlocking the project, but it is dependent on other tasks that are risky.

This is an agile project, and we won't know half of the problems and glitches that are going to come up. Nevertheless, it's good to look as far as you can through the unknowns at this stage to try and avoid obvious pitfalls.

3.2.3   *Project risks*

Having created the estimate for resources, it's important to review the risk register. Have you accounted for the likely cost of mitigating and resolving the risks that the project faces? If not, then ensure that you add an appropriate level of effort and elasticity to the estimate to deal with these. For example:

- Identify potential mitigations or workarounds. Mitigations that were previously used successfully have a high value; mitigations that are new have a low value.
- Estimate the cost of mitigation and include that cost (and the confidence level of resolving that issue) in the budget. Add low-confidence estimates with a high-risk premium (typically 100%). For example, if the low confidence mitigation is estimated at $500, then enter it as a $1,000 cost to the project. Add high-confidence mitigations with a 30% premium. For example, a $500 mitigation would be added as $650.

  Note the mitigation price is a chargeable item; the amount a customer would be expected to pay for work like this rather than as a cost to your organization. The risk premium is extra, plus the margin that your organization adds to allow it to operate as a successful business.
- Conduct a review to ensure that there are no risks with high impact (likely to lead to a project failure and loss of revenue) and low-value mitigations (no clear path to resolution).
- Have an officer of your organization (someone who is accountable in case of project failure) sign off on the budget and confirm that they accept the risk you are proposing. It's your job to ensure they are aware of and understand the risks that the organization is signing up for.

Document this process and share the documentation with the people who sign off on the risks. For example, send an email after a sign-off meeting that contains the presentation that you use to brief everyone. When the ML project runs (detailed in the rest of the book), you may want to run a review-and-update meeting with the project stakeholders every week to discuss and share the risk register.

Some risks are unmanageable. The fact is that if the data isn't there or the data isn't in a usable state due to quality or availability issues, then it will not be possible to develop useful models from it. If you are unable to inspect the data or clearly establish how the models will be developed or implemented into a useful system, then you can't underwrite the estimate. If that is the case, then further discovery needs to be done and paid for either by your organization or by the client, depending on the context. Be clear and ensure that you frame this type of project as an experiment or an investigation. Although legal provision that covers you technically should be set forth in the contract that your organization strikes, it's important that you communicate clearly with the customer.

3.3   *Pre-sales/pre-project administration*

> **Pre-project administration ticket: PS15**
> - Ensure all appropriate documents are in place:
>   - Master service agreement
>   - Statement of work
>   - Nondisclosure agreement and other formal documents as required by the project

In some projects, formal contracts are required. These include:

- *A master service agreement (MSA):* Provides for the mechanisms of payment and liability between your organization and the customer and governs the entire relationship. Many projects are covered by one master service agreement.
- *A statement of work:* Defines the effort and activity required to deliver the project and provides the legal agreement about what is going to be delivered. Importantly, it also specifies what reimbursement should get paid and when.
- *Nondisclosure (NDAs), confidentiality, and intellectual property agreements:* Depends on the MSA and in which jurisdiction you are operating.

Always hand over the development of these documents to those who are legally qualified and organizationally responsible. Never be tempted to do any of this yourself or to simply go along with what the customer suggests. In the end, it always saves time (and improves the quality and outcome of the project) if you involve the legal team early on in discussions. They will likely raise uncomfortable objections and impose annoying requirements on the interactions (for example, prohibiting ongoing work until agreements are in place), but the consequence of bringing them in to undo the damage that results from not doing this are far more impactful.

When you've created a well-founded agreement and signed off properly (often, the requirement might be that the regional CTO and the COO both sign) and it is approved and signed by the customer, work on the project is ready to start. Before you are ready to get the signatures, though, it's helpful and reassuring to go through a checklist to make sure that nothing is left out.

3.4   *Pre-project/pre-sales checklist*

Having worked through the items previously listed and described, you should be in a position to complete the pre-project/pre-sales checklist that follows. This list (table 3.1) lets you check each of the items to verify that there is adequate evidence that the task is properly completed.

Table 3.1   Pre-project/pre-sales checklist

Ticket #	Item	Notes
PP1.0	Project document repository	A space, folder, or directory on a document storage system is set up specifically for this work and all documents are copied there for reference.
		Documents produced during the pre-project phase have been stored, and there are no omissions.
		Everyone can retrieve documents.
		The repository is compliant with data retention and information security policies.
PP1.1	Risk register	A risk register is available in the repository.
		All who are authorized to access it can view the current set of risks.
		The history of retired risks and evidence for them being retired is accessible.
		The final register was reviewed with the project's stakeholders/managers/bosses, and you have ensured that the review is recorded with evidence, showing the risks as documented.
PP1.2	Project hypothesis	Has the purpose of the project been clearly described and framed as a hypothesis or an investigation?
		Is there a plausible business case that is understood by the delivery team?
		Is the hypothesis clearly understood by the team, recorded in any project statement, and are all the stakeholders aware of it and signed off on it?
PP1.3	Diligence complete	Ensure that the following are completed and available in the repository:
		Organizational map detailing stakeholders, end users, objectives, and relationships.
		Data access information including where, what, and how it can be accessed.
		Top-level solution and customer/expected deployment architectures containing the likely timetables for provision and known requirements/issues.
		Any data sample obtained and any evaluation or investigation that was done on it.
		Data protection, privacy, and ethical requirements documents that are used to qualify a lawful and ethical route to delivery.
P1.4	Top-level delivery plan	The list of high-level tasks to be completed, possibly based on the project structure in this book but customized for the actual project to be undertaken.
		Estimates of how much effort is required to complete these tasks.
		The team required and whether they are available.
PP1.5	Estimate	An estimate for the time and materials: cost of delivery plus the effort required to resolve or mitigate known risks and the appropriate premiums given those risks.
PP1.6	Presales administration	All NDAs, master service agreements, and statement of work are in place.
		All documents are validated and agreed on by the legal team.
		Documents are ready for authorized signatures (COO, etc.).

Go through this checklist with your team and make sure that they and you agree that the items are complete. One trick is to not chair this meeting yourself, but instead, get a relatively junior person from the team to host it. (Probably not the most junior as that's a bit unfair, but someone who the team respects and will benefit from the experience of running some meetings.) By getting them to set up the meeting and run it, you avoid the trap of everyone thinking that they should just agree. From your perspective, you want to know if something has been overlooked, now, before it's too late and while you can still (hopefully) fix things.

How does the whole pre-project process outlined in chapters 2 and 3 play out in practice? The next section provides a narrative that describes what might happen in real life. This is the first of the vignettes about a project for The Bike Shop, which is meant to help illustrate how the approaches in this book can be applied in practice.

3.5　*The Bike Shop pre-sales*

The (fictional) consultancy sales team identifies an RFI (request for information) opportunity at The Bike Shop (a fictional manufacturing and retail company). The collection of SaaS and on-premise packages that run the business operation require significant capital investment due to license renewals and the need for new hardware to replace the current.

By moving to a recurrent operational expenditure (OpEx) model, away from a big bang capital expenditure (CapEx) investment model, the company can free funds to invest in new logistics facilities and to renew and upgrade the company's brand and stores. To do this, The Bike Shop wants to move to a cloud-based solution.

One of the frustrations for The Bike Shop's management is that they cannot use the current systems to create a single overview of the state of the business and to generate business intelligence from that overview. After an informal discussion, you get pulled in to work on the pre-sales opportunity.

The initial RFI for The Bike Shop project does not include any details about the required application. In one of the meetings for the customers' RFI process, your team asks about it, and it's revealed that the business's key priority is to reduce spending to free up money to improve their old-fashioned distribution system. They hope to do this by increasing customer retention. The logic is that by keeping their customers longer and getting them to spend more money, they won't have to develop new markets and bring in new customers to the business.

This prompts you to suggest that it might be possible to use The Bike Shop's data to identify which customers are at a high risk of churning. Additionally, you may be able to suggest interventions that might prevent the customers from defecting. This is a standard sort of application that many other companies use. In The Bike Shop's case, their fragmented IT real estate has prevented them from being able to harness their data to do anything like that.

Later, in the discussion, the prospective customer notes that one of the reasons for the new logistics system is that the company often finds it hard to take advantage of growth and manage demand from their customers. To fulfill growth requirements, the business must hold a large inventory of components. Having too many components on hand is expensive but having too few means losing revenue. You suggest that it may be possible to make some predictions about demand, based on The Bike Shop's historical and open-source data that reveals economic and social trends. The customers seem excited by the possibilities, and after the call finishes, you work on a proposal and estimate as part of your response to the RFI.

You set up a document repository using your organization's standard tool (in this case, Confluence), and you create a backlog in your organization's Jira. The first document that you create is the project risk register. Table 3.2 shows an example of a completed register (obviously, when it's first created, it's empty).

Table 3.2   The risk register for The Bike Shop ML project

Risk ID	Description	Status	Owner
TBS1	Unavailable open-source weather/economy data of high quality	Open	You
TBS2	Insufficient customer behavior history due to data cleanse	Open	You
TBS3	Unavailable data science resource	Open	You

The next item in the pre-sales backlog is to find out more about your customers by doing some organizational modelling. First, you ask the RFI project team if they have an org chart for customer captures, and, indeed, they do. Figure 3.4 shows this chart, which you capture and file in your repository for reference.

There are two other organizational questions you have in mind as well: first, who are the stakeholders and customers for this project, and second, who are the end users? Talking to other members of the RFI team, you identify the CIO, Karima Shar, as the Director of Business Intelligence. This is the likely key stakeholder. You contact the RFI team's business manager, ask to include an item on the agenda for the next RFI update meeting with the customers, and request a meeting with Karima to discuss the potential project.

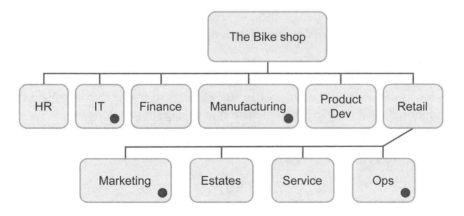

Figure 3.4   The Bike Shop's organizational chart

In the meeting with Karima, you reveal the concept for the work and ask where this functionality would be consumed in the business. Karima is able to tell you that the service team in The Bike Shop's Retail Division uses the customer churn information and that the manufacturing group consumes the inventory prediction functionality that you have described. She seems excited about the possibility and sees a lot of potential in incorporating workstreams within the overall program to migrate The Bike Shop's data to the cloud and uplift their capability.

At this point, Karima can't share any data with you but seems confident that it is available in one of the SAP data warehouses (opdis2), which the CIO runs for the business. Karima knows that some of the data personally identifies customers but don't have any out-of-the-ordinary security or privacy concerns about it. Furthermore, she has no idea what kind of a system architecture The Bike Shop would prefer to develop and deliver the proposed system.

These concepts are written into the background element of the statement of work to define the overall challenges that your team will work on. You write them in the form of a hypothesis:

- *Challenge 1:* The project will verify that it is possible to use The Bike Shop's opdis2 database and other assets to build a customer churn prediction system and will measure the performance of the system in terms of the recall and precision of the predictions made.

- *Challenge 2:* The project will verify that it is possible to use The Bike Shop's opdis2 database and other assets to build a demand prediction system and measure the performance of the system in terms of recall and precision of the predictions made.

- *Challenge 3:* You investigate an implementation that uses the data and dataflows migrated from opdis2 to a new cloud platform to provide timely, actionable information to the users in Manufacturing and Retail Service. This enables them to optimize their business decisions with regard to stock, supply, and customer interaction.

- *Challenge 4:* If challenges 1-3 are completed to the customer's satisfaction, you will implement and deliver a system that provides the required functionality.

A number of assumptions were made and raised in the discussion with the customer's representatives. You realize that if these are not documented in the statement of work, significant disputes may arise later in the project, so you create a project hypothesis document, file it, complete the ticket, and get a cup of tea:

- *Assumption 1:* Database and dataflow migration to the cloud is on track and passes its project milestones and gates.

- *Assumption 2:* You and your team can access opdis2 and other required data assets to extract the data to an approved development environment, where you have accounts and appropriate authorizations.
- *Assumption 3:* The team blends this data with open-source data in the development environment.
- *Assumption 4:* You use the application environments to make available testing and production data.
- *Assumption 5:* You need access to business experts at The Bike Shop to help clarify and improve the nature of the predictions that you make.

The next step is to review the ethics and CSR issues associated with The Bike Shop project. Now, time and money are short, so you differ about how much you should do on this, but you remember reading the following in some data protection training manual:

> *Where a type of processing, in particular using new technologies and taking into account the nature, scope, context, and purposes of the processing, is likely to result in a high risk to the rights and freedoms of natural persons, the controller shall, prior to the processing, carry out an assessment of the impact of the envisaged processing operations on the protection of personal data. A single assessment may address a set of similar processing operations that present similar high risks.*

ML technologies might not be seen as *new* by technologists, but at the time this project is being done, they are new to the vast majority of everyday people. The question then is about risk: is this a high-risk project for the subjects? Again, you consult the ICO's site and note the list of factors that indicate that this project might be high risk:

- Evaluation or scoring ✓
- Automated decision-making with a legal or similar significant effect
- Systematic monitoring ✓
- Sensitive data or data of a highly personal nature
- Data processed on a large scale ✓
- Matching or combining data sets ✓
- Data concerning vulnerable data subjects
- Innovative use or applying new technological or organizational solutions ✓
- Preventing data subjects from exercising a right or using a service or contract

You check through the items; it's clear that you will be evaluating and scoring customers to see if they are likely to stop buying from The Bike Shop. The intent, though, is not to use this to make automated decisions but to pass the information to the people who will use it in their own findings. What you are doing is systematic. All customers could be checked, but the data isn't personal; after all, having a bike isn't like having a religion.

You think that this will take large-scale processing because there are millions of customers. The subjects may be vulnerable, but what you are doing isn't relevant to their vulnerability. The technology is innovative, but you are not planning to prevent people from doing anything or using The Bike Shop's facilities.

It's probably worth creating a Data Protection Impact Assessment (DPIA), which is a way of understanding how the use of the data in the project might impact individuals. The UK Information Commissioner's Office recommends completing a DPIA to help you and the team understand the risks that you are running with this data [1].

First, you consider the nature, scope, context, and purpose of the data, and you find that it is being used for an internal process. It remains under the control of The Bike Shop. The retention and security of the data won't change. The main issue is that this is novel processing: in terms of scope, this is a record of purchasing behavior versus customer demographic information. The context is that these are customers who have a bank account or credit card, so they are not children, and their purpose is legitimate. The Bike Shop's business is to sell bikes, and that's why the customers have a relationship with the company. However, do the customers know that their data might be used to make this kind of model? Have they consented to this?

You survey the list of risks that might accrue to the individual (e.g., inability to exercise rights, restricted access services, loss of control, etc.) and determine that the only potential challenge might be a possibility of financial loss because the decisions from the data might be used to create special offers that include some customers but exclude others. You write up your initial assessment and note three conclusions:

- There is a risk that customers might not have given permission to use the data gathered so far in this way.
- The conclusions shouldn't be used to create exclusive offers.
- The initial DPIA that you have must be revisited when the project is more mature.

At this point, there is a hiatus. In this process for getting work, feedback to the RFI have to be made and responded to and so you are asked to write a few paragraphs for use in the response document, which you duly do. While you're waiting for the corporate wheels to grind over the proposal, you turn to some other work that has been gathering dust. This doesn't last long, though.

A few weeks later, you are called to a meeting and told that The Bike Shop wants your organization to make a formal proposal for a migration and data value. (Apparently, there are no other bidders at this stage, and your contribution has really energized the management of The Bike Shop to accelerate their plans and push forward with the project.) What's needed now is more flesh on the bones of what can be done and the material to draw up a formal bid for the work. You are assigned to the bid team to work on this.

Things have changed somewhat in terms of what you can do because now there are NDAs and confidentiality agreements in place between your organization and The Bike Shop, and they are committed to getting this project up and running. The questions facing you and your team now is who would work on the project if it's undertaken, and what would the work entail at a high level? In the past, you have worked with a handful of talented data scientists and ML engineers in your organization, so you consult the assignments database on your intranet and see that one of them, Rob, is currently benched. You go to the Bid Response manager and ask if you can book some of Rob's time to build a resource and project plan, and this is agreed.

You brief Rob on the project and go over the information obtained so far. Working with the templates in this book, you specify a plan that covers:

- Sprint 0 to get the project up and running. This is clear in terms of scale and scope and something that is similar from project to project, so you agree that the tasks will require three people for two weeks, probably Rob, an infrastructure engineer, and yourself.
- Sprint 1 to build the data pipelines and explore the data set in detail.
- Sprint 2 to build the models, evaluate and select the modeling approach, and complete the final models for use.
- Sprint 3 to integrate the models into an application.

Rob is clear that you need to get a better look at the data before being more concrete about what could be done with the modelling and how long the data prep and modelling phases would take. You contact Karima and ask if, now that you are preparing a bid, she could extract some data from opdis2 that shows both the way that inventory levels and how the customer histories are stored. It turns out that now that The Bike Shop is energized about the project, Karima is all too happy to arrange this. Obviously, the customer information will be anonymized.

In the meantime, Rob and you ask Karima to arrange a meeting with the potential users in Manufacturing and Retail Service to see how the model results would be consumed. Karima has settled on the idea that the models will produce information in a dashboard for the users, and at the meeting, you present some conceptual ideas about what kind of dashboard would be useful. The Manufacturing team conforms to an engineering stereotype in asking for tabular data with downloads for spreadsheets, whereas the Retail Service group wants the data to be "easier to understand."

When the data samples arrive, things look more complex than you and Rob had hoped. It seems that the data is stored in many tables that record different types of transactions and that getting a picture of what the status of the inventory or customers is on a particular day requires a lot of data wrangling and manipulation. Also, there are approximately 30 million lines in the database, representing five years of business transactions, created from two sources. Two years ago, a project to resolve data quality issues in the transaction management system was completed, so this means that there is a legacy data store containing three years of noisy data and a clean data source containing the last two years of records.

In terms of the system architecture, it looks like this will be a greenfield cloud engagement. With Rob's help, you can specify a dev/test/prod setup, and you take it to the cloud engineers in the bid team for review. Once done, you and Rob have what's needed to complete an estimate and top-level plan. Rob suggests bringing in a few people whom he has worked with previously to run a T-shirt sizing session for the tasks.

Working through the backlogs in chapters 4, 5, 6, and 7 yields an estimate that a team of five people plus yourself should be able to deliver the project in approximately 10 weeks, with a two-week sprint 0 as previously agreed. The team agrees that the risks you have picked up from the process so far are not material in terms of resources, but flag that the data permission issue is still live.

You arrange a meeting with Karima to discuss project risks and brief her about the need to restrain the use of the system from being exclusive. You also mention that data permissions may cause the system to be unusable if unresolved. Given the discoveries made about the possible state of the data, you create an additional item for the statement of work as a subproject:

Challenge 5: We will verify that data from 2-5 years ago is of sufficient quality to use when creating revenue and churn models, and we will quantify the impact that the quality of this data has on the rank and usefulness of the models that can be extracted from the available data.

The challenges are written into the work package in the bid that covers this project, along with the assumptions noted previously and those that cover data use:

Assumption 6: You need to have the appropriate permissions to use the data provided by The Bike Shop.

The final part of the description is the work that Rob and you created with the team for the estimate. In the legal agreement, this work is caveated as being subject to change as discovery occurs.

A review with the pre-sales team is held and the project is evaluated as low-risk, high-flexibility, and therefore, no explicit contingency is added to the project estimate. All agreement documents are prepared by legal counsel and a meeting is held to review and complete the presales checklist. Several small actions come up as the result of this meeting, and after all of these are closed, the documentation is sent to the authorized officers at The Bike Shop and to the consulting/delivery organization that you belong to. The documents are signed, and a sale has been made. Now the project must be executed.

3.6   *Pre-project postscript*

It's a win! The Bike Shop sale is closed, and the bid team is celebrating. This was a happy story, but pre-project activity can be an adversarial process; you are in the mix with other teams and other people using other technologies and approaches. In the corporate world, your projects are stacked up against a bunch of other projects as well. It might be that the transformation program that's shrinking the size of the administrative teams needs more money this year. It might be that your ML project to improve service productivity isn't seen as important as the ML project to get more interest on the website. In the world of consulting, there's explicit competition for business as well. Other companies may be better placed to offer lower prices or faster deliveries than you can.

Sometimes your organization will really need the project for financial or organizational (political) reasons. Your managers or the sales team may have invested a huge amount of effort to get you to the point where a project can be mooted and discussed. This means that there is a lot of pressure to be successful in the pre-project phase, or even not to do it at all and to just jump in and deliver results.

It seems obvious that you and your team should aim to win as much work as possible. This is what pays the bills after all, and it's your job to take on and deliver projects. In fact, winning the wrong sort of work can have devastating effects: burning out your team, hammering your reputation, and so forth. The cost of a team committed to a project that is bound to fail is significant. If you are in a position to say "no" to a project that you believe is going to flop, it's ethical to push back and let the customer spend their money on something else, and it's also probably in your own best interest. There are other fish in the sea; you won't burn your team or your reputation, and the customer may come back with a better idea in the future.

One of the purposes of the processes outlined in this chapter is to build a solid and factual case for doing an ML project at a particular price and on a specific timeframe. This might lead to your organization walking away from a project or to your team getting a project that's realistic and valuable to the customer. Unfortunately, it may also lead to your bid being rejected by the customer in favor of a competitor. This is a harder sort of failure to take and can sometimes come with real negative consequences for you and the team. The good thing is that when you are asked why it happened, you will have evidence to show that you were doing the right thing and also the material that you can learn from in the longer term. Step back, though. It's worth reframing and seeing that there are two sides to every story. Perhaps the customer is right; perhaps you weren't the right team to work with them. If the customer is wrong, then they've made a bad call this time. Don't worry. They'll be back after your competitor has not worked out.

Summary

- To get to a proposal for the project, the requirements need to be transformed into a hypothesis that spells out the expected outcome and key challenges.

- A structured process of estimation can then be done based on the hypothesis and the information about the delivery environment that you gathered in chapter 2.

- An useful estimate takes into account the team's structure and the commitment needed to meet the requirements.

- Get your project documentation properly reviewed and signed off before anyone mentions costs to the customer.

- If the pre-project phase fails, then it's certain that the project would have failed, and that is far worse.

Getting started 4

The idea of sprint 0 (introduced in chapter 3) is to get everything set up and ready so that the project team can walk in on day 1 and get started. In an ideal world, this phase acts as a buffer between a project that's yet to start and a project that's running and burning lots of money. It's an opportunity to discover dire problems before large amounts of cash are wasted, and it's also the time when effort can be spent on enabling the productivity of the delivery team.

During sprint 0, you will be officially working on the project for the client. This means that you will be "in the tent" and allowed access and information that you did not have during the pre-project process. Because of this difference, sprint 0 allows for some time to make requests for access, information, and accounts, and then resolving those issues without the project team sitting idly by, twiddling their thumbs, and waiting. It also gives you, as project lead, some time to agree and communicate the project's working processes and to deepen your understanding of the risks and challenges ahead. Finally, sprint 0 allows you to further check that the project is feasible and that your estimates are still valid.

4.1   *Sprint 0 backlog*

As with the pre-project phase, the backlog for sprint 0 lists the tasks or tickets that need to be undertaken to complete this phase of the project (Table 4.1). Again, as with pre-project tasks, these tasks need to be decomposed and developed further, based on the reality of the project you are facing.

Table 4.1   Backlog for getting started

Task #	Item
Setup 1	Create, communicate, and finalize the team design and resourcing.
Setup 2	Agree on and share a way of working:
	• Project heartbeat (the day-to-day way the project will run)
	• Work standards and best practices
	Agree on a common set of tools.
	Create, agree on, and share the communication plan.
	Create and share the documentation plan.
Setup 3	Build and share the infrastructure plan.
Setup 4	Undertake a pre-project data investigation.
Setup 5	Review project CSR and ethics.
	Build and share the privacy, security, and data-handling plans.
Setup 6	Build and share the project roadmap.

One of the important changes from pre-sales is that now you need to set up processes and interactions using your client's infrastructure to deliver your ML project. You need to include and integrate your working practice with their working practice. Sprint 0 achieves these three things:

- Your team is all set and ready to go with a clear agenda and with all the working systems that they need to do their job.
- You and your team are now part of the customer organization.
- You have come to grips with the project's data resources and have verified that the picture you were given about the data in pre-project is correct.

4.2 *Finalize team design and resourcing*

The project team is the engine of delivery. Without the right people, the work required simply can't be done. Because the design of the team and resourcing are one of the most important activities, during sprint 0, ensure that the right people are assigned to the project.

Team design ticket: Setup 1

- Create, communicate, and finalize the team design and resourcing.

In the pre-project phase, you created a team design to enable you to make an estimate of the costs. As part of that process, you checked that the people necessary to the team are available. It's likely that you used some sort of resource reservation and assignment system to record the team the project is calling for. If the team is reserved, then all that remains for now is basically just to "push the button" and start to onboard the team for the customer project.

Unfortunately, there are several things that can go wrong. Putative team members can be grabbed by other projects, they may have left the business, or they simply got sick. You may have to find a drop-in replacement, or you may have to redesign the team because the keystones that you used to structure it during the pre-project work and estimate are no longer there.

If your team design and resourcing plan has been derailed, then record that on the risk register. An inadequate team is a red light that needs to be dealt with. Now that the project is funded, in most cases, a rapid internal escalation will resolve the issue, either by securing the resources initially identified or by finding alternatives.

If no adequate resourcing for the original work is available, then an alternative mitigation is to replan the work. Rather than cutting your cloth to suit your pocket, you must resize your pocket to get a different cloth! Replanning can sometimes mean that appropriate resources are available to cover the requirements at different points in the project. Another mitigation is for the delivery organization (your company) to arrange for external contractors to fill in the gaps. This is expensive and will likely damage or destroy the commercial case for doing the project, but this may be preferable for your organization to protect the relationship with the customer.

4.3 *A way of working*

Assuming a project team is secured, the next step is to start to develop and agree on the project's working processes with the client. The *working process* is the set of activities that everyone agrees are required for a task to be considered satisfactorily completed.

Working practice ticket: Setup 2

- Agree on and share a way of working:
  - Project heartbeat (the day-to-day way the project will run)
  - Work standards and best practices
- Agree on a common set of tools.
- Create, agree on, and share the communication plan.
- Create and share the documentation plan.

4.3.1 *Process and structure*

Be clear about how the project will operate and how the activities will be structured and agreed on. Not only is it important to spell this out so that the team and you know what is expected, it's also fundamental for building quality into the project. If the team adopts working practices that work for them, they and you get a better result.

There is a vast library of literature [14] [4] [15] concerned with how to run (or define) an agile project. You'll find different flavors and sects that demand particular practices and behaviors: scrum teams work in sprints, Kanban teams work with continuous delivery, and so on. Deviating from the prescriptions of Scrum, DevOps, Kanban, or any other form of agile may be regarded as heresy. Although there are a lot of strong ideas about how projects should work, there is actually little evidence to support the idea that there is only one way to run projects day-to-day and week-to-week. What is clear is that different teams find different practices that work for them, and that what works, shifts with time and context.

Unfortunately, different organizations mandate different practices as management fads come and go. If a way of working is prescribed in your organization such as SAFe [15] then you need to find a way to conform to the prescribed practice. If you have the flexibility and you have found a way of working that is successful for your team and works for your customers, then use that! Having said all this, there are four things that must be made clear:

- The process and structure that will be used.
- The tools that are adopted.
- The standards and working practices required of the team.
- How everything will be documented.

Sprint-based projects are based on the scrum approach to agile, and this way of organizing a project is currently popular. A sprint-based structure is woven into this book, and this allows a narrative to evolve.

The reality of an agile project means that tasks will overflow from one sprint to another, and the project team will discover extra work and activities required to drive your project forward. For example, in a project with novel hardware, you may need detailed experiments about the performance of the cameras or sensors, for example, to understand the data that they produce. Another example is when a team must use a particular development platform and has to port a great deal of code into it to get going. Acknowledging and accommodating these discoveries by adapting the work plan as the project evolves is at the heart of the agile approach.

The sprint-based agile approach allows milestones to be set and regular reviews held to monitor progress. Decisions are required at the end of each sprint about what will need to be done (or not) next. The team now has visibility and control of the project for the next few weeks and can make plans about how they are going to manage their workloads and commitments. However, this kind of project structure is not the only way to run an agile project.

Kanban projects are run as a constantly evolving, single plan; tasks are added to the project as they emerge, and the team constantly updates and reprioritizes the task list to push through the project as efficiently and rapidly as possible. Some teams thrive by using this approach to tightly coordinate their work, and it seems to work well where the team deeply understands the domain and the project. Where systematic input from product owners and domain experts is required, the more structured is the pace of a sprint-oriented project.

4.3.2 *Heartbeat and communication plan*

Part of your role as the project lead is to act as a human message-switching device: gathering messages that need to get out to the team and delivering them in one shot, then gathering the messages from the team and processing them for one set of actions. You need to define how this is going to happen and get agreement from all directions: your managers, the customer, and the team.

People find the rhythms of sharing in a project reassuring even if they often complain that they are not getting as much out of the processes as they would like. Everyone should know how they are expected to share and receive information. There are two ways to communicate:

- Hold meetings
- Distribute documents and reports

A common complaint in a project (even when it's unjustifiable) is that we don't know what's going on. Getting a plan in place and getting commitment to it neutralizes the opportunity for carping and discontent. Conversely, the complaint of there are too many meetings is somewhat managed by the presence of a plan; you can use this to explain why there are so many meetings and why everyone agreed that it was a good idea to begin with. Of course, both types of complaints may have substance, so be careful. Be open to the idea that the amount of information sharing has become meaningless or overly detailed and irrelevant.

Sometimes you'll find that you and your team get dragged into multiple "other" meetings and catch-ups. This can be hard to manage, but it's something you need to be aware of. One project meeting a day is adequate for team engineers. Some engineers will chafe at the burden of even one meeting, but the reality is that they need to check in, and engineers that disappear for an extended time often get isolated. It's hard to take responsibility for work if you are unaware of what's happening.

More than one project meeting a day can end up quashing productivity because there's no time to get set up and settled into the task at hand. If the team and you have decided to use a sprint-based structure to run the project:

- Have a daily stand-up meeting with the product owner, the customer's technical rep or troubleshooter, and your team.
- Have a weekly review meeting with the product owner. Use this meeting to deliver a general update about the project and to review the risk register. Take minutes of this meeting, including actions, and roll those forward every week.
- Arrange for planning meetings at the beginning of each sprint with the product owner. This allows for agreement on the work assignment for the sprint. Remember, as an agile/adaptive project, there's going to be significant changes to the work as you progress with the project.
- Hold sprint closure and sign-off meetings with the team, key stakeholders, and the product owner. In this meeting, present the work that's been done and have the team demonstrate new functionality; for example, previewing working models from the data or running data pipelines, user interfaces, and so on.
- Schedule post-sprint review meetings with the key stakeholders and the product owner. Here you review any challenges or problems so they can be resolved in a sprint planning session.

It's a good idea to keep notes during all the meetings, but some meetings and some other aspects of the project need to be recorded and shared as reports. Reports are a kind of documentation, but they have a particular ranking in that they are designed to make sure that the status of the project is understood.

As noted, minutes should be taken at the weekly review meeting and then distributed to the participants. The act of doing both creates a status report on how things are going. For the sprint closure and planning meetings, your notes need to translate into agreed actions and the task board for the next sprint. A key reporting mechanism is the risk register. You can use that to maintain an agreement that there are unresolved problems or that there is movement on the problems that have been resolved.

Whichever pattern you choose, you need to schedule the meetings. This makes the participants' aware of a regularly scheduled commitment and lets them plan for it. Getting time in the participants' calendars can be difficult, but doing this now is vital to the smooth running of the project.

The pattern of meetings and communications that you define are the heartbeat of your project. Iteratively running through these sequences drives the project forward or, in a less optimistic case, they show you and your sponsors that things are not going well. In either case, this routine enables you to assemble the information and evidence, which shows that you and the team are working towards the project's goals. To achieve those goals efficiently and effectively, though, there are many tools and practices that need to be established for the project. Let's begin with tooling.

4.3.3 *Tooling*

Establish a clear agreement with all team members and with the customer about preferred tools. Often, the project's customer will mandate these. The following lists some of these tools:

- Document repository (SharePoint, Confluence, Microsoft Teams, etc.)
- Work ticketing system (Jira, GitLab, Azure DevOps Services)
- Source code control (GitHub, Bitbucket, Subversion)
- Document production (Microsoft Office 365, Google Docs, Open Office)
- Technical diagram production (Visio, Lucidchart)
- Build management system (Gradle, Jenkins)
- Dependency management system (Conda, Python's pip)
- Testing (Python's pytest, JUnit)

Sometimes using the wrong tool can mean that work must be redrafted to be accepted by the customer, and sometimes using the wrong tool will be a breach of contract. That may result in bigger problems down the line. It's worth getting this clear up front because ML projects require their own tooling. At the time of writing, this is an emerging area, but it's clear that there are significant gains to be had from standardizing on a tool to support some of the pain points in an ML development project.

DATA PIPELINING

Modern databases reflect the complex and dynamic organizations they support. Data science and AI projects demand that many of these resources are unified in an ad hoc way to create a useful representation of the data that covers a problem area. Relational databases are still hugely valuable and commonly used in data science and AI projects, but increasingly, unstructured data from sensors or in the form of natural language must be accommodated and used as well.

Large data resources may be required to support AI projects, and these can (and often do) change frequently. This requirement is not well supported by ETL tools, which were designed to support data integration projects delivering relational data warehouses. Beauchemin [3] identifies these drivers and articulates the case for a more flexible and open data infrastructure, implemented by using data pipelines.

A *data pipeline* is a sequence of transforms managed by a workflow engine and a scheduler. The workflow engine chains together a sequence of tasks in a simple program; specifically, without a loop. Technically, this is known as a DAG (directed acyclic graph).

Figure 4.1 shows an example a DAG for an ELT task. Each step on the DAG is a script that executes on a target machine, processing data in a data store or on a virtual machine. The overall DAG is specified in the workflow engine, which invokes each step in the sequence. In this case, Table *X* is loaded from System *A*, and Table *Y* is loaded from System *B*. A join is executed and then a cleaning step is run to remove null values. Each of these steps may have different internal steps, and each of these can run another workflow independently. The dotted arrow in the figure shows the kind of actions that the first step could execute.

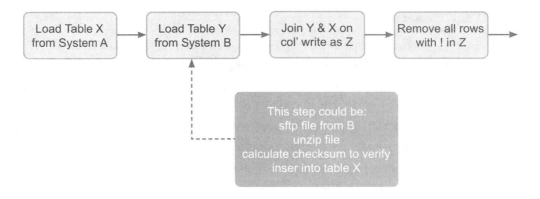

Figure 4.1   An example DAG: it's directed (D) as the information flows one way along the arrows. It's acyclic (A) because there aren't any cycles, and it's a graph (G) because that's what this sort of thing is called.

Many programming languages are used for scripting activities like this, but the idea of a pipeline engine is that it abstracts some of the complexity of managing these and chaining them together. This technology emerged along with Hadoop implementations in the form of the Oozie scheduler [1], which allows for easier management of big data resources stored in Hadoop clusters.

In 2015, Airbnb [1] needed a solution that supported the integration and management of various complex data pipelines on diverse technical stacks. Airbnb's project developed into what would later become Apache Airflow. Pipeline tools like Oozie and Airflow provide an abstraction that describes the required manipulations over data assets, and an engine allows for the execution and management of the code that's created to do this.

Large and complex libraries of data flows using this technology are rapidly becoming available, and it's common for an AI team to implement scores of processes that define the import and preparation of data for EDA (exploratory data analysis), model training, and model evaluation and production. Without these tools, this kind of work is error-prone, hard-to-manage, and extremely time-consuming. With something like Airflow, the processes are easy to inspect and well-managed, and a great deal of the bookkeeping and script management that previously dogged data projects are outsourced to the engine.

VERSIONING

ML projects produce and rely on many assets beyond code. They produce different models, tweaked and tuned to improve one aspect of performance or another. ML projects also rely on specific training, validation, and test sets. Beyond the training sets, ML projects also use complex pipelines to integrate disparate data and to produce the features that the learning algorithm processes.

Luckily, a number of specialized version control systems are now available to store and manage these things. This includes tools like DVC, MLflow, and Weights & Biases. Additionally, ML development systems such as SageMaker on Amazon Web Services (AWS) have integrated versioning components that we can use, and recent versioning filesystems such as Apache Iceberg and Project Nessie allow datasets to be identified and versioned effectively.

It is possible for the team to track model versions and other artifacts without a dedicated infrastructure and tools. Be warned, though, this rapidly becomes a huge administrative burden and can precipitate complex and frustrating configuration errors. In the worst case, your team won't be able to reproduce the behavior of the "good" model that they developed because some component of the recipe is lost in the melee of project push. This is embarrassing, at best, and corrosive in terms of customer/user trust in you and the model at worst. Being able to version the team's artifacts enables two things that are important in supporting the success of an ML project.

The first virtue is reproducibility. Being able to exactly define the components that have gone into the model, it's possible to recreate it. Having the binary of the model itself isn't enough because you might need to recreate it on a different computing infrastructure, or perhaps, some component turns out to be problematic. In that case, recreating the model with only that replacement part allows you to check that either what was done before was valid or you have a real problem.

The second virtue of being able to track all the artifacts going into a model is that it allows the testing and release of that model from environment to environment. Models depend on other components, and that dependency graph needs to be moved along with the binary.

DATA TESTING

We can improve the management of the project's data infrastructure by using data pipelining technology. This is because the processes used are explicitly and easily monitored. Failing pipelines are clearly identified and remedial action can be taken. In the most basic form of the concept, *failure* means that a bug in the pipeline has caused one of the jobs not to run—a programmatic failure has occurred. Having the data infrastructure, though, creates the opportunity to run tests to assess if there are data failures in the pipelines. By setting up and running data testing, the team can create assurance about the quality and properties of the data assets flowing into the model development and production environments.

Data errors can emerge from problems of collection (faulty sensors, poorly conducted surveys, inferior data entry, etc.), and they can also emerge from the data infrastructure that's mediating the sensors. Your system describes these errors as errors producing "bad data" and errors of data management [7].

Breck [6] suggests a series of data tests relevant to ML model development, including testing that distributions are as expected and that items determined to be excluded are excluded. In addition, Breck suggests tests that establish whether all features are correctly constructed from the source data by the pipeline code. System-level tests on the data are also proposed (for example, testing whether invariants or causal links between categories of items hold). Note that there should always be only one chef to look after a particular pot of broth.

In terms of developing the infrastructure, several projects try to show this [10], but specific problems arise due to the computational costs of data testing over large and fast data sources. Even selecting representative examples from a large data feed can impose a significant overhead, and this impacts the performance of the data infrastructure and the cost of the project. Interfacing cluster-based processors such as Spark or Kubernetes into data pipelines to test at scale can be effective, but considered and considerable engineering is needed to achieve this. It's also expensive in terms of compute cost and carbon.

This is the time in the project to decide what your policy will be on these tools. Will they cover all the bases of your team's needs? Will they be more of a drag than a stimulus for the performance of the team? The complexity of the data infrastructure and modeling process, and the maturity of the organization and domain that you are working in, have a big part to play in your decision. A project that's going to be foundational for a strategic business activity merits a big investment in infrastructure. If you're doing a proof-of-value or quick-start project, you may be better off setting up something lightweight.

4.3.4 *Standards and practices*

As well as what the team is doing, it's important to know how they are going to do it. Getting the behavior of the team right is one of the most important things you can do as a leader. Different teams work in different ways, so it's important to be sensible to the needs of your team. Adopt the following practices as a general guide for creating a smooth and positive team dynamic. The objective is to create a team ethos where everyone's insights and ideas are available, and everyone feels like they are contributing and growing as an engineer:

- Respect and politeness are fundamental. Once this is lost, people start editing themselves and stop disclosing what's really happening. Comments and suggestions must be positive and respectful. No one should interrupt (if you do, it's fine but apologize and give the airtime back to the person you interrupted).

  Everyone should listen to what others say and take it seriously. At the same time, everyone should be respectful of the others' time and make sure that they speak concisely and stick to the topic. The most powerful thing you can do is to set an example.

- Work should be recorded and tracked in the ticketing system adopted for the project. If a piece of work is worth talking about in a stand-up meeting, you should record and ticket it. In this type of meeting, everyone should have some work to talk about.

- Work or tickets should produce identifiable outcomes. Documents, code, or other artifacts (model, feature, data set, test result, etc.) can be filed in the documentation repository. It can then be pushed to a version control system and recovered by the proper team members for inspection.

- Work should be peer-reviewed. If a team member (or several team members) takes a ticket, it shouldn't be regarded as closed until another team member reviews it. This promotes a flow of knowledge in two directions: if a senior engineer completes a ticket and a junior engineer reviews it, it offers a chance to learn from the working practices of the senior contributor. If vice versa, then the senior engineer has a chance to provide pointers and support to the junior team member. Approximate peer-to-peer review also allows technical knowledge to flow through the project team.

Standards and practices also carry over to the customer. With respect to the customer and delivery value of setting a way of working, it's important to get agreement about:

- What it means to sign off when something is done. Good practice is to declare that deliverables are reviewed in one of the project meetings and sent to the product owner (the customer may want to specify that it's someone else). These then are regarded as signed off if no issue is raised, for example, within five working days.

- What the customer's responsibilities for supporting the project include. As an example, this may mean that the product owner and point of contact are present in meetings and available for discussions.

All teams should go through the process of agreeing on their ways of working. Obviously, you'll have a problem if you see a team setting low standards or creating poor practices. In that case, you must lay out a fundamental framework and enforce it. You can influence the outcome by role modeling the behaviors you are looking for from the team, but in most cases, asking questions (as opposed to imposing your answers) and seeing what comes out can be powerfully formative for them.

It's often impressive to see the depth of reasoning and insight that seasoned professionals bring to bear on questions about how folks should work together. Importantly, teams that make decisions are strongly motivated to stick with them and will likely induct and instruct new members with little prompting. Whatever the conclusions and agreements that you come to, document them and then, as much as possible, stick to it.

4.3.5   *Documentation*

Documentation has been out of fashion with some software developers for a long time. The Agile Manifesto states that "working software [is valued over] comprehensive documentation." This maxim is often taken as license to proceed without documentation, although the Agile Manifesto clearly indicates that its authors see value in comprehensive documentation as well as working software [4]. A common trope in recent years has been that code should be self-documenting and that running code beats every other piece of evidence of progress in a project.

There's a lot to be said for the "code above documents" insight. The idea that software teams should focus on getting code to run is based on a few learnings from the years of experience that people have had in developing software. For example, getting some code to work is a powerful indicator of progress and value. Another plus point of focusing on code and functionality is that it forces detailed thinking, which can expose gaps in the designer's thinking. It's quite common to surmise that designs don't work because the required code can't be written, or more commonly, that the design has left out a whole load of detail.

Recently, a more rounded view is becoming more common. The point of a software project (including an ML project) is to deliver a system that runs and is fully maintained. Without documentation, no one will know how to use the system, much less how to fix it.

Although, with time, the code can be grokked by techies, but the business won't know where to start in terms of getting the right techies to look in the right place, and there may not be time to do that. Essentially, poor or nonexistent documentation is a system killer. Developers have also realized that documentation is a great asset when making progress with their day-to-day work. It's helpful for them to be able to rely on the documentation that their team produces. Nowadays, it's a trope to point out that the person who will need the documentation to understand what you did six weeks ago will be you, yourself. Broadly, there are two types of documentation:

- The exhaust trail created by developers as they execute tasks in the backlog.
- The formal documents that update customers on progress or that constitute deliverables in themselves.

In terms of the exhaust trail, it is important that the team documents each task and files that in the repository, but these documents are not a formal delivery to the customer. Instead, this record of work provides the information needed by the team and future teams to understand the system and its evolution. The other function of the team's working notes is that they are a demonstration of the team's activity and progress, which can be used to convince stakeholders of the team's diligence and hard work. Also, if another senior engineer is asked to audit the project, a repository of scores of technical notes and working papers is a great way to convince them that the team has not been idle. Every task should be documented as a matter of course, and the technical notes retained and made available to all team members.

In terms of formal documents, there must be documentation deliverables that summarize and present information to the customer and your senior management for review. The mindful acts of documentation, if you will. These documents create agreement about the progress of the project and serve as a focus for the team in thinking about and understanding what has been done on a particular topic or activity. The plan is to develop documentation deliverables and to communicate with the client. As an example, for a typical ML project, the following documents could be delivered:

- Documentation plan
- Communication plan
- Data story
- Privacy and security plan
- Infrastructure plan
- Technical architecture
- Roadmap
- Sprint 0 report
- Data survey
- Ethics report
- Business problem analysis
- Data test plan
- EDA report
- Sprint 1 report
- Model design
- Feature engineering report
- Model development report
- Model evaluation report
- Sprint 2 report
- Application design
- UI design
- Logging and monitoring approach
- Implementation report
- Testing report
- Final project report

Optionally, it may be that you do a standalone sprint 3 report and separate out the task of preparing a final project report, depending on who is going to sign off on the different parts of the project. Some clients have stakeholders, who will agree on the completion of project parts or sprints but will want someone at a more senior level to review and own the entire project. Whatever the requirements of your specific clients, during sprint 0 you can make sure that the documentation plan you've developed meets with their approval and offers clarity about what exactly will be delivered to whom and when. Having established your way of working, it's time to focus on what you are actually going to be working with!

4.4 Infrastructure plan

This section covers the systems you need to set up to allow your team to work. Here, we come to grips with the infrastructure that is necessary to run what the team is going to build.

Infrastructure ticket: Setup 3

- Build and share the infrastructure plan.

An ML project has quite different data architecture requirements from a standard corporate data architecture. Running an ML system on a corporate data architecture and infrastructure can sometimes have unacceptable impacts on other applications. However, you may have limited or zero options, so what's needed is a pragmatic approach to infrastructure design and development.

4.4.1   System access

From the work in pre-project, you have an idea of where the data is, so now there are two steps to take: first, question and confirm the information, and second, get to the point where you have access to a set of technical interfaces (APIs, SQL queries, filenames, etc.). It may be that this information is not available from the folks you talk to, or you were told that the data is in a particular database. You need to dive into any lack of clarity about system access fast, because a lack of the proper access to the data resources will likely almost halt technical activity on the project until resolved.

Immediately initiate discussions to pin down the access and permissions that are needed to get to the data. When you have this information, start the processes that grant access. Bear in mind, that not only will the team have to apply for access, they will probably have to do some training to be qualified or certified to handle the data. It is likely that this will require between 2 and 8 hours per team member to complete, but identifying and scheduling the training required to onboard to the customer's infrastructure is a priority. This is one of those times where it's really worth asking all the obvious or dumb questions that come into your mind about the process and requirements because one of them may reveal a critical blocker for your team's productivity.

In some cases, access to the environment that's used to host the data may be restricted to specific laptops with specific builds, which prevents (or limits) data egress. In this case, make arrangements for the team to have access to the laptops or to the workspaces that enable them to connect to the data servers.

Arranging these permissions, training, and accessing the needed systems always takes longer than expected because the processes for addressing this tend to be low-priority and underfunded. Sometimes, the process for doing this doesn't exist or is being run for the first time. The lesson is the quicker and more energetically this step is addressed, the better off the project team.

4.4.2   Technical infrastructure evaluation

In chapter 2, we shared a specification of the dev/test/prod environments for use in the project. This should have been completed with respect to the best available information about the customer's environment. In most cases, the pre-project engagement involves competent technical and security architects from the customer and an accurate picture of what is available.

Unfortunately, when you ask, it can turn out that what was hoped to be used just doesn't exist. It could be that the pre-sales team were unable to involve the proper technical expertise from the customer or that the technical environment is an at-risk item in the statement of work. It could be that the assumed infrastructure is just not available because of a mistake or a misunderstanding. Let's say it was assumed that when the project started, there would be a GPU server to use in production. By asking some questions, you may quickly discover that, in reality, the GPU server is on order, but it won't be delivered and commissioned for nine months!

If this kind of issue is uncovered at this stage, then you must think inventively and create a workaround with the team, or the customer needs to change the infrastructure provision, or the project should be scuttled. This is where you can renegotiate the scope of the project: is there another approach or viable application that doesn't need a GPU? Get the details of the infrastructure that was promised and the infrastructure available on your risk register and start working through the required mitigations and changes to scope as soon as possible. Ensure that the customer acknowledges the delta right away after its discovery.

On the other side of the requests for access and the process that provisions them, there's certainty about the infrastructure that the team will use. Write it down and document it!

4.5   *The data story*

Yet again, data, data, data. This is one of the vital differences between what you would focus on in a sprint 0 for a normal software project and what you need to do for an ML project. Setup 4 tasks you to do another data investigation. But, why now?

> **Data story ticket: Setup 4**
> - Undertake a pre-project data investigation.

In the pre-project process, we mentioned how important it is to obtain a data sample in the pre-sales phase of a project, and we also noted the importance of figuring out whether the use of the data is ethical and legal. Sprint 0 is the first chance for paid work (protected and licensed by commercial agreements), undertaken to understand the customers data. Ronald Fisher, inventor of modern statistics, was a bit of a strange man but, apparently, he said:

> *To consult the statistician after an experiment is finished is often merely to ask him to conduct a post-mortem examination. He can perhaps say what the experiment died of.*

> — R.A. Fisher, Presidential Address to the
> First Indian Statistical Congress, 1938

This is relevant here for a few reasons. You and your team are asked to build a picture of the operating domain of your customer, which yields the data for modelling. What's available defines how good a picture you can make. If you are lucky, everything will be cleanly laid out in a nice data table for the team to work from. More likely, you will need to assemble the tables your modelling team needs from various not nice, not clean parts, so you need to get deeper into the issues that your team faces. As you work through the project, you'll need to understand several iterations of this process.

Before the team comes onboard and before access to the data is available, it's time to build a narrative story about the data, using your time and project mandate as the main tools. In sprint 1, you'll need to create a data survey investigation from the system's point of view. A data survey pins down what data is in which resource and how it can be made available. Then, after you complete the data survey, the team will be able to do a proper EDA to find out what's really in the data sets.

Next, the modelers come in to do all the fun bits. If this iterative process of locating and digging into the data is followed, you can be hopeful that they won't find huge derailing problems with it, which stops the project in its tracks. For now, without technical access fully in place, the best way to reduce the risk of this happening is to develop a data story.

The data story is a history of the components of the data set that the customer wants you to access and to use. At this stage, the story that you get will be the customer's view of what the data is made up of and how it got there. This is often different from the technical reality. However, this view is important and useful because it articulates the corporate memory of key events and drivers that have made the data what it is.

Frameworks for this are available, which you can use to structure the questions that are asked about the data. For example, to understand data assets, use the 5W1H+R framework [16]. This is based on the long-standing idea that journalists use to get to the heart of a story; they ask questions about why, who, what, when, where, and how. Additionally, the 5W1H+R framework introduces the idea of asking about the data's relationship to other data in the infrastructure. The data's lineage and provenance are crucial and so need to be understood and exposed.

The full 5W1H+R framework poses 27 questions that cover aspects of data governance, integration, and compliance. If the metadata for all 27 questions is available, then use that to understand the assets. It's quite likely that you will discover there is no preprepared data catalog or the MDM system or catalog is incomplete. The main questions to ask to cover this context are:

- Why was the data created and how was it intended to be used?
- Who owns the data and who can grant access to it?
- What are the privacy and security concerns relevant to the data?
- What are the source systems that were used to get the data set?
- How is the data stored in those systems? Can it be easily queried?
- What are the types of data stored (unstructured, tabular, relational)?
- When were the data and systems created? What were the major episodes in the life of those systems (for example, outages with data loss, repurposing for business change, aggregation of other systems into that one, replatforming, etc.)?

- What is the origin of the data that is on the systems (for example, gathered from sensors, keyed in by operatives, website logs, mobile phone histories, bought from data brokers, transaction logs, etc.)?
- What is the scale of the data assets? What is the profile of data scale over the history of those systems (for example, a system might have started with small transaction volumes but scaled to large volumes over several years)?
- What is the sense of data quality in each of the components? Does the customer trust it?

The 5W1H+R framework is useful for extracting information about the data, but it focuses on supporting data governance tasks. Modeling and, by extension, using the data for ML raises further questions. Even so, there are (at least) four ways that the story of the data you will use affects your ML models:

- *Motivation and context:* Why the data was collected.
- *Collection:* The mechanics of the data collection and the measurements made.
- *Lineage:* The process that has brought the data into its current form and storage.
- *Events:* What happened to the data.

4.5.1 Data collection motivation

It's not surprising that why the data was collected plays a big part in what you can do with it. After all, when we were in science labs at school, it was drummed into us that the kind of experiments we do returns different (and limited) results. Shining a torch down the cellar stairs to avoid tripping offers vastly different information than turning on the lights and seeing all the wine bottles on the shelves. The person with the torch might not have seen any wine bottles at all.

More relevant to the work that you will do is the fact that a data set that is collected as part of a controlled experimental study is different from a purely observational data set, and to create valid inferences from differently motivated data collection exercises requires different approaches [2]. By definition, the distribution for a variable that is deliberately selected will be different from the natural distribution of the variable.

A simple way to think about the impact of collection motivation on a data set is to imagine the picture of a butterfly collection. Often, we are more interested in the rarest cases of anything and will throw away data about the common cases (however, in the case of the butterfly collection, expect rarities to be overly represented). Additionally, the butterfly collector probably didn't collect other insects that live with butterflies, and maybe they have arranged them by color or size. These are rather arbitrary parameters. Perhaps all the specimens were collected in the summer months, perhaps the date of collection is recorded, and the place—or perhaps not.

A data collector behaves differently from an ecologist or an entomologist. The data collected in corporate systems is subject to similar biases, however, which is neither good nor bad, but it does affect the information that is available for models. This needs to be understood and allowed for.

4.5.2   *Data collection mechanism*

A good example of the impact that stems from the data collection approach is the concept of *total survey error*, where the sample data is always slightly or somewhat different from the whole population or a bias is introduced in the way questions are asked or in the way the interface is designed [13]. Data that has been collected and repeatedly updated (like personnel records or inventory) often has systematic errors due to the interface used by the people entering and updating the data. For example, where a choice about a particular parameter is picked from a list by the data-entry user, it's often the case that the first item on the list is chosen disproportionately.

Alternatively, imagine a website UI that asks for sensitive information from users, and you are asked to find the makeup of the site's users, but a proportion of the users refuse to give their details. It could be that this proportion is evenly distributed. More plausibly, people with sensitive characteristics are less likely to respond because, sadly, in our society, they have learned that giving away their identity can be damaging. The point is that there would be bias in the data about the site users, although it is representative of the users who are willing to reply to a sensitive characteristics survey!

Data captured from sensors has a different set of problems. This is carefully considered and treated by engineers and physical scientists in specific contexts, where the data collected from sensors must be reliable [12]. Calibration and rigorous installation standards such as those reported in the NASA assembly guidelines [11] are used to prevent sensor errors. Nonetheless, network sensors can stop responding or can be installed in the wrong location. In the worst case, sensors can be correctly installed, apparently functional, and yet deliver erroneous results. To understand the sensor data in the data set, the team needs to incorporate a view as to the processes and checks that verify sensor data in the organization and in the implementation of the systems that you need to understand.

4.5.3   *Lineage*

Data sets supplied for analytics projects are often several steps removed from the questions, logs, and sensor readings that they report. Data can be generated at such a pace and scale that special real-time databases are required for collection. Scaling these databases to hold data long-term or to support analytic queries can be expensive and complicated. It's commonplace for such data to be mirrored into cheaper storage infrastructures called data warehouses.

In big organizations, it's easy for politics, cost constraints, regulations, and general incompetence to generate many of these general data stores. This creates a sprawling Byzantine data architecture. Another force that creates a sprawling data architecture lies in the actions and mechanics of capitalism. Large companies are often sold, taken over, or split up. Data warehouses and data lakes are acquired, inherited, or mirrored as a consequence of all this financial engineering. Finally, regulation can result in unnatural and complicated data architectures as particular data is partitioned or mirrored to enable and promote competition. Because of this set of dynamics, the origin of the data that's in a particular table can be unclear and complex to decode.

Finding the lineage of a data table is much easier if the customer implements a data catalogue or a data lineage system such as Alation or Collibra. Alternatively, organizations may make use of the metadata management facilities and processes in their data architecture, so there may be a master data model available to use as a road map for understanding the origin of the data at hand.

At the time of writing, some research is emerging on the provision of tools for automatically tracing data origins through a data estate by using *data discovery* techniques. For example, using measures of entity relatedness such as social network analysis [9] or embedding vector similarity [8]. Tools that support and automate this process will be extremely helpful when or if they develop and mature. But it is likely that this kind of sophisticated practice will take a while to implement into all data architectures, so any previously collected lineate information should be grabbed with both hands. If there is a spreadsheet that tracks the data in the organization, that's better than nothing.

In the worst case, if there isn't a preestablished global view of the data in the architecture to work from, then it's necessary to map out at least the part that you and your team will be working from. From your perspective, what matters is that the ultimate source of the data sets be pinned down. Not only does this help you get to the bottom of motivation and collection issues, but it avoids the same data being used to generate multiple signals into the same model or set of models.

The processes used to lift and shift the data around the data architecture and the processes used to map it into different formats also must be understood. Scripts and pipelines can generate data that's interpreted as being a feature of the domain but is actually an artifact of the engine that's collecting and aggregating it. For example, you may discover that sensor data collected every 10 minutes has timestamps, which are applied every six hours as the data is pulled out of the operational data store and put into the data warehouse. These timestamps are meant to be used to check that the data pull worked (probably by using a count to check that the right numbers arrive), but they have then been used subsequently at the actual data collection times. It is amazing how many errors occur to people when they get home from work, when they go to bed, or when they get up and how well the systems work the rest of the time. (Although, in this scenario, no one can explain what happens at noon.)

It's extremely hard to get to the bottom of all the assumptions and myths that create a view of the data and what it can be used for. It's not unusual for late revelations about the origin and meaning of a field in a data set to change the interpretation and value of the models that an ML project creates. It's impossible to eliminate the chance of this happening, but it is possible to reduce and manage the risk by locating or gathering the information that's available and then questioning why the assertions about lineage should be trusted.

4.5.4 *Events*

Various calamities can befall data stores over the years. Underinvestment can mean that room to store data runs low, leading to data being tossed out. Sometimes this happens systematically; sometimes it's done randomly. Accidents happen as well. Some data can be lost due to a poorly written query, and no one notices until it's irretrievable or a hardware failure occurs and corrupts the table over time. Insidious events and errors such as poor rounding or type conversion can lead to noise being gradually introduced into the data.

Data stores are subject to quality improvement exercises, re-architecture, and replatforming. There may have zero impact on the data and its use to represent the population of interest for modeling, but this can all go horribly wrong. The changes and features introduced to support a new use case can be accompanied by bugs or may require updates, which has an impact on the data. Data fields can be migrated from short integers to long integers, or floats. Sometimes this will be done well, yet the data is unimportant, and sometimes rounding or simple corrections for storage types (for example, moving from 32 bit to 64 bit) can introduce noise.

Understanding the chain of events that the customer thinks defines the evolution of the data set can explain strange and striking results that the team gets when they are creating a model. It's challenging but getting the full extent of this picture saves a lot of time chasing exciting but illusory patterns. Being careful and thorough now prevents your team from wasting time later.

The information that you gather about the data is also important in deepening and changing your view about the ethical aspects of the project. Where and how the data was obtained bears on what you should do with it: what it might not say as well as what it does say. The recent debate in AI and ML about the behavior of language models and the ethics of using them are strongly informed by the source of the data that underpins them [5]. Collecting and documenting this information and taking it into account as best you can is going to be important if someone challenges you about the appropriate use of the model and the safety of its users.

4.6 *Privacy, security, and an ethics plan*

As noted, developing an understanding of the motivation for data collection, methods used to collect the data, lineage, and the events that affect the data set in storage help form a picture of the ethical implications of using the data. Having said that, the technical questions that are important to the modeling team are necessary but not sufficient to get a full view of the ethical, privacy, and security issues that your team needs to deal with. Setup 5 in the sprint 0 backlog needs to be undertaken to build a fuller picture, allowing you to make informed decisions about these vital issues now as well as later in the project.

> **Privacy, security and ethics plan: Setup 5**
> - Review project CSR and ethics.
> - Build and share the privacy, security, and data-handling plans.

In the pre-project work, the ideas and hypothesis to drive the project were qualified to ensure that they were legal and ethical. For example, we did a DPIA for The Bike Shop. As more information emerges, and as you gain more access to the customer and their issues, sprint 0 brings the opportunity to address these issues in more detail. This lets you pose questions like:

- Were all the data tables for the project gathered for the same purpose? Is the purpose of the project appropriate for all the tables?
- Were all the data tables gathered in the same legal jurisdiction? Does being from or subject to a particular jurisdiction exclude some of the data?
- Are there any exceptional data subjects in the table that should be excluded or treated differently for security and privacy purposes?
- Can you put adequate data-handling processes (anonymization, aggregation, encryption) in place on the infrastructure for the project?
- If your team and the application have access to all the data sources, should they?

Validate and document your findings on the CSR, privacy, security, and ethics aspects of the proposed system using the answers to these questions. The pre-project activities should have identified relevant experts and authorities in the customer's organization so use these points of contact to open discussions.

4.7 Project roadmap

> **Project roadmap development ticket: Setup 6**
> - Build and share the project roadmap.

The project roadmap is the high-level plan that drives the project. Essentially, it's a mirror image of the project hypothesis and estimates that you created in presales. The roadmap tells you (and the team) what tasks will be executed when and the dependencies that need to be resolved to unlock and open the different phases of work. Developing the road map now is useful because:

- You're in possession of new information about the project's delivery context. This is information about the client organization and the data stores that has not been available until now.

- You know what the team structure is going to be and when the team will be able to work on the various elements of the project.

The roadmap must follow the general structure presented in the rest of this book:

- Data acquisition and project infrastructure building: Sprint 1 described in chapters 5 and 6.
- Model building, evaluation, and selection: Sprint 2 described in chapters 7 and 8.
- System integration and productionization: Sprint 3 described in chapter 9.

However, different components in this general pattern can be dragged forward or delayed, depending on your circumstances. Importantly, you need to reach an agreement with your client stakeholders about a change of course so they understand why you are (or are not) spending their money in the way that you planned.

In sprint 1 (chapter 5), for example, we proposed to start work on the system's UX features. All things being equal, this is a smart thing to do because it better establishes nonfunctional requirements for the models. This is important when it comes to evaluation and selection of the models, and so, there is a dependency that can be satisfied by getting the UX work underway quickly. Also, building UX designs brings the project to life and engages the customer.

If you have serious doubts about the integrity of the data or the possibility of effectively processing it for the modeling team, however, then it's not a good idea to waste time on the customer's model, which will be work that's completely superfluous. In the same vein, it might be a sensible decision to take a "quick and dirty" approach to the data infrastructure, building initially to rapidly prototype some models. This could drive all the technical risk out of the project, but at the price of requiring a lot of rework and potential delay later on.

As you gain more experience, these kinds of decisions become far more obvious and straightforward to make. The most important tip is that getting through this process should be done in collaboration with your client: build a shared understanding of why particular focus points are required. Agree on how these issues will be dealt with and overcome.

Building the project roadmap now also provides you with the opportunity to cross-check your estimates and assumptions for the project. Be realistic about your estimates in the light of what you have now discovered about the technical infrastructure and the data that's available for modeling. Flagging the complications and difficulties that may emerge at this point and making decisions about how they should be mitigated (possibly by reducing the projects scope, increasing its budget, or by reconsidering the project altogether) can be painful. However, it's much less painful than hoping for the best and ending up with a project that fails.

4.8   *Sprint 0 checklist*

You can complete the checklist in Table 4.2 with the delivery team to ensure that the elements of sprint 0 are put in to place before the project starts. The objective of sprint 0 is to ensure that the conditions for the team to work effectively and efficiently are met. Everyone involved in the checklist meeting should be invested in making sure that every item is covered usefully.

Table 4.2   Checklist for sprint 0

Item	Notes and examples
Description of data	Does an adequate life history for the data resources exist? This is a discursive description of what the data is (domain, source systems, scale, timeframe, etc.).
	Does the overview seem consistent and sufficient?
	Has the data description been validated with any data experiments or with any other method?
List of supplied data tables and other data sources	Name of the table and a description of contents (e.g., customer master, customer type hierarchy).
	Name and description of other data sources (e.g., sensor, aggregated sensor platform) and connectivity details.
Limitations or problems	Description of known problems with the data.
	Document any unexplained or unclear steps in the data's origin.
Business uses	Outline of known business uses of this data to date (how the customer currently uses it).
Documentation plan	Ensure that a date for delivery is defined for all mandated documentation and that it is feasible for these documents to be created and delivered on time.
	Ensure that resources are allocated for the delivery of the documents.
Project roadmap	Provide a high-level breakdown of how the ultimate outcome of the project is to be achieved.
Communication plan	Ensure that adequate touchpoints with the project's stakeholders (internal and external) are established.
Infrastructure plan	Resourcing and time are in place to deliver the required working environment and development infrastructure.
Team design	Delivery resources are identified and available for the project to be successfully executed within budget.
Project heartbeat	List planned meetings across the project duration, the purpose of each meeting (sprint-planning, retrospective); include the daily stand-up schedule and attendance list.

4.9   *Bike Shop: project setup*

The Bike Shop project is defined and sold to the customer, delivering on five challenges:

- *Challenge 1:* The project will verify that it is possible to use The Bike Shop's opdis2 database and other assets to build a customer churn prediction system and will measure the performance of the system in terms of the recall and precision of the predictions made.
- *Challenge 2:* The project will verify that it is possible to use The Bike Shop's opdis2 database and other assets to build a demand prediction system and will measure the performance of the system in terms of the recall and precision of the predictions made.
- *Challenge 3:* You will investigate an implementation that uses the data and data-flows migrated from opdis2 to a new cloud platform to provide timely, actionable information to users in Manufacturing and Retail Service. This enables them to optimize their business decisions with regard to stock, supply, and customer interaction.
- *Challenge 4:* If challenges 1-3 are completed to the customer's satisfaction, you will implement and deliver a system that provides the required functionality.
- *Challenge 5:* We will verify that data from 2-5 years ago is of sufficient quality to use when creating revenue and churn models, and we will quantify the impact that the quality of this data has on the rank and usefulness of the models that can be extracted from the available data.

You've celebrated the win with the bid team, and everyone is looking to you to get the project up and running. Your organization assigns you to the project and allocates a resourcing budget. You are told to work with the resourcing managers to bring an appropriate delivery team together.

The first thing that you do is to call Rob and check that he's still available for the project. You breathe a sigh of relief that he's not been snapped up and immediately flag him for The Bike Shop resourcing system. Rob recommends a data engineer, Kate, as being free to work on the setup sprint. You then ring Kate and ask her to meet for coffee to talk about working on a project. In the meeting, you outline the prospective assignment to Kate: working to support Rob, setting up the infrastructure, and starting the work on the data investigations for The Bike Shop. Kate's keen to work on the main project, and you decide that she'd be a great fit.

You flag Kate as required, and her manager tells you that she's now billing your project. Rob messages you to let you know that he's meeting Kate later to get her working on the system access requests.

You need to find three other people to make up the team. You set up a meeting with Rob and together you review the work plan. The two of you decide you'll need two ML engineers and a data scientist until the final four weeks of the project. For the final four weeks, you'll need a UX engineer and an application developer but will retain one of the ML engineers and, of course, Kate and Rob. You contact the relevant resource managers and ask who would fit the assignments that you have.

Although the assignments are short-term, the resource managers are quite positive because their experience is that this kind of project can be motivational for their reports. Quickly, a list of names rolls in. You review all the CVs and set up get-to-know-you chats with all of the candidates that you and Rob agree are qualified.

The candidates prove to be excellent, and you ask Danish (a data scientist), Jenn (an ML engineer), and Sam (also an ML engineer) to join your team for four weeks along with Clara (a UX engineer) and Miguel (an application/data engineer) for the last four weeks.

You know that the form that system is going to take for the users will be important. It's agreed at a high level that you'll need a set of dashboards (ones for inventory with more detail and for customer churn) with a focus on ease of use. You decide to get Clara to spend a week early in the project pinning this down. As it happens, Clara and her resourcing manager are open to this idea because Clara wants to go on a holiday during weeks 6 and 7.

This good fortune prompts you to check the leave cards for the team, and you discover that Rob has a week's leave booked in week 4, and you have two weeks leave booked for weeks 7 and 8. This is inconvenient and disruptive, but a moment of reflection tells you that people, including you, need time off. These new gaps give you the scope to book Sam for the last four weeks of the project. Table 4.3 shows the resourcing plan to date.

You work with a member of your organization's operations team to calculate the cost of the proposed resource plan, and you are relieved that it comes in well under the target cost for the project. In fact, you are left with some contingency that might be used to retain Danish for weeks 7 and 8, which could be a good thing, given the volume of work required.

Table 4.3 A crude resourcing plan for the project now that resources have been identified

Resource	W1 (0)	W2 (0)	W3 (1)	W4 (1)	W5 (2)	W6 (2)	W7 (2)	W8 (2)	W9 (3)	W10 (3)
You										
Rob										
Kate										
Danish										
Sam										
Jenn										
Clara										
Miguel										

You sit back in your chair and think about what you, Rob, and Kate have to do in the next eight or so working days. You've moved as fast as possible, but the clock is ticking, and you've got lots to do. There are two things you can get out of the way quickly though: the documentation plan and the communication plan.

You work from your standard template and decide that Karima would be a great fit as the customer's product owner, so you message her and ask her if she's willing to pick up that role on the project. You also ask her who on The Bike Shop side can work as your day-to-day troubleshooter to facilitate delivery.

Happily, Karima is on board to be product owner for the project, and she knows a great person, Niresh, a delivery manager in her organization, who can be a day-to-day technical point of contact. Niresh knows The Bike Shop systems like the back of his hand, and Karima is totally confident that if a problem can be fixed, Niresh will fix it. You write two drafts and send the comm's plan and the documentation plan to Karima and Niresh and ask for their comments.

Using the pre-project organizational map, you get Niresh to introduce you to the Data Protection Officer at The Bike Shop and to the Security Architect who's responsible for signing off on this project. Before meeting with them, you, Rob, and Kate get together and work out possible privacy, security, and ethics catches. These include the data permissioning issue identified in the project contract and the need not to make the system exclusive of particular customers. When you meet the Data Protection Officer (DPO) and the Security Architect (SA), you brief them about the project and plans. You share the briefing slides with the DPO and SA after the meeting, along with the actions and notes that you acquired (typically, these are for more information and detail, which will come out later in the project).

Rob and Kate now have a clear understanding of the infrastructure to be used, and you have a strong idea of what data will be acquired and how it will be manipulated and exploited. The next step is to get Kate and Rob to set up the project infrastructure. There are two chunks of work to do here:

- Rob needs to design the dev/test/prod stack that's going be used. Rob can draw on the components that he and the team will have access to in the customer's infrastructure to complete the design. Then he and Kate can request access permissions.
- Kate needs to design and set up a working infrastructure. Again, to do this, there needs to be the necessary permissions.

To complete the work, Rob and Kate get the necessary permissions and begin setting up their respective environments. A complicating factor is that The Bike Factory project was sold as part of a wider migration. The overall concept is that the company's data assets need to be migrated to the cloud, and the new data asset will enable the deployment of new applications such as churn management and inventory prediction (which you will be developing). The date for the data migration to be completed is week 7 (W7 in Table 4.3). Before that point, the data will not be available in the new production environment.

The implication of this discovery is that a workaround is needed to get the team working effectively before the production database is available in the cloud container that's being commissioned for The Bike Shop. Rob talks this over with the technical architect of the migration project, and they agree that a one-time copy of the opdis2 data asset is the most feasible approach.

This avoids all the complications of managing the data feeds and dependencies that are the core of the work in the migration project and provides the assets your team needs. Niresh and the Security Architect are contacted and agree with the plan. The result is the design in figure 4.2. The migration provisions the production (prod) environment and that will then be used to provision the test environment with the appropriate subset of the prod environment. In the meantime, a one-off copy will support development (dev).

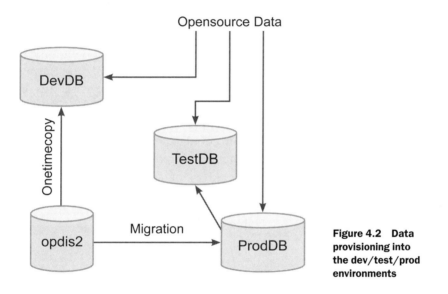

Figure 4.2 Data provisioning into the dev/test/prod environments

Once Rob understands how the data is provided, he is able to identify the set of services that are needed in each of the environments. His next task is to figure out how the assets produced in the dev environment will be commissioned into the test and prod environments. A scripting system is needed to define the test and prod environments. This will then be read by an interpreter in the new The Bike Shop cloud and deployed without manual intervention.

Rob defines the dev environment as requiring two high-specification development instances that the modeling teams will use and a test instance that the ML engineering team will use to create and prove instances of selected models.

The strategy for the prod environment is to use the cloud environment's cluster management technology to instantiate and run the model instances on demand. These will spin up in milliseconds and can be used for inference episodes until the demand drops, when they will be automatically decommissioned. Rob advocates this approach as cheap and robust. The demand for the instances will be created by a workflow triggered by a table refresh event in the new prod database. The dashboards can then be used to review the data tables that are updated by the models. This sounds quite complex, but Rob assures you it's the modern way to go.

Now that Rob has completed the infrastructure design, Kate can look at system access, so you ping her with your resourcing plan. This will let her know who to get access for on the dev machines. Kate is also tasked with setting up the document storage area on the customer's infrastructure and getting access to the customer's work ticketing system. Source code control is to be done using industry standard tools, and Rob specifies a model/experiment management tool and a data versioning system.

You and Rob leave Kate to her assignments and start working through the process of creating the data story. This involves running several meetings with data architects and the system users. By working through the list of people who understand elements of the opdis2 system, a picture emerges.

The data warehouse itself was created from aggregating three operational databases. These represented three operational areas managed by Manufacture: Europe, Americas and Asia, and ROW (rest of world). Although the data was not marked as originating from any one of these assets, the data was marked as relevant to a particular country; each record has a country field. Figure 4.3 shows this flow.

Overall, it was determined that the team could expect approximately 40 million rows of data, extracted from three tables in the data warehouse. The three tables in opdis2 identified as potentially useful are:

- The Main BW table, which contains transaction lists (sales that had been made).
- The Product Hierarchy/SKU table.
- The Currency table.

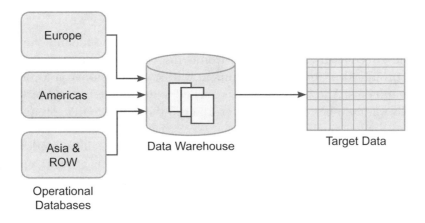

Figure 4.3   Three operational databases used to create the tables in opdis2

The data owners identified the Product Hierarchy and Currency tables as required to aggregate and to normalize the information in the transaction list. The Product Hierarchy/SKU information was important because it permitted a sensible grouping of items such as parts, racing bikes, utility bikes, and so on. This arrangement allows predictions to be made over items sharing common nodes in the hierarchy. Items might be sold individually but rarely and frequently as a type of thing, so understanding these aggregations is key for providing useful information to the business. The Currency table was identified as important because this allowed the value of the sales to be normalized.

The main concern is to figure out what happened during the data quality project mentioned in pre-project discovery, where it was discovered that this was completed 18 months before the current project. This means that data older than this is likely to be different in character and probably noisier. Talking with Niresh reveals that there were extensive changes and deletions made to the Main BW table in opdis2 during the data quality project, and he feels that, although the project was seen as a success, it's hard to pin down actual improvements to the overall data. It's more likely that things were tidied up, but there doesn't seem to have been any metrics applied to the state of the data before and after the exercise. This reinforces the need for the team to try to quantify and characterize the differences before and after the changes when they do get access to the asset.

This information forms the basis of the data story document that you write up. You review it with Kate and Rob and after some comments and improvements, you file it in Kate's new repository. You notice that she's filed the communication and documentation plans in there for you already, so you write her a thank you note.

You set a conference up with Karima, Niresh, Rob, and Kate to go through your idea of how the project should run. The roadmap that you describe is easily agreed on. There needs to be some upfront UX work and, at the same time, a lot of focus on understanding the impact of the data improvement done as part of the data quality project. You walk through the projected next three sprints, and it is agreed with a nod from the participants. Then you come to the working practices, and you describe your proposed project heartbeat:

- A daily stand-up call
- The weekly stakeholder meeting
- End of sprint show and tell (biweekly)
- End of sprint review (biweekly)
- Sprint planning meeting (biweekly)

Niresh and Karima are a bit taken aback; they had not expected such a significant commitment of time to the project. You note that this is all up for constant review, and if they feel that it's wasting time, some of the meetings could be run without them. However, you ask them to try your schedule for the first few weeks. If it becomes clear that the meeting schedules and pace is unnecessary, then things can be changed after that. It's going to be important that everyone communicates clearly at the outset of the project when the team is "storming and forming."

Kate and Rob really enjoyed the review of the data story. They're keen to keep up the practice, and they also want to be careful to ticket and record their work. Kate writes a short team manifesto and files it in the document repository:

- A ticket is created for every work item.
- Something concrete is produced for every ticket and retained by the team.
- Work is completed only after it's been reviewed.

You sit back on the afternoon of day 10 of sprint 0. Everything is complete, and you've got time to do your timesheets and catch up on the emails that you've been ignoring. On Monday, Danish, Sam, Jenn, and Clara join the team. Rob's just demoed the dev infrastructure, and he's got credentials for the team members to use first thing Monday morning. It looks like you and the team are ready to rock!

Summary

- Administrative processes need to be started early, before the people that need to use the systems or get into buildings are billing the project. Actually, doing the work to determine what needs to be asked for is a good first step, asking for it all is a great second step.
- You need to make sure that the customer understands what is going to be delivered, and how and when it is to be delivered.
- Ensure that lines of communication are open, and everyone knows how they are expected to share and get information.
- Your team needs to have a shared understanding of how it will get work done.
- Check that the development environment you need can be set up and is operational for all team members.
- Make sure that there is an understood path to production.
- Delve into the life story of the data that your team will be using.

Diving into the problem

In sprint 1, the team puts in place and starts using the infrastructure to support the delivery project, then they open the data that's going to underpin the ML project. In order to crack the data open, they will use the infrastructure (particularly the pipelines and testing systems) that they construct.

5.1 Sprint 1 backlog

The sprint 1 backlog provides tasks that are described in this chapter (S1.1 - S1.4) and in chapter 6 (S1.5 - S1.7). With sprint 1, you prepare for the core ML activity of creating and evaluating useful models using ML algorithms. The work is to dig deeper into the data resources and develop the team's expertise and capability to use them for modeling. You also need to build the supporting infrastructure that lifts and shifts the data from where it's resting to where you need it.

Table 5.1   Backlog for sprint 1

Task #	Item
S1.1	Undertake a data survey; scan and inspect appropriate tables for completeness, coverage, and quality.
	Conduct data tests to address bias, poisoning, quality, coverage, and accuracy (of labeling).
	Write up and review the data survey.
S1.2	Develop a business application description.
	Develop the application user story backlog (S2.1, S3.1).
	Validate the application description and user story backlog with users.
	Identify and validate the ML model performance requirements.
	Create UX designs.
S1.3	Aggregate and fuse relevant data into an integrated picture.
	Implement and manage data pipelines.
	Design and implement data tests.
S1.4	Commission and adopt a model repository.
	Identify and record all artefacts for use in ML pipelines.
S1.5	Plan and design EDA.
	Write and share the EDA report.
S1.6	Check ethics in light of the emerging understanding.
S1.7	Define and implement the model baselines.

The first step to delivering this sprint is to deepen your (and the team's) understanding of the data. We'll cover that in the next section.

5.2   Understanding the data

Your team is on board and funding is in place to work on the client's problem. In sprint 0, you acquired an overview of the data resources for the job. Now, the task at hand is to do a rapid but systematic evaluation of the available data resources.

In this book, this task is called a *data survey*, but it could be called an inspection or an overview. It's a fast, structured investigation, which produces results that you can document, discuss, and share to build understanding and insight. Most importantly, this creates a checkpoint for obvious problems with the data.

> ### Data survey ticket: S1.1
>
> - Undertake a data survey; scan and inspect the appropriate tables for completeness, coverage, and quality.
> - Conduct data tests to address bias, poisoning, quality, coverage, and accuracy (of labeling).
> - Write up and review the data survey.

Because you built a narrative about the data in sprint 0, you have a map for the team to work with, even if it's labeled "there be dragons!" But, as they say, the map is not the territory. Now, you need to use your data story in combination with your carefully assembled team of data ninjas to find more dragons.

It may be that you don't yet have the team, access, or infrastructure to start work on the core problems such as handling the data, articulating an understanding of the problem or creating the infrastructure to support work to solve these issues. If you lack required permissions and access, you are in trouble; the team can't work and can't progress. There may be some scope to work on the UX, but in reality, the team can do little until this is sorted out.

5.2.1 The data survey

There are three steps to the data investigation that this book recommends. We did the first step, the data story, back in chapter 4. The data story elicits and records the recommendations and information about the data resources that are available. Now, we need to do the data survey, which validates the data story and provides more information about the nonfunctional and system properties of the data assets. Later, when we have the data in the right place, the exploratory data analysis (EDA) looks at the statistical properties of the data. With the EDA, we find out what can really be done with the data.

The purpose of the data survey is to reduce uncertainty about the contents of the data resources. The data story will be full of assumptions and assertions about what is in the data sources and where it comes from. Now, we need to check that the assumptions made in the data story are plausible.

What are the drivers for a structured and systematic investigation? First, it's relatively cheap in terms of time and effort. The queries that need to be written for this are easy enough for any data engineer, and the queries should all run fast. This may not be true for the later EDA exercise and almost certainly won't be true in the modeling phase. The engineering required for that phase may take a lot of thought, and the queries may take a while to run, test, and debug. The relatively low effort spent on the data survey now avoids expensive mistakes later.

The second nice feature of the survey is that because it's simple, quick, and cheap, it can be comprehensive. In contrast, an EDA can uncover a huge number of avenues for investigation in an interesting data set. The team won't get through them all; in fact, they will probably only have time to explore a relatively small fraction of the data set properly.

A narrow investigation means that potential show-stopping issues can lurk unde-tected. suddenly appearing at the end of the project, derailing everything, and embar-rassing everyone. A broad but shallow survey lets you and the team make rational decisions about where to focus deep and time-consuming EDA effort. As for the survey itself, the following checks on the data are a good way to start:

- Can all component elements described in the data story be identified and located in the customer's system? If in the worst case, you don't have access to the system, can a technical support person or a data catalog be used to provide a proxy for determining that the data is there?
- Can you get a count of records for today or last week or last period, and can you get a file size in bytes (Tb, Gb, Mb, Kb) for the data assets? The size and structure of each data resource identified should correspond to the expected values, given the data life history. Sometimes, the table scans to determine if all the required records are present can't be done on the operational infrastructure. Smaller que-ries, however, are often possible without disrupting the data system.
- Are the oldest and newest records in the data as expected, given the customer's description?
- What are the largest and smallest values in the key columns, the basic aggregates (mean, median), and the range of data?
- Are there changes in scale, format, or type in the records for periods before and after major events in the data set's history (migrations, replatforming, data qual-ity programs, federation, and integration episodes)?

To explore the idea of a data survey, imagine an illustrative project to manage an intel-ligent building. One of the tables might contain temperature data from a bunch of sensors, and you and the team want to integrate this with data on sunlight, building usage, and climate to create an energy-saving control system for the building. If the team has access to a good data management system or a data catalog, then they should find that the required databases and tables are in place and have the expected number of records and storage sizes. Even so, it's worthwhile to cross-check what the records show in case the metadata is out of sync with the actual data store.

In the next few paragraphs, we'll see an example of how useful investigating what's actually in the data tables with simple ad hoc queries can be. The investigation shows that the data is as reported in the DBMS and is available for queries. We'll use a few snippets of SQL to illustrate, but don't worry if you can't read the code, the text explains what's happening.

These investigations run like a stream of consciousness as you find oddities and check your understanding of the data. What's important is to make sure that these four points are probed: it's all there, it's the right size, the records look like you expect them to, and any major issues are uncovered. There are three types of data in the resources that you will need to use:

- *Numerical fields:* Represent measured quantities such as sizes, weights, densities, frequencies, wavelengths, times, concentrations, or temperatures.
- *Categorical fields:* Represent labels that are applied to things such as colors, genera, species, textures, or product identifiers.
- *Unstructured fields:* Represent images, text, or sounds. Examples of unstructured data include product descriptions, example images, sequences or timeseries, social media messages, customer support emails, conversations between traders, or incident notes.

The next section provides examples of how you might treat each of these fields in a data survey exercise. A common way of starting the survey is to get a list of all the data tables that exist in the different customer databases. Unfortunately, different databases use different tools and commands that can be used to perform the survey. For example, we can access the tables in an Oracle database with the following command:

```
select table_name from all_tables;
>TABLE_NAME | OWNER |TABLESPACE_NAME
TEMPERATURE_READINGS | SYS | SYSTEM
INCIDENTS | SYS |SYSTEM
```

This command shows that there are two tables available: temperature_readings and incidents. Temperature_readings contains numerical data so we will use this as the first table addressed in the survey.

5.2.2 Surveying numerical data

For the smart building, it makes sense to start by checking that the right number of records are in the temperature_readings table. This is done using a `select count(*)` statement.

```
select count(*) from temperature_readings
>262944000
```

Does the result make sense? We are looking at about five years of sensor records, so there will be a leap year in there. The count then is 5 * 365 + 1 = 1,826 days, so 262,944,000 / 1,826 = 144,000. That's a nice round number. If it reminds you of 1,440 (24 * 60), it's almost as if 100 sensors have reported without fail every minute for five years of perfect 24-hour days! A bit odd if you think about it for a minute, but because of this, there's approximately the right amount of data in the table.

There's more to check though. Let's make sure that the records are actually useful. Instead of using a `select count (*)`, we'll use a `select *` in the following code snippet, which means "get everything." Of course, getting everything would be tedious because reading thousands of records can be painful. For this reason, we'll add a `limit 1` clause to the statement, which means "start getting everything but then stop as soon as you have one":

```
select * from temperature_readings limit 1
>(21,2021,September,17,00:00:10,04.3,tx,op)
```

At least one of the records is useful. Often, rather than setting `limit 1`, it's more sensible to scan a handful of the records (maybe 10 or 20) to check the data. We can do that by changing the `limit` number (but you knew that!). It also might be smart to use the `where` clause to probe for records in different years. Hopefully, the data schema is available and understood, but if not, then why not check it too and record the outcome?

In the query results from temperature_readings, 21 is the sensor number, followed by the year, the month, the day, and the time of the reading: `21,2021,September,17,00:00:10`. In the example, it's unknown (by anyone) what produces the *op* at the end of the results; this isn't unusual in data projects. However, what you found should go on the project backlog as an investigation item. It might be that *op* means *out of parameters* and indicates that the sensor is broken. Alternatively, *op* might mean *operational*, an indicator that the sensor is functioning properly. The point is that someone needs to check this soon.

Having established that there are useful records in the database, the next thing to check is that there's meaningful information in it. The dependent variable here is `temperature`. It's shown as 04.3 in the previous record. A sensible check is to see if the dependent variables are really recorded in the data. For example:

```
select count(*) from temperature_readings as tr where
tr.temperature!="null"
>262583041
```

Hmm, that means that there are 360,959 (262944000 − 262583041) null temperature readings in the data set—about 0.13%. That's not much, but it's something that the team needs to know.

Also, how many of the temperature readings are 0 or not? The temperatures recorded could indeed be 0.0° C, but in many data systems, (not so) smart programmers replace "bad" readings with 0 to make their data pipelines work smoothly. A count of 0.0 values is worth doing:

```
select count(*) from temperature_readings as tr where tr.temperature==0.0
>1890030
```

Which, again, is not an unreasonable number, overall, 360959 + 1890030 = 2250989, so less than 0.86% of the data might be junk (however, the 0.0 values could be real!). Even if there are pathological concentrations of noise created by these missing values, their overall rarity means that it's likely that the results of the modeling will not be completely invalidated. Obviously, some scenarios could make these problems more pressing. For example, it could be that the null values appear when temperatures go over a certain value only (as the sensor fails, for instance).

Depending on the significance of the table and the time available to build the survey, it might be that you attain your goals with such simple queries, and the task is complete. Perhaps the project is dependent on many tables with many dependent variables, but there's nothing complex jumping out. If this is the case, then getting a view of the quality of the tables and databases at a high level could be the right allocation of effort.

On the other hand, if the scale of the work is more manageable and you have ample time, or if there is a higher level of caution in the data story about the data quality, then delving deeper would be smart. In this case, you might contemplate doing the following (based on the smart building scenario):

- Check that ranges that cross 0 work as expected. How many negative temperature readings are there? Should there be any?
- Check the limits of real-world attributes such as temperature. How many readings above 60° or below −35° are there?
- Determine what are the entity counts. For example, how many records are from sensor 21? How many sensors are recorded? How many records have "op" and what different values are there in that code field?

Additionally, in the work that you did to compile the data story, you may have already uncovered some known issues with the data. Now is the time to focus on those and to dig in. Looking again at the smart building example, let's imagine that there was a known change in sensor design after the first year of operation. The question is, did the change make any difference to the data that's present? We saw that there are 360,959 null values in the data set. What's the distribution of them year by year:

```
select count(*),year from temperature_readings as tr where
tr.temperature!="null" group_by year
>(0,0,0,0, 360959)
```

About 0.5% of the data in the first year is null, and the first year is the year that the sensors were changed. That's something to further investigate and take into account when modelling. It may be that that year's data should be disregarded altogether. The job of the data survey is to find problems, and it informs the team as to what they can expect in the data resource. The survey shows them that what they were expecting is there or not.

The previous examples deal with numeric values. Of course, numeric data will not be the only data that you will need to use, so what kind of actions should you take to survey categorical or unstructured data?

5.2.3 *Surveying categorical data*

With categorical data, it's often important to know the distribution of records across the categories. In the smart building example, there is a sensor type code, which was seen when we ran the query:

```
select * from temperature_readings limit 1
>(21,2021,September,17,00:00:10,04.3,tx,op)
```

The unknown is `op`, but `tx` is a type of sensor. How many types of sensors are there? The data about sensor types is categorical (manufacturer ID), so getting a sense of it requires a slightly more complex query that first gets all the distinct sensor types from the temperature_readings table and then counts them:

```
SELECT Count(*) FROM (SELECT DISTINCT sensor_type FROM
temperature_readings);
>7
```

The number 7 is low enough to make it worth enumerating them:

```
select distinct sensor_type from temperature_readings as sensors;
>Sensors
A1
A2
Tp
Tn
Tx
Xr
UNKNOWN
```

The appearance of UNKNOWN is an issue that we will need to investigate, including what the different types of sensors are. At this point, however, we can stop this line of investigation because the EDA exercise may commit significant resources to dig further. Remember, the data survey is about establishing what's important or difficult about the data that needs further scrutiny, not necessarily about doing that scrutiny now.

If the sensor types are determined to be important, then in the EDA exercise, we should look at the number of each type, how many different readings each produce, the impact that the different qualities of sensor have on the data, the range of readings from each, the outliers each type generates, what granularity of temperature each sensor registers, and so on. The point of the data survey is to establish what these questions are, which is what we've done now. When the survey is reviewed, the issues and questions can be prioritized for the EDA team to follow up on.

5.2.4 *Surveying unstructured data*

Dealing with unstructured data in the survey is different. Delving into the properties of a set of unstructured items requires deep ML techniques. We'll cover investigating unstructured data in more detail as part of the EDA exercise in chapter 6, but these approaches are often too involved and time consuming for a data survey. In the survey, we need to map out the issues and problems that might be lurking in the data. Some will be irrelevant to the models that the team develops and the applications that consume them. The important thing is to know where they are so that they can either be investigated and resolved or avoided.

With unstructured data, it's important to establish what useful unstructured data resources are available and to assess their quality. In the smart building database, there is an incidents table that needs to be included in the survey:

```
select count(*) from incidents;
>1781

select * from incidents limit 1;
>23-05-2021, CRITICAL, 360, "HVAC failure…", "affinity engineer..")
```

The query shows us that the text fields are incident_description and resolution. Let's gauge the quality of these:

```
select incident_description from incidents limit 5;
>"HVAC failure meant loss of cold air for floor 12 to 25",
"HVAC intermittent for several hours, users complaining",
"HVAC reported as making rattling sound",
"Loss of cold air on 5th floor, seems isolated",
"Users reporting excessive heat on 5th floor"
```

It seems that there is potentially interesting information in these snippets. It might be hard to translate that into data because parsing out which floor the problems are occurring in may be challenging. On the other hand, it's probably going to be easy to relate some of these incidents to strange sensor readings.

Typically, you would do this kind of inspection over more records because it's easy to scroll through scores or even hundreds of records to see if they do (or do not) contain rich-looking information. It would also be normal for the analyst doing the survey to check how many records are empty or contain the word *NULL*. A quick inspection might also show other indicators of useless records (such as "." or "n/a"), which were used to gloss over mandatory fields in their administration application.

Similar approaches can be used for other types of unstructured data as well. Skilled analysts can quickly extract and render hundreds of images from a database and scan them for issues. For instance, a selection of 100 images might contain 90 that are simply of blue sky. This might be normal and expected and still indicate useful data, or it might be a problem.

Spotting regularities, patterns, and oddities in unstructured data quickly allows you to ask more questions and to delve down more deeply into the data. Perhaps the 90 blue sky images show up in the analyst's query because there's some quirk in the database that makes them appear in a random selection. The EDA team can get to the bottom of this and provide the evidence that you need to show your sponsors that there is or isn't an issue. The point is that you will do this all before you've committed serious time and resources to the modeling and evaluation activities.

5.2.5   *Reporting and using the survey*

The data survey needs to be documented and reviewed before it can be used. Table 5.2 lists as a suggestion the items that could be recorded in a survey report. Typically, there will be many pages of uninteresting findings, reporting on the existence of tables with the right number of records and good integrity, for example, so it's useful to attach a cover sheet to the survey with key deltas recorded. This alerts everyone to the main foibles that were found in the records.

Table 5.2   Data survey report contents

Item	Note (examples)
Description of data	Discursive description of what the data is (domain, source systems, scale, time period, etc.).
List tables provided	Name of table and list of attributes.
For each table:	
Known problems	Relate the description of known problems with the data.
Number of entities	If it's possible to live count the records; otherwise, taken from a data catalog.
Sample entity	A fresh sample taken from a table.
Number of records with nulls	Possibly focused on attributes of interest.
Number of records with 0 values	Possibly focused on attributes of interest.

Specific queries to investigate known or revealed data integrity issues	`Query 1`
	
	`Result`
	
	`Query 2`
	
	`Result`

A survey report is useful for the team; they would have to find this information themselves to use the data, so it saves repeated work. It also creates a talking point about the data properties. Additionally, more queries to investigate the integrity of the data as is will get added into it over time as different people raise suspicions and bright ideas about the data. Gradually, the data resource becomes a well-described entity for the project.

The most important use for the survey, however, is to allow the team to determine where to spend effort during the EDA exercise. The survey provides a map, showing what infrastructure is needed to allow for the questions that need to be resolved before building a model. The survey document also becomes a handy way to start data testing. (Data testing is needed to support the implementation of data pipelines for the modelling and for subsequent production exercises.) Finally, the survey may already have uncovered problems with the data that jeopardize your project. If this is the case, then get them on the risk register and make the client aware of these.

5.3　*Business problem refinement, UX, and application design*

Moving on from the data survey, the next step in sprint 1 is to develop a deeper understanding of the business problem. Documenting and understanding business issues provide the information that enable the team's work on the project and data infrastructure to be efficient, directed, and purposeful.

Business problem refinement ticket: S1.2

- Develop a business application description.
- Develop the application user story backlog (S2.1, S3.1).
- Validate the application description and user story backlog with users.
- Identify and validate the ML model performance requirements.
- Create UX designs.

Understanding a business properly is a daunting challenge that can consume months or years. A technical team typically only gradually evolves a deep appreciation of the demands and constraints on a business, and it'll take a long time for them to really see the heart of the issues that are most important. Yet, pinning down the business problem that the team is addressing must be done, and the team must develop a view on this if it is to be successful. To accelerate eliciting and documenting the core business issues, it's necessary to adopt a few tactics and tricks.

In the pre-project, you built a project hypothesis, and in sprint 0, you turned that into a project roadmap. These flesh out your team's mandate for the work that you're delivering, and the customer reviewed both. In addition, you created user and model stories while doing the project hypothesis. These outputs should be helpful in beginning the work that is needed to create an effective application design, but there's a lot more to be done!

To make progress, the team needs to use the information they have so far to talk to the next layer of experts and users. Agile practitioners say, "a story card is a promise for a conversation" [3]. The user stories you compiled in the pre-project phase can be further developed and formalized into story cards. *Story cards* lay out the application concept, who is impacted by it and how, and what the story does for the organization. Table 5.3 shows the contents of a typical story card.

Table 5.3   The contents of a story card for an ML project. Note the final five rows, which establish how to go about creating this.

Item	Notes (example)
Concept	A simple explanation of the top-level area the project addresses; for example, customer service or inventory management.
List of stakeholders	Jo Bloggs (IT), Sam Smith (Proc), Arthur Aske (Logistics)
Business priorities	The list of focus areas for the business: customer service uplift, revenue, cost reduction, growth, diversification, capital efficiency, cash flow, competition, social responsibility, for example.
Impact statement for business	How the solution delivers value; what problem it solves for the customer. For example, this analysis provides insights of interest to the Primary Products division and. . . .
Impact to business priorities	States the link between the impact statement and the business priorities of the company. For example, these insights inform purchasing and manufacturing how to better drive revenue and improve capital efficiency.
Data resources	Identifies the data resources the system will draw on, both for training and for production. Describes how the data will get to the model in production.
Model concept	Describes the model to be used, what it does, and why it's expected to work.
Functional/nonfunctional requirements	Relates how good the model must be at Its job. I low much throughput, latency, and availability for the model? How much does serving it cost?
How it will be used	Explains how the effect delivered will be materialized as a business activity. What will be done with the information from the model or the decisions from the system? Also provides information via visualization and a dashboard for decision makers.
Problems and issues	Notes factors that could derail the implementation of the system or prevent it from being useful.

Documenting organizational aspects like this provides context and explains the story's purpose. Also, documenting the model's data and why it's thought that the model will work or can work shows that the work to be done is purposeful. The team sees a feasible way to employ ML to deliver the business value that is hoped for.

The last three components of the story card describe the model's constraints. Functional and nonfunctional requirements spell out the performance that the model requires to be useful for the client:

- Functional requirements typify the ability of the model to produce valuable classifications or predictions.
- Non-functional requirements spell out the need for the model to do so quickly, economically, and robustly.

The next part of the card asks for documentation about how the model is to be used. This is something that must be clarified now. If there isn't a point in the business process where the output of the model can be created, picked up, and used, then even if the model is perfect, it will be perfectly useless. Finally, problems and issues should be considered and notated. Are there any factors that negate the value of the model in the business process? For example, if the model produces some advice for a user, but when the user most needs that information, they are typically busy, then work is needed to make the model's output effectively consumable.

The process of gathering the information required to populate story cards can be time-consuming and challenging, so it is important to prioritize. Because you are working on an ML project, you need to place extra emphasis on some elements of the story card. For example, the data resources section of the card is key, so it's useful to relate what's said in discussions on the stories to what's known from the data story and survey. Issues that are identified when developing these cards can usefully feed into the survey document and on to the EDA for clarification.

Beyond emphasizing the data aspects in the story, the model's functional and non-functional performance requirements have a strong bearing on the designs that we will develop in chapter 7. These include:

- *The required latency and responsiveness:* How fast will the model need to be to produce predictions from the data for it to be useful?
- *The expected throughput for the model:* How many cases can be dealt with per second or per day?
- *The expected mode of use:* Will it run in batch mode (for example, updating millions of records in a database overnight) or online (for example, responding to a user on a web site)?
- *The required robustness:* How often can a failure of the model be tolerated?
- *The model's accuracy:* How accurate do the different stakeholders believe a useful model should be?

  Model accuracy is a complicated concept, and there is a lot to do to properly evaluate and measure it (see chapter 8 for a long and tortured discussion of this). For now, it's important to get an understanding of the depth of the challenge the team faces.
- *The number of mistakes:* What kinds of mistakes will the different users tolerate? What mistakes erode confidence in the model? How costly is a false negative classification versus a false positive one? (As an example, if the model misses an incidence of a disease in a sample, how costly is that compared to the model falsely detecting a disease in error?) What consequences will these mistakes have?
- *The performance criteria:* How is the system's performance related to business value? At what point does the system's performance (or lack of) destroy value? Are there any thresholds where diminishing returns kick in? When is performance improvement unimportant?

For each story created and gathered, you need to consider two things: validation and interaction. First, the story card needs to be validated. You need to run through it with the people who are impacted and make sure it reflects their concept of reality. Additionally, ask yourself, are these the stories that money should be spent on? Rigorously prioritize and prune the stories to understand the minimum set that creates value.

The demands of the stories on the models developed are also important. Stories that impose challenging demands on the models are likely to be expensive. Eliminating them, if possible, makes the project much more viable. The question is, "is this important and valuable enough to justify focusing the project on the requirements of this particular story?"

Second, the UX experts in your team need to work up ideas about how the users will interact with the system, and ultimately, will interact with the models underpinning it. At this point in the project, the team should have a good, if still necessarily vague, idea of what the final product should look like. The benefit of developing UX concepts now is that by producing the wireframes and mock screens, you start to bring the concept to life for its consumer as well as the team. This creates engagement and builds a shared understanding of what's possible, what it's going to do, and what it's going to look like. (Chapter 9 has an extensive discussion about the style and structure of the applications that can use ML.)

These findings can be written as an application description and reviewed with project stakeholders. This creates and documents a joint agreement about what the application might look like and how it might behave. The requirements in the report that you've extracted also need to be validated with the modeling team, your data scientists, and your data engineers. Potentially, this creates either red flags and risks for the risk register, or green flags and negotiation points with the users when agreeing on the requirements that the team can deliver. It explains which stories are in, which stories are out, and what it is that the models need to do to deliver them.

At this point, it's appropriate to make a comment about agility, as in "this is an agile project." The set of selected stories and the projected application remain as discussion points. They cannot be concretely agreed on yet because the models do not exist and may never exist. Instead, they are an agreement that this is the first set of things that the team will build; if all goes well, then these are the best options for spending the client's money. If performant models cannot be extracted from the data, then the story cards need to be reshuffled, and you need another take on solving the customers problems and creating business value.

A clear set of stories describing the value and approach to modeling sets the scene for the development of useful output from the project. In order to support this, there's more background work to do. The next task that must be tackled is to develop the first set of data pipelines. The pipeline takes the raw data and transforms and moves it to the environment that the team will use to explore and manipulate it for modeling.

5.4 Building data pipelines

The data pipeline infrastructure is the lifeblood of an ML project. The availability of useful, clean data and the ability to transform and enrich data rapidly in response to changes or new results is hugely enabling. Having a flexible and easy-to-manage pipeline infrastructure makes the team more productive and responsive to the project's requirements. Importantly, it helps them cope if things go wrong and approaches and algorithms don't live up to their expectations. Task S1.3 defines what needs to be done at this stage. Because this task delivers the data pipeline to the team's development environment, work to replicate this pipeline or to reuse it for test and production data flows is required in sprint 1.3.

> ### Data pipeline ticket: S1.3
> - Aggregate and fuse relevant data into an integrated picture.
> - Implement and manage data pipelines.
> - Design and implement data tests.

Data is often distributed in a complex ecosystem of containers, databases, data marts, and data warehouses across intranets, clouds, and organizations. Managing the collection and the manipulation of these data assets can quickly become overwhelmingly complex.

Before the EDA exercise (in chapter 6), the team needs to build an infrastructure that lets them examine and process the data quickly and conveniently, and they want the results of the investigation to be reliable and reproducible. This work can then be built on to create a system that distills the available data into forms that can be readily used to train and test models. Normally, this means using a series of aggregations and transformations to reduce many (possibly hundreds) data assets into a single table or stream of relatively simple records for consumption by a few algorithms. Data needs to be rebalanced to cope with uneven distribution of the types of items present, enabling a robust model to be extracted by the ML algorithms.

In the case of unstructured data, this often needs to be rendered to a standard format or size, and for corrupted items, it needs to be filtered and distorted. Data augmentation is a process of using transformations and alterations to create examples for training [5].

Later, in the development process, the team extends the pipelines to service the algorithms that the data scientists want to use and evaluate. As the models are tested and compared, novel manipulations can be tried to improve and fettle the results. Constructing the data infrastructure to accommodate these additions and changes is essential for promoting agility. Before the team gets to that though, they need to bring together the data tables that contain the raw information and provide it in a way that is consumable. The task is to:

- Create a live and maintainable resource. It's possible to use this resource to both work on up-to-date data and to reproduce past results from specific checkpoints.
- Identify and deal with any problems in the source data. This sets a solid foundation for the next phase of the project.
- Create an asset that reflects the reality of the domain that it represents.

The pipeline must support all the required phases of processing to achieve these three objectives and to create a usable training data resource. Figure 5.1 shows an overview of the process required to support data engineering for an ML project. The process in figure 5.1 has different names and is often presented with different nuances and divisions between stages. One of the most familiar framings is ETL (extract, transform, load) in the context of data engineering. This process presented here emphasizes the particular requirements of an ML project. From figure 5.1, you can see that the data must be:

- Ingested from its sources. These can be data streams from sources such as RabbitMQ or Kafka or can be from data files stored as XLXS, CSV, or Parquet formats. A common ingestion requirement is to use SQL queries to pull data from several tables and databases. Another ingestion requirement is to bring data from different infrastructures into a target infrastructure. Often the data is brought in from different cloud environments, SAS applications, or on-premise data stores into the cloud infrastructure. Once there, it can be conveniently processed by the ML processing facilities that are often available on demand in a cloud environment. It's important to note, though, that restrictive security requirements pertaining to a particular data set can drive data from disparate environments back into the on-premises infrastructure where the sensitive data resides.
- Once data is ingested into the target infrastructure and data engine(s) that are used to process it, the data must be manipulated and laid out for use in creating models. Sometimes this step is called *integration* because often the requirement is to create a single table that can be passed to an ML algorithm to create a model. Often, though, it's better to create intermediate tables and data stores that put the acquired data into convenient and accessible forms for the modeling team. Manipulation of this data includes cleaning it and creating features from different aspects of the data.
- Having laid out the data for the modeling team, it's important to ensure that the data can be appropriately and easily accessed by the right members of the team. IAM frameworks for many infrastructures can be used to provide this kind of infrastructure, ensuring that only the members with the right credentials can access the resource.

  Beyond access control, the other requirement is to set up a serving system to read the data appropriately. This might be an SQL query, access to a large data file, or an API that the team uses to request training, test data, or data streams. A great practice is to provide documentation that lets the modelling team self-serve from the resource created by the pipelines.

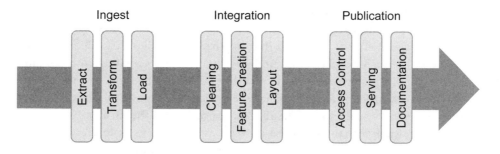

Figure 5.1   The processing requirements delivered using the dev environment data pipeline infrastructure. This provides the data resources for the ML modeling team in sprint 2 and beyond.

There are two pitfalls that can cause serious issues in an ML project if they are not avoided at this stage. First, building a data set from a variety of sources can create statistical problems, and second, failing to address this task in a disciplined way as an engineering problem can create technical debt and mire the team in detail and difficulty later. The next section addresses the statistical problems that can arise when data from multiple sources is integrated to create a training set for ML systems.

5.4.1   Data fusion challenges

A relatively new practice constructs modeling data sets from multiple data sources to build the data picture. Traditionally, statisticians gathered data using a single process (a survey or a sampling protocol) for a specific purpose. Independent experiments to create and gather data were done to reproduce or invalidate previous studies. Meta-analysis was used to combine the results of multiple studies of a phenomenon and to gain greater confidence about the results. Although retrieving and using other people's data is difficult and expensive, it was generally accepted that this approach proved easier and more fruitful when getting new primary data.

   The context of data being stored and available for reuse and repurpose is new. Starting in the 1970s, data sets were systematically prepared and stored in digital archives for replication and reuse, but the computational resources to manipulate them didn't exist. Nonetheless, statisticians studied the process of recombining data under the name of *data fusion* [1]. Nowadays, it's common for data to be acquired and recombined to create new insights, but there are some problems with this process.

   Combining data from a particular part of the population with data from general observations can introduce bias. You can gather data as part of an experiment that you use to study parts of the populations to detect a particular effect. For example, you might use a test negative protocol to ensure that a control group and a target group are selected from the same part of a population. These studies yield controlled, high-quality data sets, and it's tempting to combine them with observational data to model some population-level behavior. Unfortunately, the selection protocols that control bias with respect to one variable versus a set of cofounding factors noise that interferes with the result) can introduce bias with respect to other variables.

One of the most significant ways that bias is introduced is when we take data from different time periods and treat that as part of a single asset. When the data was collected is often a hidden feature; perhaps data sets were created from operational snapshots, which themselves contain records from different ranges of time. For example, you might collect aggregate retail data as a snapshot for several years and store it on the same date each year. This might all look consistent on first inspection, but because the day of the week that the snapshot is taken varies (for example, the first of April might be a Tuesday one year and a Friday the next), prime trading days can be shuffled from one period to another. Poor practice in the modeling process that consumes this data can lead to models that have significant distortions and then fail to work in production.

Rare entities in data sets can either create distortion by appearing disproportionately in samples because of random chance or they can create blind spots for modeling because they are missing from the data asset. Moreover, you can over-represent rare entities because they are more noticeable in data than normal entities and because they are more important to the client organization. For example, repeat and serious offenders appear disproportionately in criminal databases because petty offenders are not of interest to police. It's less likely that the police will record petty crime, but that doesn't mean that it's uncommon. Building profiles of offenders from police records does not create representative profiles of all offenders, just the ones the police are interested in. This might mean that using this data to prevent crime can prove ineffective because the interventions predicted as successful may be inappropriate for the majority of criminals.

Sensor data sets may contain data gathered with different qualities. In fact, the *same* data set can contain data with different qualities. For example, you might want to sample some sensors every minute and some sensors every hour. Some survey data may have values of agreement in the range 1-5 and some from 1-10; some tables may contain the average temperature for an area, whereas others may have samples of temperature within an area.

Understanding the semantics of the data sources at this level is crucial for deciding whether it's meaningful and useful to combine them. Normalization errors can make a big difference to the models you derive from subsequent fused data sets. Just bolting the data together blindly may not be a good idea. There is no substitute for developing a strong understanding of the domain and thinking through the issues that might create a distorted distribution in the data set. Luckily, your team is in place and the work that you have done provides the information and awareness of these potential distortions: you need to qualify the processes as being well-founded and reflective of reality. At a minimum, it's worth checking that:

- The data entities were collected on the same basis, whether that's with a principled selection or with general observations.

- There are no hidden variables (such as offender identity or time of collection) that hide distortion.

- Sensors capturing the entity's behavior haven't quantitatively or qualitatively changed over time.

There will be times when data that violates these strictures is useful, and you will be able to develop valuable models using such data. If so, then it's important that you deliberately exercise your judgement and decide that's the case rather than relying on blind luck!

5.4.2 *Pipeline jungles*

Now, let's return to the second challenge that can emerge as you construct the data infrastructure for the project: failing to address the task S1.3 in a disciplined way as an engineering problem.

A common malady in ML projects is the emergence of a pipeline jungle [4]. This creates significant technical debt, leading to a situation in which the project is difficult to manage and both technically and functionally unreliable. Pipeline jungles emerge in projects where significant glue code for the data transformations and aggregations are constructed in an ad hoc way with no regard to management and maintenance. No team wants to create a pipeline jungle, but they emerge incrementally over time, creeping up on the team until they suddenly find themselves enmeshed and mired in complexity. The process reminds me of a famous quote about bankruptcy:

> *How did you go bankrupt? Two ways. Gradually, then suddenly.*
>
> — Ernest Hemingway, *The Sun Also Rises*

Some common issues can precipitate the start of a pipeline jungle. In some cases, specialist data infrastructures need to be handled by the team to cope with the scale, speed, or special properties of the data used in the project. For example, old proprietary data warehouses sometimes stored their data in arcane binary formats, which can be difficult to exfiltrate data without other proprietary export tools. The skills to deal with these tools may be beyond your project team, and you may have to collaborate with experts in the customer organization.

Specialist tools can be a necessary evil, but they may be the only way to make the data available for modeling with acceptable performance characteristics or to provide compliance with software licensing terms. When using specialist or proprietary tools and adapters, it's a good idea to wrap them within a standard pipelining tool, ensuring that the pipelines are integrated into the generic infrastructure. Because the wrapping and the integration work may be an overhead for the team, it's tempting to hack a one-time process to get the data you need but be warned: that way madness lies. Doing it properly means that you have control over how data flows and the ability to spot issues and fix them as needed.

Another driver is a failure to document and version the pipelines as for any other code. Data pipelines can turn into one of the most significant code investments that the team will make, so treat it as such. Pipelines need to be documented with respect to how they work, but they also need to be discoverable and well known. If you use a pipeline management and scheduling tool such as Apache Airflow, then pipeline discovery and identification will be looked after for you. Be alert for exceptions or special cases that somehow get missed. Make sure they are corralled; for example, by wrapping them with a single-step pipeline and the standard tooling. The single-step pipeline calls to the tool that you used for that component of the infrastructure. However, it will do so from the pipeline infrastructure.

Finally, as for other code pipelines, pipeline steps must be instrumented and tested. Each step and pipeline should report when it is invoked and whether it succeeds or fails. Failure conditions can be asserted by creating timers or timeouts that fire when an operation or pipeline takes too long or when completion occurs suspiciously fast. Setting these constraints catch problems that evade data testing because sometimes the data tests aren't as good as they should be. Often, however, the data tests don't pick up a problem in the technical execution of the process. For example, a data set that should be appended if certain conditions are met might appear to pass tests for distribution or integrity even when the call to the database to retrieve the appending data fails. However, because the failure occurs very fast (because the join is tiny) or after several timeouts (because a connection can't be established), this should alert the team to a problem.

5.4.3   Data testing

As well as building pipeline tests, the team should invest in data testing. There is a tripwire to step over with data testing, though. Data tests can prove expensive and slow to run. This is unsurprising because there is often a lot of data, and tests can involve a lot of cross comparisons, which are computationally expensive. If you can't afford data testing that's exorbitantly expensive or that brings the pipelines grinding to a halt, it must be deployed strategically.

The level and target of data testing is a matter of judgement, but obviously, as for tests in normal software, the more *high-quality tests* that are implemented, the more the team can be confident of their work and their results. Types of data testing commonly implemented include:

- *Tests for duplication:* A common problem with a data pipeline is the replay of data from a source that encountered a problem exfiltrating data and then was programmed to start fresh. Duplication can also come from bugs in loop conditions in code that copies data (for example, a loop variable that doesn't update on the last iteration of the loop or after some condition) or from manual cut-and-paste mess ups. Note that you may not even be aware that way back in the data's story, someone cut and paste into a database, but this happens a lot!

- *Tests for volumes:* Over time, volumes of data should be somewhat predictable. Use this fact to create a check on what's arrived and what's expected to be implemented. Try to establish bounds and bottom limits on what's reasonable.

- *Tests for preconditions in input data:* This kind of test establishes that the input to a task is as expected. A partial and incomplete list of tests of this sort include testing that all expected columns are present, testing that the columns contain the same number of non-null data points (for example, if sensor x is off, then reading x is null), and statistical testing that shows that the distribution of data approximates the expectations (the standard deviation of the data is within a certain bound, for example).

- *Tests for postconditions:* This test determines if what is produced is as expected. As for the previous tests for preconditions, you can establish something about the output of a data pipeline.

- *Tests of constraints from precondition to postcondition:* Check that the expected relations between these conditions hold. For example, all non-null preconditions have a non-null post condition or that the same number of 0's is present in the pre- and post-process data (if that is what is expected).

- *Tests of performance:* As mentioned, the data pipeline steps may have nonfunctional instrumentation: the amount of time, memory, cost, and number of invocations, for instance. These parameters are useful for monitoring the development infrastructure and will be important for monitoring the production infrastructure in the deployed ML system, but they can also be exploited for testing. These tests can be absolute (the task should complete in less than three seconds, for example), or they can be relative (the task should complete in no more than two standard deviations of the time for the task to normally complete). In the worst case, steps in the pipeline do not complete due to nonfunctional stresses or run out of order, creating significant corruption.

- *Tests for reactions to* extreme values, test null, NaN, large_number, small_number and 0 behaviors.

Ideally the testing infrastructure feeds into a monitoring system. It's important that system-level failures (such as a database becoming unreachable) are logged and notifications and alerts distributed. Automated alerting means that the infrastructure team can rapidly respond and sort things out before the ML team has to put down their tools and play table tennis instead.

5.5 *Model repository and model versioning*

Task S1.4 requires the team to build the model management and versioning infrastructure. This allows an agile, yet controlled development and deployment of the ML models that will be developed in sprint 2.

Model versioning ticket: S1.4

- Commission and adopt a model repository.
- Identify and record all artefacts for use in ML pipelines.

During system development, it is expected that each model will require a large number of iterations to find the appropriate combination of training process, hyperparameters, algorithm, architecture, and so on. In order to manage the experiments generated by a typical iterative modeling process, you need to implement a model repository. The repository records the specific model created during a particular iteration or experiment, the parameters (data, features), hyperparameters, algorithm, architecture, and other model components, along with the evaluation metrics for this iteration.

An evolution of the model chosen and the information that informed the decision making that drove the evolution are important factors that determine how the model will behave in the future and how governable the developed system will be. Recording the models' evolution can inform investigations into the system's future stability, failures, and blind spots. By maintaining this information, the system becomes accountable, and you can document your choices with factual evidence. You'll use the model repository to record the following:

- The identity of each model, which is the name that links to the binary or declarative specification that is used in testing and production (but ideally, both).
- The evaluation results that were created for the model during the development process.
- The test results (if any) that were created for the model during qualification and selection.
- A list of all technical artifacts used by the model and those that were used to develop it (for example, foundation models or features).
- The status of the data pipeline (running or not) and the data pipeline identities that were used to provide the training, validation, and test sets.
- The test results and monitoring information created when the pipelines were used to build the training, validation, and test sets.

Beyond implementing the model repository, the team must commit to using it. The core task of modeling has not yet started, but early experiments, off-the-book tests, and baseline developments are information that should be captured because this sets the context for the rest of the project.

5.5.1   *Features, foundational models, and training regimes*

Providing a model versioning system is important because it provides control and automation for the team when they build, evaluate, and integrate models in production. As mentioned, there are other artefacts that the team will likely use in the project. The infrastructure to handle these is going to be important to the smooth delivery of the project as well.

You should record and track explicitly all the tools and components that the team uses. The editors, interpreters, compilers, libraries, and virtual machines all need to be recorded and approved by the customer. Many clients have architectural compliance policies that cover the validation and selection of libraries and tools for software projects; these almost always have exception processes to allow a new tool to be adopted if necessary. You can't dodge these processes, so use them to either get assurance that your toolset is compliant or to get it formally registered as an exception.

The development of reusable foundation models created a new class of artifact that is pivotal to an ML project. It's good to check licensing conditions and to make sure that the customer knows the model that's used, and it's essential that it's registered in their repositories and catalogs. Also essential is making sure that you use the right versions of the foundation model in all processes and pipelines. Generating embeddings using one model and then trying to match them using a different model generally creates poor results. Using a hash function such as MD5 [2] to create a unique identifier for the model and then embedding that into the model-serving code as an on-load check guarantees that the correct model is used in production as well as in development and test environments.

Of course, the team will use specific libraries and tools to provide the algorithms that will extract the model from the data. Versioning is again, important. Watch for anomalies like the team adopting a nightly build or downloading a build in defiance (or ignorance) of corporate policies. Expect builds to be explicitly checked by security teams before production and understand that a rogue build may not only result in a corporate slap on the wrists (or your summary dismissal) but also in a dependency issue that then prevents deployment.

Another pitfall that can arise is testing builds to avoid issues with licensing costs or to get over the lack of particular hardware in tests. For example, a virtual machine used in testing may dispense with floating-point calculations in order to enable rapid completion of integration or system tests. This is a normal thing for deployment and platform teams to set up, but if the test virtual machine or library somehow makes it into the production build, then the production system won't work.

5.5.2 Overview of versioning

ML is a fast-moving area, and new components that support an ML system are emerging rapidly, so it's impossible to enumerate every required item to be versioned to make a solid production system. However, implementing some systematic tests and processes in the project to control versioning helps. Tests that you can use to develop confidence in the system's versioning include:

- Using checksums to establish that the right information is present in the artifact.
- Using signed binaries to establish that the right owner and source of the artifact is in use and that it can be trusted.
- Sampling known values from the binary, then checking that they are correct.

In many projects and settings, taking these steps to identify, register, secure, and validate the project's dependencies may seem like overkill. You can be assured it really is worthwhile! This enables problems to be tracked, discovered early, and quickly resolved. It will also allow the CI/CD processes required for rapid and effective production to be smoothly implemented. Build management systems like Jenkins, GCP Cloud Build, and AWS Code Build need to be hydrated with the right versions of all components to deliver the right configuration for the system into production. Good control of the component versions allows configurations to be rapidly updated and delivered. If you end up doing it by hand, then expect very slow going.

With data pipelines, data testing, and model and feature stores in place, commissioned and adopted by the team, it's now feasible for the team to dive into the data. Once the team can easily manipulate the data in place, they can get a real sense of what it is they've got for modelling. Everything is now in place for work to begin on the EDA and then on the model.

This chapter covered the work the team needed to do to come to grips with the real technical problems that they are going to face before delivering the project. We discussed mapping out the data resources and understanding what issues need to be further explored and checked, building insight into the business issues that can be resolved, setting up data pipelines that support the exploration of the data assets and their use in modelling, and commissioning the model versioning infrastructure. In chapter 6, we'll look at the rest of sprint 1, including the EDA process that will deepen the team's insight into the statistical properties of the data set and the development of the first baseline ML models. At the end of chapter 6, you will find The Bike Shop narrative that covers all of the work in sprint 1.

Summary

- A data survey establishes that the expected data resources exist and have a level of integrity that will allow the team to meaningfully work on them.

- By developing story cards and UX prototypes, you'll generate a deeper understanding and agreement about the direction of the project and the requirements on the ML modeling activity that's at the core of the project's hypothesis.

- Model repositories and versioning infrastructures for all the artefacts required in the project development need to be established, commissioned, and adopted (turn them on and use them).

- Systematically build a data pipeline infrastructure to support agile development of modeling later in the project. The pipeline must provide support for ingesting the data, transforming it for use, and providing access to it for the modeling team.

- Take careful note of the motivations and approach to data gathering for the data resources that the project uses.

- Establish infrastructures for data testing and data pipeline testing to provide assurance during model development and into production that the team is working with the correct data.

EDA, ethics, and baseline evaluations

6

This chapter covers

- Undertaking an EDA to discover the statistical characteristics of data
- Exploring unstructured data properties using foundational models
- Checking the project's ethical, privacy, and security aspects
- Building baseline models to get feedback about the potential for success
- Providing support for estimating performance of more sophisticated models

In chapter 5, we learned about the work required to get a data resource that the team can work with for modelling. Now the team can dive into the data to understand its characteristics and discern what can and what can't be done with it. To do this, the team needs to work in a structured way, exploring the data, investigating it with a range of tools, and documenting and sharing the insights learned.

An important part of this work is for the team to look again at the ethical issues surrounding the project. This is essential because ethical concerns can shut down lines of investigation and development. It's important to determine if that's going to be the case before wasting the client's money on development that will never be used or exploited.

117

Finally, the team and you will develop the baseline models that demonstrate the bottom line of performance, which you can create with off-the-shelf and quick-to-implement approaches. This is done to gauge the possibilities for more time-consuming and sophisticated approaches and to ensure that these methods deliver the value that justifies their use.

6.1 *Exploratory data analysis (EDA)*

Everything is in place for you to undertake the work in the S1.5 ticket from your backlog.

EDA ticket: S1.5

- Plan and design EDA.
- Write and share the EDA report.

So far, we've built a narrative about the data the team will use, and the team has checked that it exists and appears to be as expected. We've got system access and set up a data pipelining infrastructure. The information about the data sets and credentials to access them can now be used to bring the data into a place (or if things are difficult, places) where it can be analyzed. If the data is in a state that is amenable to analysis, the next step is to use analytic methods to systematically create an understanding of what we have and what we can do with it.

This process is commonly known as an exploratory data analysis (EDA). This practice was developed in the 1970s (at the dawn of the data age) and championed by John Tukey [12]. Originally the focus of an EDA was to enable practitioners to move from working in comprehensive end-to-end studies to working with "found" data. Nowadays, we use EDA in a variety of ways, here as a prelude to an ML modeling exercise.

6.1.1 *EDA objectives*

With the team prepared to look at the statistical properties of the data, an understanding of what information might be available for consumption by ML algorithms can emerge. At the heart of EDA are some simple questions:

- Do individual data examples make sense? Are there really customers like the most extreme examples in the customer data set? Customers might have hundreds of transactions a week, or maybe there's a majority of customers with few transactions or no transactions for weeks on end. If you find the typical customer, does that customer's revenue and number of transactions look appropriate?

- What is the distribution of the entities? This question builds on an understanding of the typical entities and the most extreme examples in the data, then uses that to decide if the data overall makes sense. Are there gaps or dead spots in the ranges of data that can't be explained? Are there gaps that should be there but have surprising values? Typical examples are holiday seasons and weekends appearing in the data set. If a retailer is reporting high traffic on Christmas day, then there needs to be an explanation as to why; at least, it's worth checking that the business stakeholders think that makes sense.

- Do the aggregate statistics of data items make sense and relate to the data's context? For example, do the total transactions in a transaction table add up to the total revenue of the company? Do the total number of transactions in each calendar period look appropriate?

- Do the relationships within the data match expectations? For example, in a demographic data set, are there children who are older than their parents? In a growing company, are there any periods in the past that have more revenue than in the current trading period?

The philosophy of EDA is to let the data speak for itself, but unfortunately, the clock is ticking. If you have time, an open-ended exploration of the data is a strong approach, but it's difficult to do on a tight schedule. Instead, using the raft of questions raised from the data story and data survey, you and your team can plan a structured exercise to develop the understanding that you need.

It's a good idea to write out the set of specific EDA activities that you want to conduct, listing the activity, the method, and the reasons that you are looking at the data in this way. Then, jot down what you expect to find. By doing this, you create a paper trail that shows the professional approach taken. Working with the team, you will also be able to efficiently prioritize and control the work that needs to be done, making sure that you focus the resources and time that you have on high-priority investigations.

As well as developing a general understanding of the data, the EDA exercise enables the team to effectively revisit the design of the data pipelines. You built these in chapter 5 to provide data for the team to work on. Using these for the first time, the team will have some feedback about how they're performing. Later, the team will use these to create the test, training, and validation data sets for modelling, so as noted in chapter 5, they are fundamental to the modeling exercise's success.

You may need to tweak the performance and behavior of the pipelines in response to the feedback that the team provides after generating the first view of the data. The EDA exercise itself will have an impact on the structure of the pipelines as well. For example, if the validation sets used to determine the training performance of the model are not representative of the target domain, then it's likely that the training process is under-specifying what the model should represent [4].

The variance of the key properties of the data set determine how large the validation set needs to be. The spread of the variance of key variables or properties of the data set are also helpful when determining the ordering of data during training [9]. There are three types of tools that the team can employ to come to grips with the data:

- *Summary statistics:* Calculations that reduce data to a few easily compared attributes such as its mean or median values (although, there are a lot of values that can be calculated!).

- *Visualizations:* Represents data as a visual map with the objective of showing its overall characteristics.

- *Model based:* Uses a foundational model to map the data into a summary or visualization domain to gain some understanding of its properties. When you and the team handle unstructured data, such as images or text, then a model is required to reduce the real-world features in something like an image to a format that a human can interpret.

6.1.2 Summarizing and describing data

A summary statistic is a single number that gives a picture of a set of numbers. For example, a series of numbers such as {1,2,3,4,5} can be described as having a mean value of 3 and a median value of 3. Although a great deal of information is lost by describing this set as having a mean value of 3, in some contexts, that's the important information about all the numbers in the sequence. As another example, the bags of flour on a warehouse pallet might have various exact weights, but the fact that their mean weight is 1.5 KG provides almost all the information that a buyer needs to determine the price for the pallet.

Within a modern computing environment, we can summarize numeric data by using data frames-based processing (suitable for a relatively small data set that can be stored and processed on a single machine) or by using SQL or other structured query languages. Examples of data frames tools include Python's pandas, dplyr in R, or Data-Frames.jl in Julia. These tools provide powerful data manipulation and summarization mechanisms that can rapidly provide statistical insights both on instances of data and aggregations. These are often preferred by data scientists and engineers because they provide programming conventions and constructs that are more convenient and powerful than raw SQL. These tools often provide a `describe()` function that you can use to create a standardized initial report of the characteristics of numeric data. To find out more, check out the following resources:

- For information about using Python's pandas, try Reuven Lerner's book, *Pandas Workout* [6] or Boris Paskhave's book, *Pandas in Action* [7].

- For a detailed description of using dplyr for an EDA, see Ryu's *Cran-R EDA* vignette [8] or the wider overview given in Hadley Wickham's book [13].

- SQL provides some of the functionality of a data frame-type system but in the context of a database engine. In some cases, moving the data into the machine's memory that uses pandas or another data frame system is inconvenient, and sometimes, the scale of the data makes it impractical. Modern database engines can often run highly optimized and parallelized SQL queries over the data that is stored in them. This means that aggregating and summarizing data for an EDA is practical for even large data sets. SQL is often seen as lower level or more complicated to use than a data frame language. Conversely, there are many engineers who have developed deep skills in SQL and may prefer working with it in contrast to data frames.

Choosing the statistics that best describe a particular data set can be daunting. It's not clear what will be important before starting the investigation, and there are a host of different ways to calculate the qualities of different types of data. Helpfully, there are automated ways to cover all this ground. The Cran-R EDA vignette [8] describes the function `eda_report`, which automatically generates a report covering univariant, distributions, and target-based (characteristic) analysis.

Although creating a summary report is a good way to get some orientation and an overview of a data set, alternatively asking questions that are directed based on the team's knowledge about the data and their needs for this can be even more illuminating. Let's revisit the smart buildings example. The team member looking at the temperature_readings table might write the following query:

```
select count(*), year from temperature_readings group_by year

>(52560000, 52560000, 52560000, 525704000, 52560000)
```

The sensor readings are spread out evenly across the years, although one **(525704000)** has 140,000 more readings than the others. This is not suspicious because the year in question is a leap year, so there is an extra day. However:

```
Select count (*), month from temperature_readings group_by month

>(0,0,0,0,0,0,0,0,0,0,0,26944000)
```

Eeesshh! All the readings are badged as being done in December, not good. At this point, you realize that there is a global problem with the data. Perhaps visualizing what's going on will clarify what's really going on with it?

6.1.3 Plots and visualizations

Although creating summary statistics using queries can answer specific questions and give general information about a data set, visualizing elements of it using, for example, scatter or ridgeline plots (in the case of time series or other sequences) is powerful. Summary statistics, no matter how well constructed, can be deceptive, so building visual descriptions of the data set is a useful way of gaining a clear understanding of its properties.

One way of using visualizations and plots is to explode summary statistics. As an illustration of why this can be an important step in an EDA process, it's worth being aware of Anscombe's Quartet (see figure 6.1). While the data in each of the four plots have different joint properties, they share some identical summary values: the mean of x_n is 9, the mean of y_n is 7.5, and the x_n and y_n Pearson correlation is 0.816. Other summary statistics are identical as well. Whereas a detailed statistical investigation of every property of the data set might find the gaps between reality and belief that something like Anscombe's Quartet can create, it's often easier to spot this by plotting everything out and seeing how the data points relate to one another.

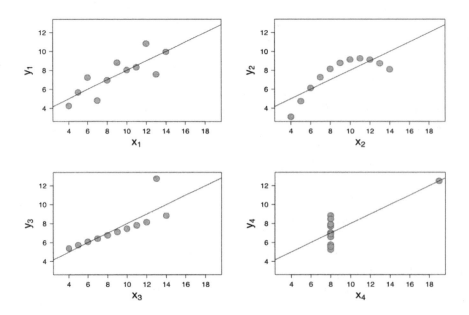

Figure 6.1   Anscombe's Quartet. Anscombe.svg: Schutz (label using subscripts): Avenue, CC BY-SA 3.0 (https://creativecommons.org/licenses/by-sa/3.0), via Wikimedia Commons

Another way is to look at data that contains deceptive covariant behaviors. Figure 6.2 shows the relationship between the size of a tip and the size of the check at a restaurant (image from Wikipedia, original work [3]). One might expect that the checks would be clustered around the diagonal fit, representing a linear relationship. As the bill gets bigger, so should the tip proportionately increase in size. However, there is a significant dispersal with mid-sized bills and poor tips and of tips for larger checks.

In the context of an EDA exercise, a plot like the one in figure 6.2 shows the team that they need to be careful to account for the differences in dispersal between the top end and the bottom end of the range when designing their data sets for modeling. Just sampling at random might not provide the information that the algorithms need to create an effective model.

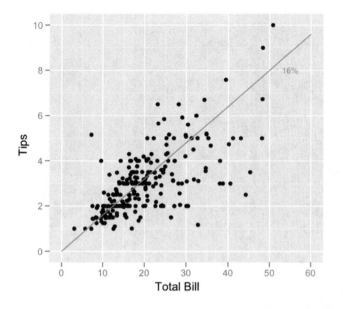

Figure 6.2 **Tips versus bills (checks) at a restaurant from the Wikipedia EDA page. By Visnut, own work, CC BY-SA 3.0, https://commons.wikimedia.org/w/index.php?curid=25703576**

In the smart building example, we saw that the month field for the temperature data wasn't meaningful. Let's plot the number of temperature readings in the day field. We can get this out of the data with a query like:

```
select count(*), day from temperature_readings group_by day

>[1.00000000e+00 7.21986000e+06 7.21985800e+06 7.21984900e+06
 7.21985200e+06 7.21985300e+06 7.21985200e+06 7.21984600e+06
 7.21986200e+06 7.21985500e+06 7.21986300e+06 7.21984800e+06
 7.21986100e+06 7.21986300e+06 7.21985600e+06 7.21986400e+06
 7.21985300e+06 7.21985600e+06 7.21984600e+06 7.21985200e+06
 7.21986200e+06 7.21985200e+06 7.21986000e+06 7.21985900e+06
 7.21986400e+06 7.21985400e+06 7.21986200e+06 7.21985900e+06
 7.21986200e+06 7.21986200e+06….
```

The result is a big array of large integers, so the thing to do is to rewrite the call with a Python function and pass it to your favorite plotting library (in this case, matplotlib). Figure 6.3 shows the result as a range from 0 to 7, but this looks a bit odd at first. You quickly see that the Python plotting tool decided to scale the y axis by 10^6, so it shows that there are 350+ day values with a bit more than 7 million readings, and the one on the far right looks like it's got about 1,800,000 readings. A few seconds of thought brings some good news. The day attribute is a day-of-the-year, and day 366 is February 29, which is about one-quarter of the other values because it only happened once in the life span of the sensor network.

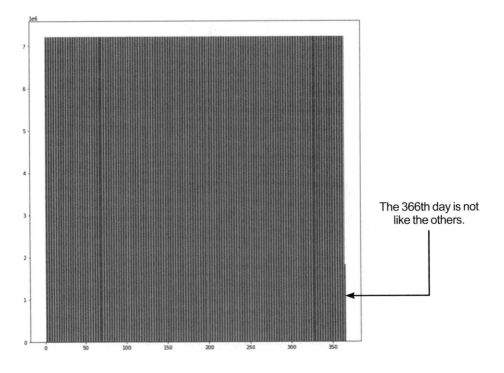

Figure 6.3   Distribution of sensor readings over day of year

It's clear that each day of the year has (approximately) the amount of temperature data that would be expected if the sensor's data was logged per day, and the month field was ignored. We can also see that the distribution of data across the years is correct, so it looks like we have data for every day over the period that the data set was collected.

One more obvious avenue for exploration is to look at the statistics of the temperatures that have been recorded. Although we have a large number of readings, by taking a relatively small sample randomly from the whole population, you can get representative statistics.

SQL, pandas, and dplyr are all well-integrated with powerful plotting and visualization engines such as matplotlib and ggplot. In practice, especially during EDA and with large data sets, visual exploration should be done using small subsets of the data. Plotting millions of points is going to make a mess of any high-res screen, but it also can challenge more powerful modern processors and GPUs.

Efficient processing and binning techniques can help, along with plotting probability densities rather than single points. While sampling can be misleading and problematic, it's also simple and, in the context of using it to visualize drawing a sample and plotting some part of a data set, it can be a useful approach. Some investigations do require the entire data, though. For example, looking for anomalies or looking for problems with integrity can fail because a small subset doesn't catch any candidate "baddies".

6.1.4   *Unstructured data*

What if your project consumes unstructured data such as photos, videos, or text? ML algorithms are useful here too because they can uniquely process unstructured data into useful abstract models. It's meaningless to apply statistical thinking to unstructured data. The median photo in a collection isn't easy to define, and if you do define it and pick it out, it probably isn't going to inform you about the properties of the other photos in the way that the median entity of a population of, say, customer records will. Nonetheless, it's useful and possible to explore the quality of the information in unstructured data resources.

It can be helpful to use pre-canned or quickly constructed ML to explore a new unstructured data resource, but it's also possible to use human perception in a systematic way. Consider the example of a prelabeled image data set. The properties that may be of interest are:

- *The number of images that correspond to each label:* Are the classes balanced? Are there any labels that are severely underrepresented?
- *The orientation of the labeled items:* In Torralba and Efros [11], images were sampled and shown to be dominated by particular side on and showroom presentations. Furthermore, coffee mugs are often shown with the handle orientated to the right (try a search online for yourself).
- *Image positioning:* In [11], this is called capture bias. How often do labeled items appear in parts of the image?
- *Environment:* Are some backgrounds repeated and associated with some images? Apocryphal stories abound about models that were built to search for tanks, being trained with images that showed tanks in the snow and tractors in the sunshine. Consequentially, it's claimed that the model labels everything in the snow as a tank and everything in the sunshine as a tractor.
- *Coverage:* Is the label set complete with regard to the images in the data set? Are there images that are unlabeled? Are there items that are shown in several images that are not labeled? Are there (surprisingly) missing labels? Let's say the images are of household tools; you might have screwdrivers, hammers, and wrenches, but are there saws or pilers?

These investigations were done with human eyes applied to the result from queries over the labels in the imaginary data set. Yet, what if there are no labels, and more to the point, are there ways to use ML to help with EDA before we use ML to solve our business problem? The good news is that you can use a prebuilt foundational model to transform the data into a form that allows you to explore it.

Facebook, Google, and others use ML to create models of general domains like English text and everyday images (scenes from everyday life rather than from telescopes, microscopes, and satellites). These models can be problematic, and care is required when using them, but for an EDA exercise, employing them advisedly is low-risk, and over unstructured data, these models can provide insight that is not available from any other source.

An appropriate foundational model is straightforward to use to get some overview information about the data set. We can use many foundational models to generate vectors (large, ordered arrays) of floating-point numbers, which the community calls *embeddings*. These represent the position in conceptual space where the model has determined the unstructured data item occupies.

If you are working with a data set of photos, then select a foundational model such as EfficientNet [10], or for text, use one of the BERT-derived models such as all-MiniLM-L12-v2. Download these from one of the many open-source repositories that store and distribute them and use them to generate embeddings for all or a reasonable subset of data. The embeddings are typically 768 or even 1,024 floating-point numbers. They represent high dimensionality spaces. Understanding or consuming the embedding directly is not useful, but the team can get some sense out of them indirectly.

One straightforward approach is to use a dimensionality reduction mechanism such as T-distributed Stochastic Neighbor Embedding (t-SNE) or principal component analysis (PCA) to visualize the distribution of the data items in your embedding space. This can sometimes be informative, but the level of dimensionality reduction and information loss can be large. Alternatively, the embeddings can be indexed with a system like FAISS (Facebook AI Similarity Search) [5] or Annoy [2], then you can use the nearest neighbor query functionality to extract some structure from a corpus.

There are openly accessible texts of Shakespeare's plays, so it's simple to use these to show how we can use this kind of foundational model/index system to support exploration of unstructured data. If the plays are supplied to a parser and split into sentences, these can be fed into a model like all-MiniLM-L12-v2, where you give each sentence an embedding:

```
array([ 8.19933936e-02,   9.97491628e-02,   6.05560839e-02,   6.95289299e-02,
        4.54569124e-02,  -5.78593016e-02,   2.58211885e-02,  -5.37960902e-02,
        1.54499486e-02,   1.98997390e-02,   3.31314690e-02,   4.48754244e-02,
       -1.08558014e-02,   2.36593257e-03,  -1.36038102e-03,   5.81134520e-02,
        4.76119894e-04,....
```

```
= Indeed, there is Fortune too hard for Nature, when
     Fortune makes Nature's natural the cutter-off of
     Nature's wit.
```

When these were indexed, we used FAISS to find the nearest neighbor in another play:

```
Nature and Fortune join'd to make thee great:
     Of Nature's gifts thou mayst with lilies boast,
     And with the half-blown rose
                    (King John)
```

By iterating over all items in the index, we can create a matrix that shows the strength of the links (neighborliness) between all the plays. This can be visualized as a heatmap as in figure 6.4.

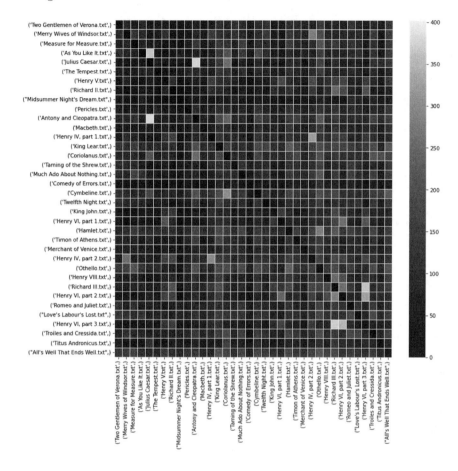

Figure 6.4 **Heat map of nearest neighbor connections in Shakespeare's plays using all-MiniLM-L12-v2**

The heatmap may or may not provide some insight into the unstructured data. Certainly, *The Comedy of Errors* looks to be distant from the other plays, and *King Lear* and *Othello* seem to be well connected. We can apply other filters to the neighborliness data, though. For example, we can run a filter to extract only connections that are 2 or 3 standard deviations above the mean link value. In this case, a graph like the one in figure 6.5 can be rendered, which shows the clustering of *The Hollow Crown* plays on the left and the strangeness of *The Merry Wives of Windsor* on the right.

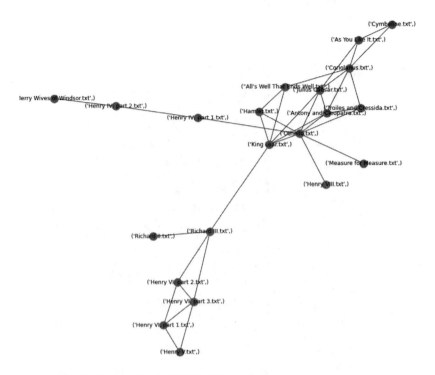

Figure 6.5   Finding significant (0.05%) links between plays

6.2   *Ethics checkpoint*

> **EDA ticket: S1.6**
> - Check ethics in light of the emerging understanding.

At this point, it is appropriate to deploy some of the ethical evaluation tools that have been developed in recent years to systematically check the issues that might arise. Currently, the IEEE, the Ada Lovelace Institute, and Microsoft have tools and systems to evaluate and track ethical issues in AI and ML systems.

We discussed this kind of tool in chapter 2, where it was suggested to use an impact assessment to understand the ethical implications of deploying the system that is under consideration. At that time, you and the team had a minimal understanding of the proposed system. Since then, you've checked the data and have developed a deeper understanding of the business requirements. Now you are in a much stronger position to review the ethical, privacy, and security issues surrounding the project.

In a recent survey of ethical impact analysis tools, Ayling and Chapman [1] note that there is a wide spread of these tools in terms of what stage of a project they can be applied to and what aspects of ML ethics they address. Ayling and Chapman also discovered deficiencies and gaps, and this and the plethora of available tools makes it likely that further development and a consolidation of the approaches in this area is inevitable. When a well-defined and relatively complete methodology for understanding and documenting the ethnical impact of ML systems comes into use, you should adopt it. At the time of writing, however, there some clear requirements for an impact assessment:

- Involve all project stakeholders including the users and the people impacted.
- Understand the costs versus the benefits to those impacted.
- Focus on the lifecycle of both the project and the system to be developed.
- Know how the impact of the system is to be measured and understood as it evolves.
- Look at the adequacy of the mechanisms that will be used to govern the system.

To some extent, these requirements (and others from future, well-developed ethical evaluation systems) are in the hands of you and the team at this point in the project. You are still in control of what the system will become, so you can still influence and develop those aspects of the system that define the outcome of the system.

It may be that the costs of the system to those exposed to it will outweigh the benefits. If this is the case, then this needs to be surfaced on the project's risk register and mitigated while that's possible. Likewise, the governance aspects of the system could be inadequate (given what you now know about the client organization and the business aspects of the system). Again, you can use the risk register and project backlog to address this.

The ultimate success and value of the system developed is defined by its ethical impact. Unethical systems are likely to not only end up as valueless, they may well become a total liability. No one should intentionally develop an unethical system! Use this opportunity to take deliberate steps to prevent you and your team from becoming involved in an accident.

6.3 *Baseline models and performance*

It's common to see performance evaluations presented in isolation from their application and domain. For example, a team might produce a classifier that's 99% accurate, which is great, but, without context, who knows if it's useful or interesting? The majority class might be 99% of the examples in the test set, so the classifier might always predict that class.

When estimating performance, there are many ways to get past that sort of gotcha (to be discussed in future chapters at length). It's important to quicky establish where the model's performance sits in comparison to what it needs to do for the business. It's also important to understand performance in comparison to simple models that predict a majority class, for example. If your models don't do better, then you're wasting your time.

> **EDA ticket: S1.7**
>
> - Define and implement the model baselines.

It's possible to rapidly develop a baseline model over a relatively small sample of data (enabling quick iteration), using simple modelling techniques such as decision-tree learning or low-dimensional perceptron's. Simple models can often overfit (memorize the data) or may be badly under-specified (not modelling the data's complexity), but in this phase, that's OK! We're looking for indications of the challenge and want to establish bottom lines for the system's performance.

A nontechnical route to baselining comes from business analysis: an expensive sophisticated model that predicts customer churn needs to work better than a hand-crafted classifier that looks at the month that a customer's contract expires, the estimated household income, or the monthly expenditure. How much better? We can answer that with another question, how much will the model have to improve to provide the return on investment that is required to pay for the project?

Projects that take the naïve position of being a tiny bit better than an unintelligent, simple system may look great in development. Somewhere along the road to production, however, they are almost certain to fall by the wayside.

6.4   *What if there are problems?*

The EDA exercise described in section 6.1 is what is often called a "sunny day story". The conclusion, however, glosses over the problems, diversions, and dead ends that we typically encounter in a project. It would be surprising if complications and problems don't trip the team up more than once while they obtain and explore the customer's data. For example, it's quite normal to try SQL endpoints, only to discover that they don't exist. Sometimes they are behind a firewall that can't be reconfigured. Or the team may be shocked to discover that the credentials they've been given don't work, and the admin is unavailable due to illness or annual leave. This is to be expected and can be overcome quite easily if the team and project have the right level of customer sponsorship and support.

A more serious issue is the discovery that the data resource is quite different in character and content than what was portrayed by the customer when the project began. There are three "rainy day paths" to walk in this situation:

1 Take the road to disaster.
2 Renegotiate the project's objectives.
3 Stop the project.

The first path is the road to disaster. You continue with the project as if the data is what you expected and use it to build the models and answer the questions that underpin the project. Perhaps something will turn up, and the data resource will be restored and recovered, and all will be well. Experience suggests that it won't, and the project simply fails.

The second path is to renegotiate the objectives of the project with the customer, given what you now believe can (or cannot) be done. The key thing is that you and your team can speak to the real concerns and value that you understand from the engagement thus far. Doing this enables you to map out a new route to success, based on the data that is available. This new project may be more expensive and less ambitious, or it may be just as tight and ambitious but somewhat different. In either case, the customer must come on board and accept the change in direction and outcome. The assumptions that were baked into the statement of work about the data and the system are critical at this time because it provides an opportunity for renegotiation. This opens the door to the third path.

The third path from an unhappy discovery about the data resource is to simply stop the project. Again, the assumptions in the statement of work are the mechanism that enables this. Even though you are contractually able to take this path, it can still be a commercially and professionally painful decision to make. Although in this ultra-tight, ultra-compressed project structure, you've completed one-and-a-half out of three sprints, which will be paid for, the purpose of driving so hard and moving so fast is to develop this project in more profitable and interesting ways and to win more business once you succeed. That's not going to happen now, and the work burned to find that out is effort that could have been spent on other, better opportunities.

Suppose the ethical assessment that you conducted revealed unsurmountable issues. It may be impossible to build a system of the type desired without causing unacceptable harm to previously unidentified stakeholders. In this case, it's simply impossible for the project to continue. Your job is to identify these issues. You've driven out risk as quickly as possible, things are not great, but it is what it is. Getting out now may be the only sensible thing for you, the team, and the client.

The rest of the methodology and this book focuses on the happier prospect: you complete the EDA without substantial issues. The data that you hoped for is available, and the team understands it and can use it. You have established and documented the data constraints and understand the business constraints and opportunities, in addition to the constraints imposed by the customer's system.

Having collected these constraints, now we must solve them to find the right solution for the customer. It's at this point that the models at the heart of the system need to be designed and developed. The team has the tools to work with, an understanding of the model's constraints and requirements, and the assets that enable development of the data and foundational models. Putting all these things together and using them is the next step in the project and the task of sprint 2, where the modeling team gets to work.

6.5 *Pre-modeling checklist*

Having addressed the items of work for sprint 1, the team should pause and run through this predevelopment checklist. The goal of doing this is to ensure that adequate preparations are made, the necessary resources are in place before beginning modeling work, everyone has consumed and understood the relevant information created in this sprint, and any outstanding issues are addressed.

Table 6.1   Pre-modelling (PM) checklist for sprint 1

Task #	Item
PM 1	Access to training and validation data obtained.
PM 2	Data survey conducted, and data checked to be as expected and useable.
PM 3	Data pipelines implemented and versioned.
PM 4	Appropriate data testing in place.
PM 5	Appropriate repositories and versioning infrastructure created to support recording and managing all artefacts.
PM 6	EDA undertaken and results recorded.
PM 7	Baseline model created.
PM 8	Ethical assessment conducted.

6.6 *The Bike Shop: Pre-modelling*

The data resources for The Bike Shop project are in legacy SAP instances, managed on a corporate intranet behind The Bike Shop's firewall. The team needs an interface to SAP using the proprietary data services bridge to deliver the data to the cloud data warehouse in advance of the migration project. The Bike Shop owns and manages the cloud data warehouse on their cloud landing zone. To use the cloud landing zone, the team needs to be granted credentials as The Bike Shop's contractors. The steps required to access the data for The Bike Shop are as follows:

1 Secure a license for the data services bridge.
2 Get contractor IDs for team members.
3 Using their IDs, the team members must attend a corporate onboarding for security training and confirm that they accept all data policies for The Bike Shop.
4 Acquire and install the two-factor authentication and VPN clients.
5 Implement the data services bridge in the cloud landing zone.
6 Configure the cloud landing zone firewall to allow traffic to the SAP servers.
7 Configure the corporate firewall to allow traffic from the cloud landing zone.
8 Configure the SAP servers to accept the connection from the cloud landing zone.

9 Execute the agreed on one-off copy.

10 Ingest and format the data in the data warehouse into an appropriate schema.

Although that's a fair amount of work, there's more of an elapsed time component to these tasks. They are dependent on provisioning the services, the physical processes that deliver the components, and the time spent by team members in training courses and briefings for security conformance. Additionally, the data transfer can take time due to the cost of corporate interconnects. (Typically, these are an order of magnitude slower than consumer connections because of traffic management and quality-of-service liabilities and requirements that corporate businesses impose on their network providers.) Despite these bottlenecks, the team checks with the migration manager working on The Bike Shop contract at your organization to ensure that this process is front-loaded at the beginning of the sprint and that the data arrives in the cloud data warehouse on day 2.

6.6.1 *After the survey*

The data survey for The Bike Shop raises significant questions about the source data. Although the data covers the appropriate time span (five years), and the appropriate number of records for each year and month are distributed as expected, the team discovers a problem. There were large numbers of duplicate records in the data warehouse table and significant mismatches between the record counts in the three original data tables and the aggregate table. They noted these issues for further investigation and resolution.

During the survey, it was also noticed that almost all the records were from week 4 of each month. You ask the product manager to check why this is. It turns out that this wasn't an issue of an unused attribute (as for the sensor data). In fact, it was a business undertaking. The finance teams processed records to meet deadlines each month, completing their work at the end of each month. A cross-check is undertaken to count the distribution of records against the countries of origin. This verifies that the distribution of sales records for each country are in line with the relative importance of each country for the business. You prepared a report on the data in the data warehouse and send it in a notification via the document repository (as per the communication plan for the project) to the customer and to the team.

In the meantime, the team spins up dev, test, and prod environments in the Bike Shop's landing zone (as per the infrastructure plan). Infrastructure as code (IaC) is used to rapidly instantiate all the components and services that the backbone team needs for project delivery. In this case, there is no bespoke infrastructure and there are no problems of scale that will delay the build. Verification of the build is done with straightforward inspection, and an infrastructure report is prepared, filed, and communicated (as per the agreement on policy). A workshop with the business stakeholders is held to determine how they will consume and make use of the system. The agenda of the workshop ls as follows:

- Overview of proposed solution (including a mock UI) to understand what is to be built.
- Review of user stories developed during the pre-sales phase.
- Review of project challenges in the statement of work (SOW).
- Questions to move the project forward:
  - What are the entities that predictions should be made for? Countries? Regions? Product lines? Individual products?
  - What configuration options are required?
  - What controls should be provided for the user to manipulate and experiment with the models?

The workshop proved to be challenging; several of the required stakeholders failed to attend, and it's now apparent that the sponsorship for the project rests with the CIO and the team. This means that there will be a lack of business input in the project's direction, which ultimately diminishes its value to the organization.

This common experience is driven by the difficulty that operational managers have in valuing and grasping innovative initiatives for their business. Operational managers that own profit and loss (P&L) lines and that are accountable for their success are generally incentivized to deliver incremental performance improvements and to see strategic changes or changes to organizational focus (such as investing in different product lines or investing in different markets) as a threat to their business. They are, therefore, unlikely to invest in this kind of initiative.

In the case of The Bike Shop, innovations were often identified by a mechanical engineering development group under the control of the Director of Manufacturing. This group owned an innovation budget that was ringfenced by corporate management to enable the business to keep its product lines competitive. Unfortunately, this group is disinterested in supporting IT innovation. As companies and the economy digitize new structures that incentivize the participation of business stakeholders in IT, innovative projects become more and more important. But, for The Bike Shop project, that time lay in the future, and the team has to deal with the reality of the business's disengagement.

To overcome this, the team works with the product owner to reach out to the grass roots of the organization and set up meetings with people who can give insight and validation about the system. These mid-level managers can be engaged by the CIO team because they are involved in the business-as-usual implementation and upgrade initiatives and are, therefore, incentivized to maintain a good relationship with the CIO group. They have operational expertise and are also younger and more interested in technology than the senior stakeholders who were initially identified, so they are a good source of information. On the other hand, these experts are not able to sign off on the features and concepts they endorse. A series of meetings yields a stable set of user stories and alignment on the mechanism and output that the finished implementation should provide.

With agreement on the user stories, challenges, and features, the team develops and validates the backlog tasks S2.1 and S3.1. At the same time, information is now available to allow decisions to be made about what open-source data can be used to supplement the sales and inventory data from SAP. Economic indicators and country-specific news stories sourced from Reddit are selected. Discussions with the subject matter experts verify the team's findings about the aggregate data table in the SAP data warehouse.

Additionally, there appears to be issues with the aggregation process used in the data warehouse, which means that large numbers of records in the origin tables are likely not present in the aggregate table. After discussions with the CIO team, it's decided that importing the three regional tables and creating modelling from those is the only way to create results with any degree of integrity. These decisions allow the team to design and develop the pipeline to move and transform the source data into coherent data, suitable for an EDA and then modelling.

Figure 6.6 shows the ingest pipeline developed by the team. There are five steps in the pipeline that are broken out as workflow elements. First, the pipeline is started (a), so the first thing to do is to notify those in the team that are responsible for the pipelines that one has been started, and log that the pipeline is running. Step (b) pulls the data from the three SAP instances into staging storage on the cloud.

The next step (c) runs the SQL queries that generate a normalized value for each transaction in The Bike Shop's chosen global currency. (It could be $, £, or €, but £ was used in 1991 and adjusted as a relative value as well as an instantaneous value versus a modern basket of currency.) This step creates a set of three new tables containing all the original records with extra columns.

Step (d) joins these three normalized tables and chooses only distinct rows from them. This is because, in the preliminary discussions with The Bike Shop subject matter experts, it was mentioned that different regions often duplicated the record of a particular sale. Because the application under development is not aimed at determining local compensation, which is why the duplications occurred, and is aimed at gauging underlying business performance, these duplications must be removed.

Step (e) runs some simple checks over the resulting source table. The number of rows created versus the number of rows in the normalized and source tables is recorded, along with the amount of time taken and any exceptions raised in the logs from steps (b) and (c). The ingest is determined to be a success or a failure according to these checks, and a notification is sent to process subscribers, along with updates registered in the project metadata stores.

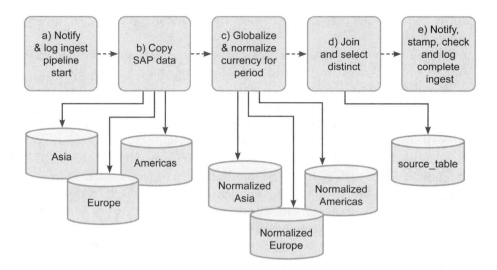

Figure 6.6   The Bike Shop data ingest pipeline with four atomic steps

Danish and Rob lead a discussion about modelling requirements, and the idea of bringing in open-source data to supplement the information in The Bike Shop databases is revisited. It's decided to use weather forecast data to develop the demand models with the idea that a forecast at some point before a prediction can produce insights about whether customers will want to get out cycling or whether they will be intent on sheltering from the rain on buses.

On another tack, the team wants to use newsfeed data as a source of general customer sentiment and then use that to predict sales. They identify these data sources in the version control system, and it's determined that a language model is required to support the sentiment extraction. The team designs a selection exercise and adds it to the backlog. One of the data scientists then runs the exercise. A model is chosen, and the data scientist documents and reports the choice and the reasons for it to the team. It's also identified in the versioning systems.

6.6.2   EDA implementation

The team is ready to do an EDA to build an understanding of the actual data that's available. As discussed in 4.7.1, the EDA activity focuses on making sure that the source_table has high integrity and that the data in source_table has sufficient information to make modeling plausible and valuable. They also want to gain a good understanding of the data and its characteristics so it can be shared with the team. Two specific integrity checks are identified:

- Is the sales data in the data set plausible and in line with the revenues reported by the customer to markets?
- Do the currency conversions and normalizations make sense?

In terms of modelling, the question becomes is there even coverage across the relevant markets and products? If there is some bias in the data from market to market or if there is a bias in data between product lines and business divisions, then a potential exists for these effects to be more important in derived models than in the underlying drivers and in the difference between business performance and practice. Additionally, the team needs to understand the distribution of activity between regions and between product groups

Identifying these objectives, the team places the EDA activity in the backlog. Two of the data scientists take on several subtickets covering each of the activities mentioned and start to work on individual activities to close these. The team also includes a subticket to bring the results together in a report. The EDA integrity checking reveals that, although the data in the source data tables shows the predicted problems, the deduplication and new join process seems to have been effective. Figure 6.7 shows the aggregate sales in the data extracted without deduplication, where a naïve normalization was used.

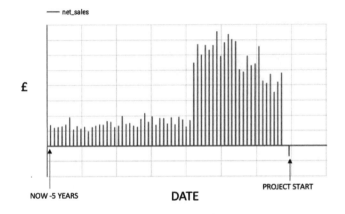

Figure 6.7   Naïve normalization and deduplication sales data

After deduplication and with proper normalization, the picture is much more plausible (figure 6.8). Cross-checks to published revenue figures reveal minimal deltas (in the order of 0.1%).

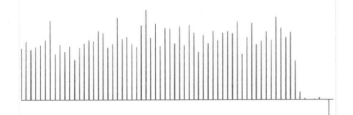

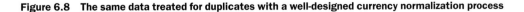

Figure 6.8   The same data treated for duplicates with a well-designed currency normalization process

The team investigates the negative revenue observed in the latest period and the negligible revenues for the more recent periods leading up to the project, and they determine it to be caused by cancelled orders (input as negative revenue by the sales teams). The lead time for orders to be booked as confirmed sales is long, which causes a systematic distortion. The Bike Shop adopted these practices to prevent corporate revenues from being overstated, so they are a necessary feature of the data. The team introduces reconciliation factors to compensate for the pipeline lag and to deal with the negative revenues in the current period.

Simple projections from the data are used to answer the other questions about the data created in the backlog. A team member then creates an EDA report, based on the results of the sub-investigations conducted by all team members. This report is reviewed, filed, and distributed according to the communication plan.

A review meeting is scheduled to further address the data privacy and ethics issues surrounding the project. At this stage, no data privacy issues are identified by the team because no personal data is identified in any of the data sources used. Now that the team is familiar with the project and the objectives of The Bike Shop, they can use the IEEE use case matrix to gain insight into the key ethical concerns that are likely to be relevant to this application (see figure 6.9)

Usecases		Human Agency and Oversight	Technical Robustness and Safety	Privacy and Data Governance	Transparency	Diversity, non-discrimination and fairness	Societal & Environmental Well-being	Accountability
Product and Customer	Personalised Marketing Offers			X	X	X	X	
	Next Best Action			X	X	X	X	
	Loan and Deposit Pricing			X	X	X		
	Credit Adjudication				X	X	X	
	Customer Sentiment Tracking	X		X			X	X
	Customer Lifetime Value			X		X	X	
	Customer Segmentation			X		X	X	
Risk	High Frequency Trading/Robo-Advisors	X					X	
	Cyber Security		X	X			X	
	Fraud Detection		X	X		X	X	
	AML		X				X	X
	Model Validation and Bias Detection		X		X	X		X
Operations	Robotic Process Automation	X	X					
	Operational Efficiencies	X		X				
	Expense Management	X				X		X
Corporate	Talent Acquisition			X	X	X	X	
	Talent Retention			X	X	X	X	
	Audit		X	X				
	Collections	X		X		X	X	
	Customer Service			X		X	X	

Basic	**Developing**	**Advanced**	Leading

Figure 6.9   Ethics assessment matrix for The Bike Shop, based on an IEEE use case matrix

The team identifies the proposed application as being relevant to operational efficiency Although there is no personal data in the application, the team sees the data governance issue as significant. If the data in the application is not well managed, the results could be misleading. The matrix also identifies human agency and oversight as critical concerns. The team notes this and determines that these concerns should be addressed in sprint 2, ensuring that the modelling techniques accommodate tooling for insight and interaction with the predictive analytics. In addition, they plan to use controls that allow the predictive analytics in the system to be disabled and to use trend-only or steady-state forecasts instead. An ethics report is prepared, filed, and communicated to the team.

Now that the data set is in hand, the team can undertake some simple modelling work to create baseline information supporting the evaluation of the models to be produced and to provide the team with feedback about the challenges ahead. Danish quickly implements a regression model for both inventory demand and customer churn rates. This provides a baseline performance measure. The results from it show that there are some strong signals in even the limited data sets and sample that Danish used. In a quick test, the model predictions correlate well with the observed fluctuations. Danish produces this model quickly because he's operating on top of the first version of the model CI/CD pipeline that the team built. He also made a lot of assumptions about the data, so everyone is aware that the problem is far from solved.

A note about the significant elements of the data survey, application definition, EDA, and ethical report outcomes is prepared and presented at the sprint review session. It's used as the basis to request sign off for sprint 1 by the customer. The backlog for sprint 2 is developed and agreed on, thus initiating sprint 2, which we'll discuss in the next chapter.

Summary

- By undertaking EDA, it's possible to develop insight into the potential for developing models that meet the requirements of the project.
- We can systematically explore unstructured data as soon as the data set is available for analysis.
- Use graphics (plots and charts) to explore and illustrate the data features. Visual methods are revealing, and communicating what is discovered is important for people who work on the project in the future.
- Simple methods (counting, sizes, labels, etc.) provide some insights into unstructured data. Modern methods (embeddings, mappings, etc.) further characterizes these data sets. Explore what's possible with the current state of the art.
- Address ethical considerations explicitly as the data sources and types become clear. Remember, failing to think about this aspect of the project can waste a lot of money as well as compromising the team ethically.
- Building simple baseline models can provide validation of the potential for modelling and a way to measure progress.

7

Making useful models with ML

This chapter covers

- Transforming data for processing
- Injecting information with feature engineering
- Designing the model's structure
- Running the model development process
- Deciding which models to retain and which to reject

Sprint 2 is the rollercoaster ride that we've been working toward; finally, we're going to do some ML! The success or failure of this phase of the project is the pivot point for everything else. Although we created the conditions for success with the work in presales, sprint 0, and sprint 1, all this work will be for nothing if we can't implement useful models. Creating a model is easy if you've done the hard part of getting and preparing the data. A simple model can involve writing a single line of code or pressing a button on a user interface. However, creating a useful model is much harder.

What makes a model created with ML useful or useless? The traditions of ML say that a useful model is one that generalizes well: the model can effectively deal with data that it was not trained on and that it copes with unseen circumstances. But, in fact, there are a bunch of other traits that make models useful, or if they don't have them, useless.

Table 7.1 lists the qualities of a useful model contrasted with a useless model. To deliver a useful model, the team needs to generate many features from the data, create a large number of candidate models, properly evaluate them, select the one that's going to be the most effective, and explain all this to the people who are impacted by the model or to the regulators and the auditors. This process must be professionally executed and managed. Furthermore, without a rigorous evaluation process, your model may prove to be brittle in production, or it may be that you face difficulty in convincing your stakeholders that you have made responsible and appropriate choices about the model.

The three drivers of the entries in table 7.1 are the need to do modelling work that is aligned with the needs of all the stakeholders in the system, to build on solid foundations, and to ensure that the result is solid. A solid result is not just a great model, but it's a model that others can verify as being great. Now, the team needs to generate the assets that allow that verification to take place.

Table 7.1   What makes a model useful or useless?

Useful	Useless	Commentary
Created from a well-understood and well-prepared data infrastructure.	Developed from ad hoc data resources prepared with little control or thought about quality.	If you don't have a process that ensures quality, you won't know if the data you are working with is good.
Created in response to a well-understood requirement and meets that requirement.	Created because it can be; unclear if it meets any requirement.	If you don't have established sponsorship for the case that the model supports, then the work required to get sponsorship may be prohibitive. You probably don't have the level of insight required to second-guess a stakeholder's view on business value and then prove that you are right.
Created with regards to ethical considerations.	Created without thought about ethical impact or regard for the people impacted.	Models with ethical issues are eventually killed by the business. The further down the road to production, the more damage they do.
High-quality feature engineering creates strong performance.	Low-quality or no feature engineering.	Poor feature engineering means that model performance in tests is likely to be disconnected with the user or real-world expectations and requirements.
Purposefully designed.	Arbitrary design.	If the design is arbitrary, it's likely the model will be brittle.
Thoroughly evaluated.	Not well evaluated.	When the model is poorly evaluated, no one knows if it works or not.
Model selection process is purposeful and transparent.	Model selection is arbitrary.	With an arbitrary selection, who knows if you got the right one or why you picked it?
Defined modelling process used.	Modelling process is arbitrary.	A defined process for modeling allows for accountability with respect to model choices.
Well documented.	No documentation.	Because documentation promotes transparency, it also enables problems to be identified and fixed.

7.1   *Sprint 2 backlog*

In sprint 2, the team implements systematic and professional modelling and evaluation processes. By using an organized and documented approach, the team avoids some of the pitfalls and common problems that produce poor quality models. At least, that's what is to be hoped! Let's look at those tasks for sprint 2 before we dive into the details.

Table 7.2   Backlog for Sprint 2: modelling and evaluation

Task #	Item
S2.1	Create a feature engineering plan, then share and review it with team.
	Implement a feature-engineering pipeline.
	Design and add data augmentation.
S2.2	Create the model's design and document it.
	Consider the forces acting on the model's design.
	Decide on the decomposition of tasks to create your overall design.
	Choose component parts based on the required inductive biases given your data.
	Develop composition schemes that fuse your model's output.
S2.3	Agree on the modeling process and set it up:
	• Commission and use an experiment tracker.
	• Commission and use a model repository.
	• Identify and reject obviously poor models.
S2.4	Implement and commission the test environment.
S2.5	Develop a set of tests to determine the model's functional performance.
	Determine the measurements to use over the test scenarios.
S2.6	Test nonfunctional features.
S2.7	Use the evaluation data to determine the model to use.
	Employ an explicit mechanism to use the model test/evaluation data to choose the model that used in production.
	Account for how component models will be combined in your design.
	Account for nonfunctional requirements.
	Account for the qualitative aspects of the model.
S2.8	Write a model delivery report.
S2.9	Determine and document model selection.
S2.10	Review and obtain customer sign-off on model selection.

7.2   *Feature engineering and data augmentation*

> **Feature engineering ticket: S2.1**
> - Create a feature engineering plan, then share and review it with team.
> - Implement a feature engineering pipeline.
> - Design and add data augmentation.

Feature engineering and selection is a core part of the ML pipeline. The raw data that's assembled might make little sense to an ML algorithm without some preprocessing to create consistent, useful, and informative features. Before modelling starts, the data set needs to be enriched and transformed to provide the appropriate features for the algorithms to consume.

Systems of feature selection and engineering are available for use. For example, in their book *Feature Engineering and Selection: A Practical Approach for Predictive Models*, Kuhn and Johnson [7] provide an analytical perspective for identifying, creating, and selecting features. In this framework, they use mathematical and technical considerations to restructure data, making it more amenable for consumption by ML algorithms. A systematic approach to feature engineering is helpful in identifying and solving technical issues with data. In particular:

- Identifying and removing biases created by the same information across multiple fields in the data set.
- Resolving biases created by skews of distribution and differences of scale.
- Handling hierarchical data and the information distributed within the hierarchy.

As well as resolving technical problems with the way the data is presented to the algorithms, we can use feature engineering to encode human insight and common sense for the machine. For example, it's common sense (for folks raised to understand the Gregorian calendar) that December is followed by January, and it seems reasonable to assume that December is represented by the number 12 and January by the number 1. But given the information that there are three days, 12/30, 12/31, and 1/1, how can a machine be expected to deduce that the first day of January follows the last day of December?

Another example deals with data that includes an orientation or a direction, often represented as a scalar value between 0' and 360' or sometimes as a compass direction or relationship between different points. If we treat this data as a linear quantity, then items with a bearing of 359' and 1' appear at the opposite ends of the scale. In reality, they are close, and both are almost exactly due north (0'± 1'). We'll get better results if we reframe the data to account for this circularity.

Feature engineering is the process of transforming the data in such a way that it makes sense to an ML algorithm (for example, the information that 1/1 is preceded by

12/31 and that 359' is next to 0' is included as knowledge for the machine). Instead of embedding knowledge as some sort of extra reasoning rule, a feature engineer rewrites the data so that it's part of the information that the ML system works with.

Given the three days, 12/30, 12/31, and 1/1, we can solve that irregularity by representing the date as a distance from a point. If we take Midsummer's Day and then New Year's Day (1/1), New Year's Day represents the value 182 (often), the last day of the year (12/31) is 181, and the second of January (1/2) is 181 as well. The point here is that all these examples are similar in value, so this transform makes more sense for the things that are similar.

We can use the smart building example to show how rewriting orientations can be useful. As we saw in chapter 4, the building sensors record the temperature on days 1–366, where day 366 accounts for a leap year. Figure 7.1 shows the mean temperature per day for each day of the year.

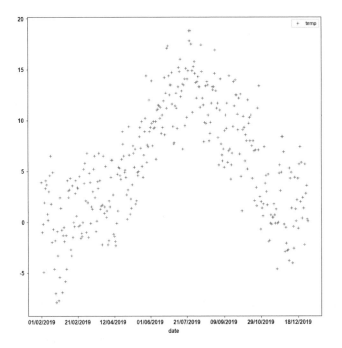

Figure 7.1   Temperatures plotted by day of the year (data for Suffolk Wattlesham weather station, 2019, from UK Government).

Figure 7.2 shows two new features: one giving the distance in days of a candidate day from Midsummer's Day and another with the mean temperature for that day divided by the distance from Midsummer's Day and normalized from 0.0 (Midsummer's Day) to 1.0 (Midwinter's Day) if there is a leap year. That's 183 days, so the day after midsummer has a value of 0.0054.

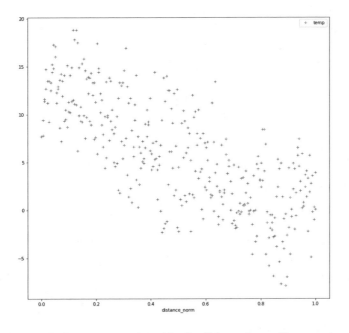

Figure 7.2   Temperatures plotted for the distance from midsummer (scaled 0.0 – 1.0)

We can also create features for some unstructured data sources by using pretrained foundation models. In chapter 4, we used a foundation model to explore the unstructured data in the text of Shakespeare's plays. We can use the same approach to create features from unstructured data, which we can then feed into ML. This is a different tack from doing ML directly over some unstructured signals, where the regularities and patterns are created in the foundational model's training. We then use these results to represent the data in a more consumable form for the modeling process. With Shakespeare's plays, we used the all-MiniLM-L12-v2 sentence transformer to create a concept of novelty and difference. We then extracted a concept graph to relate similar themes.

We can use similar approaches (and other more direct uses of foundation models) to create useful features and to fuse information from unstructured and structured data sources. For example, the Shakespeare example showed how to find similarity in a space of unstructured documents (the plays). Let's take a new problem that involves textual data.

In this scenario, an email to accept a new customer is passed into an approval process. It's discovered at a later stage that the email was sent to the wrong person and should have been handled differently, wasting a great deal of time and effort. Your team informs you that they think it's likely the text classifier misbehaves on emails that are new or strangely framed.

Corner cases of this kind can end up consuming a disproportionate amount of cost in the final process, and it might be so bad as to destroy the user confidence in the triage system. After the EDA process, the team thinks that a feature that determines outliers in the training set would be useful in terms of cleaning it and wants to build a high-quality classifier that determines appropriate topics. They construct a simple feature to provide a new-weird/not-new-normal signal for the system. As before, the data is indexed using embeddings from a foundational model. The email's novelty is rated by getting the second closest email in the index (ignoring the identity match) and using the similarity distance to rate how close this email is to it as this pseudocode shows:

```
results_array = array [length(emails)]
for email in emails :
    match = index.search (email)
    results_array[email.id]=match.D
```

email.id is the index of this email.

match.D is the distance that the index has returned.

The results array contains the distance to the closest match in the index for each email. If you find the standard deviation of this array and set a threshold of two times the standard deviation plus the mean, then you can filter out the strangest 5% of the emails for training. If you use this feature for the topic classifier itself, then you can create an "Other" label and the classifications for the remaining topics will be stronger.

Developing high-quality features for a domain can be time-consuming and difficult. A lot of experience and domain insight is required to get good results, and this is the reason why feature stores are valuable assets. If a previous project develops a way of expressing the position of a sensor in a building that provides insight and information, then that's a huge win. In addition, creating a consistent way of using data in an organization is helpful in terms of ensuring that the behavior of ML algorithms is consistent and well understood. If your project is a trailblazer, then hopefully the feature store that you develop and leave behind will be a lasting asset for the client.

7.2.1   *Data augmentation*

There is an apocryphal story often told about an early ML system that was purportedly developed to identify tanks in photographs (the exact application it was developed for is always vague). The story's punchline is that the ML system learned not to recognize tanks but, instead, to recognize snowy ground because the only shots with a tank in were taken in the snow. The story is almost certainly fiction, but there is a point to be made: if an ML algorithm only has a narrow data set to learn from, then what it can learn is restricted. Although it might be able to learn a robust classifier from the information it receives, it's also likely that there are traps that it can fall into, where it learns to use coincidences in the data to make a classification. If there are different examples, however, it could be that the misleading coincidences become much rarer.

To fix this issue, Shorten and Khoshgoftaar [13] developed the technique of *data augmentation*. Data augmentation is a process of using transformations and alterations to create extra examples for training. We can use this technique to make ML models more robust when only a narrow set of examples is available in the original training set.

Figure 7.3 shows a set of image augmentations. The original image example (a) is rotated as per (b), (c), and (d), although we can generate more rotations. Also, extra objects can be added into the image as per (e) and (f), other sorts of noise (g), inversion (h), scaling (i), and repositioning within the frame or scene (j). In (k), the image is mirrored, providing another example of a cat for the ML algorithm.

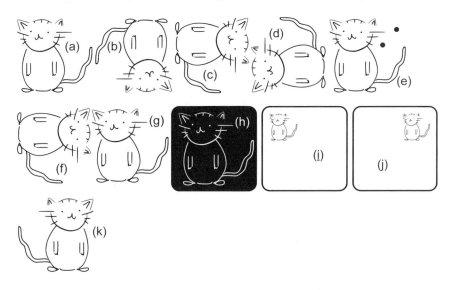

Figure 7.3   Augmenting an image of a cat with simple manipulations (Wikipedia commons, https://commons.wikimedia.org/wiki/File:Black_and_White_Cat_Sketch.svg).

We use augmentation processes such as the one shown in figure 7.3 to make models that are more robust and general. The idea is that a model that focuses on a coincidental feature will be less likely to be chosen by the ML process if there is a wider variety of signals in the training data. We can also apply similar augmentation processes to other forms of unstructured data. For example, we may want to add spelling errors to text samples, replace non-stop words (words that aren't regarded as stop-words/ discardable by NLP parsers) with synonyms, or pass sentences through an auto-translate system to change its phrasing. For image recognition systems, we may want to use alternations for contrast and brightness, as well as many schemes that introduce noise and distortions.

Whatever the need, we can apply new features and data augmentation approaches iteratively during the modelling process as the team's investigations proceed and new information about the behavior of the algorithms comes to light. How that process of iterative modelling is managed is discussed in section 7.4. Once the first set of features is implemented, the next step for the team is to create the model's design.

7.3   Model design

> **Model design ticket: S2.2**
> - Create the model's design and document it
> - Consider the forces acting on the model's design.
> - Decide on the decomposition of tasks to create your overall design.
> - Choose component parts based on the required inductive biases given your data.
> - Develop composition schemes that fuse your model's output.

Before the models can be built by ML algorithms, they must be designed by the data scientists and ML engineers in the team. As an analogy, it's worth remembering that rocket engines are designed to take advantage of the technology and fuel available to power them to achieve the results required. If your rocket engineering team can't access exotic metals and high-quality fuel, their approach will have to be much more pragmatic and constrained than if they had lots of titanium and synthetic chemicals. Similarly, ML models are designed to deliver functionally and nonfunctionally, given the data that's available and the production environment they will operate in.

7.3.1   Design forces

In sprint 0 and sprint 1, you exposed and clarified the requirements and constraints on ML modelling for the business application you are developing. A range of forces should have been articulated in your user stories to act on the model's design that's going to underpin your team's approach to providing a solution. Some examples of these forces are listed here:

- *Quantitative performance:* A few examples of qualitative performance measures include a good F1 score, precision and recall, or sensitivity and specificity. (Chapter 8 has a detailed discussion of these different performance measurements if this is the first time you've come across them.) It's worth being careful with specific measures, but essentially, you can measure the quantitative performance of the classifier by how effectively it does its job.
- *Explanation/transparency:* The classifier that gives the best numerical evaluation might not provide a sufficient explanation for its decisions or be transparent enough in its workings to allow its use in a particular context or application.
- *Latency:* The latency of the classifier should be appropriate to the application. For example, you may need to execute the classifier within a fraction of a second of the data becoming available for an interactive application. On the other hand, you can transcribe a movie's speech to create subtitles in a batch job overnight.
- *Cost:* If you need to execute a classifier millions of times, the cost of the infrastructure that you use to run it can become prohibitive.

- *Data privacy/security:* Inferences made from the classifier's behavior might disclose secrets or confidential data.

- *Reuse and data sparsity:* There might not be enough data to train some types of classifiers, so there may be prebuilt classifiers that you can download and use without training to execute some part of the project where there's insufficient data.

- *Project risk/time to develop:* Training classifiers from scratch can be difficult and risky, and unexpected behaviors may mean they can't be used. Downloading pre-trained components or using simple models can reduce project risk at the cost of overall performance.

- *Robustness in production:* A highly tuned solution might be brittle and fragile in the real world.

Today's ML practitioners have a range of algorithms available to deal with the complex functional and nonfunctional demands of modern applications. Given this wealth of resources, can you just pick a solution out of a toolbox that resolves the particular forces in your project? Sadly, the world just doesn't work that way, and things are a bit more complex.

7.3.2 *Overall design*

It is important to choose the right algorithm for the data and the problem at hand, and there is a huge amount of literature available to support your choice. For example, Kevin Murphy provides detailed, in-depth explanations of a wealth of algorithms in his book, *Probabilistic Machine Learning: An Introduction* [10]. Often, though, it isn't a simple case of picking the best option from all the available candidate algorithms because:

- There is no best option. Instead, you are faced with trade-offs.
- Nothing quite fits the application, and you must choose, at least, a bad option.
- The best option isn't going to work for your model's context. Your team doesn't understand it, you don't have the time to implement it, the hardware platform won't support it, or (commonly) it requires too much attention and intervention in production, and it won't get that from your users.

What can we do to overcome these everyday challenges? One pragmatic response to these challenges is to implement a composite model that brings together several techniques to address different parts of the data in a way that a single model is unable to do (quickly and reliably in a time-bound project). For example, you may require an automatic translation bot to interpret a sentence uttered in one of several potential languages into English. It is technically possible to implement this model as a single, deep network, and the performance of the single network may be superior to specialized single-language networks. It might be less risky, easier, and quicker to break the problem into parts and to use a more well-worn and tested solution.

A different issue is created by a challenge that requires several disjoint models to be developed, which work independently in different parts of a business process. For example, in a customer service flow, it may be that your system needs to recognize the language a customer speaks and then offer the right support information to them, based on the challenge they face. With these challenges, there are architectural choices that you can make to break the problem into bits and algorithms that can be made to solve each part. How are those choices made, though?

7.3.3 *Choosing component models*

Data scientists use their expertise and experience to select the right ML algorithms to produce the right model for the problem at hand. Nothing substitutes for experience and insight, but there are some useful heuristics, which are good to have in mind during this process. Although these rules of thumb and general principals may not correspond to the best technical approach, they can be useful in terms of managing the project's risk during its modelling.

Two of the most basic determinants of the model is the type of data that the algorithm consumes and uses and the type of output that the model produces. If the model needs to produce a graduated control signal from 0.0 to 1.0, and it can only produce a binary signal of on or off, then the model is useless. If the ML algorithm can't "see" in color, then the model it produces will be in black and white. Fundamentally, the question is, can the algorithm model the output distribution effectively? This is a fancy way of saying is there any output from the model that it is technically unable to produce? Is it able in principle to produce the correct proportion of output? If not, then you need to stop the team and get them to use approaches that can.

Given that the algorithms you choose are capable (in principle) of creating a model of the distribution that you are after, then well-known algorithms should be preferred to novel algorithms where possible. A new algorithm may be state-of-the-art and may perform a little better than the old stager that everyone has used forever for problems like this. Moreover, a new algorithm may also be undertested and not well-understood. If nothing else, a well-known algorithm should be benchmarked against the newest and shiniest approach advocated by the modeling team. If their new "gee-whiz" ML magic outperforms older and better-known architectures and approaches, then great! If it doesn't, then the older approach will be a source of great comfort to you.

In general, it's best to use a simpler algorithm if you can effectively address the modelling problem with it. Sophisticated, deep-network architectures, however, can do things that other algorithms can't. Despite this injunction, you may find that the team has no option but to dive into new waters, especially when dealing with domains like images, sound, and natural languages.

Deep networks can create models for complex unstructured data, but these are usually considered not to be transparent or explainable. There are mechanisms that use deep networks because their functional performance is great. This can be explained to humans effectively, but these mechanisms are always inferior to more straightforward, transparent models, such as association rules or decision trees. If transparency is a design force, you may have to balance it carefully against the functional performance of the system.

Deep networks can be expensive to train and expensive in terms of latency and cost when used in the production system. Remember that the team burns a lot of C02 when they run a data center's worth of GPUs for a week to create a model that can be used to improve a building's energy efficiency. This might not be a good thing for you to have to tell your sponsors about.

These general principals are just good common-sense design heuristics. We choose our models because they will produce the required output from the input. This likelihood goes by the luminous title of *inductive bias*.

7.3.4 Inductive bias

We can create ML models using different algorithms and approaches, but each of these introduce some bias into the process. Consider the sensors from the smart building example. The sensors have the following attributes that describe each of them: age, manufacturer, and installation. Installation has two values, internal/external; age is a scalar from 0 (new) to the number of days that the sensor has been installed. There are five different manufacturers, and half the sensors failed in our data. Because of this, we would like to make a decision tree that predicts which sensors are likely to fail.

We have some choices to make about how we'll construct the tree. Which attribute should we test first? What tests should we apply to which attribute? In this case, a sensible test to start with might be the installation attribute. Is this sensor internal or external? In some situations, we might see that 80% of the external sensors fail and that less than 20% of the internal sensors also fail. Figure 7.4 illustrates the effect of a split on some data with the installation attribute.

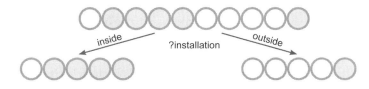

Figure 7.4 Splitting the training data using the installation attribute. Outside sensors (right) fail much more often than inside ones.

Even though our choice is commonsensical, in some ways it's arbitrary. Figure 7.5 shows an alternative split using the age attribute, which creates a clean division of data. Now we see that all sensors that have been installed for longer than 100 days always fail. A split using *test age* > 100 creates a left-hand node that only contains failed sensors.

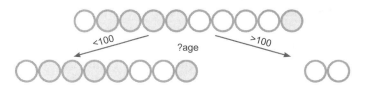

Figure 7.5 **Splitting the data using the age attribute to yield a pure node on the left branch. No further tests are required on this tree.**

More sophisticated choices have been developed, which are backed by well thought-out reasoning as to why they are appropriate or not. These arguments almost always come down to a variation of Occam's razor, which tells us to choose the set of splits that tend to make for the simplest decision tree in preference to the infinity of other ways of determining class membership. An algorithm that uses one criterion for splitting a target set at a node in a decision tree, such as an information theoretic measure like the J-measure [9], might be more likely to discover a particular regularity in the data rather than an algorithm that utilizes another criterion, such as statistical significance or simple counting [2].

Often, we use XGBoost [1], other boosting algorithms, and random forests to creating effective and robust models over tabular data. Unfortunately, they create complex classifiers that are hard to understand. This can make it difficult to use them in applications where decisions based on models should be transparent and readily explained.

If an XGBoost model is too detailed and complex to be used directly, it can be used as a denoiser, screening out the noise that confuses simpler models. To do this, we need to train an XGBoost model and then use the output as the target variable for modeling with a simpler decision tree or an association rule discovery algorithm. Alternatively, you can use XGBoost as a baseline to gauge how much the choice of a simple explainable model is costing you in terms of model effectiveness.

For unstructured data such as images and text, XGBoost is less successful and less applicable. The development of a variety of hierarchical architectures for deep networks means a range of biases can be created when selecting a particular architecture. Choosing the correct bias means we can sometimes obtain a much lower loss from less data in return for a much lower burden of training and inference computation.

Figure 7.6 shows five different types of deep networks. These are hierarchical arrangements such as multi-layer perceptron's, grid networks designed for computer vision tasks, recurrent networks [5] designed for speech and text-based tasks, graph networks [4], and attention-based networks such as transformers [11].

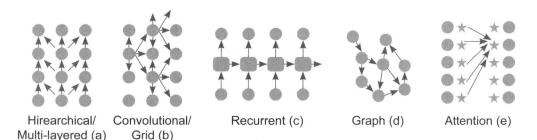

Figure 7.6 Inductive bias in ML algorithms (adapted from Jumper, Evans, et. al. [6]. The sequence (a) through (e) is determined by the order in which these biases gained popularity in the ML community. The arrows indicate the propagation of signal across a network or in a graph.

The network structures in figure 7.6 were developed in response to the need to process different types of data. For example, figure 7.7 shows a perceptron-type network using a hierarchical structure. This consumes the data from an image one pixel at a time, but because the context of the pixels is as important as its content, the perceptron doesn't do well. The information in the image is largely stored in the relationship of the pixels to each other, and the perceptron can't capture that.

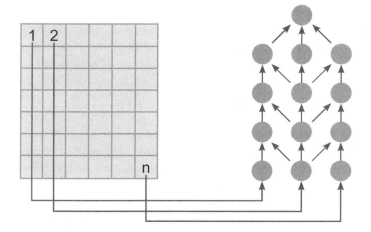

Figure 7.7 What images (pixelated on the lhs) look like to a hierarchically arranged network (rhs). The order of the image is lost and effectively randomized with pixel *n* fed to the right most input of the network, distant from the pixel above it or diagonally adjacent to it, this makes the task of object recognition hard for the system.

On the other hand, we can construct convolutional networks [8]. (shown as (b) in figure 7.6) to consider localities. *Convolution* is the process of propagating information locally in the network, providing normalization and filtering of activations at a local level. A learned filter is passed in a sliding window over the network, determining how signals should be propagated from pixel to pixel, and information is pooled between layers. Convolutional networks became the favored architecture for image recognition problems after large scale training sets and compute engines sufficiently powerful to harness images on these types of training challenges became available.

7.3.5   *Multiple disjoint models*

Many projects require that several models be constructed to support different parts of the AI application. The models' results do not feed into one another but are consumed by a human or as separate input to a decision-making system. For example, a credit risk model might be made up of several disjoint models that represent different types or drivers of risk. One might model fraud, and another, dependencies that make the applicants risky, whereas a third one might model economic trends. These models' output can be composed together to create a single score, or they can be displayed separately to a credit controller.

If your team is working on one integrated system, the divergent requirements of different models can have a significant impact both on the complexity of the system required (in terms of the inference and the data layers for production) and on the performance of the system (in terms of quantitative and nonfunctional performance). We need to balance the allocation of resources to each of the models to ensure that the overall value of the system is maximized.

Remember, though, resources include both the time and the processor power allocated to the production models, as well as the time and the team's effort during development. An easy trap for a team is to spend weeks polishing one model at the expense of not focusing on other models, which could yield far more benefit with a bit of work.

7.3.6   *Model composition*

An alternative setup is to use models in sequence to perform an overall reasoning process. Sometimes, we chain models together because we need to capture further intervention or outcome. For example, a decision must be made regarding the control of flow for some reagent in a process, and the outcome of mixing must be observed before making another decision about heating the solution. This situation is known as *model composition*, and its design process is more complex than for two isolated, independent models.

Alternatively, it may be that we can sensibly break a single task into a set of dependent models, although there are cases where a single model is the best option. Often, problems can be quickly and reliably solved with the pragmatic approach of breaking the problem into a number of steps and learning each of these individually to create a chain of inference for the model.

As an example, think about the challenge of translating a sentence into English. The first step is to recognize the source language. The next step is to determine the meaning or intent of the sentence, then the final step is to render that meaning or intent into English in the most elegant way possible. It is possible to imagine a single network that encompasses all three tasks in a meta task called translate (and, indeed, these do exist and have definite advantages). It may, however, be easier to build three different networks that do each of these steps and chain them together with the appropriate glue and management logic. This approach has the following advantages:

- We can more closely manage the technical risks of each subproject as it builds a component model rather than the risks of a large and challenging E2E (End 2 End) network.
- Reusable elements like pretrained, off-the-shelf networks or data sets may be available for the subcomponents as these may represent more general tasks than the E2E solution.
- We can test individual components in isolation, enabling easier troubleshooting and debugging.
- We can build in parallel individual components, potentially shortening development time (although this assumes that the cost in the engineering time for building a better single network is larger than the cost of integration).
- We can engineer partial solutions into an overall system that provides business value.

If there is some success in developing some of these components, and if these components can be integrated into the business processes and used to support its decision makers, we can deliver a successful project. The trade-off is that there are also downsides:

- The composite model might not perform as well as a single bespoke model.
- Managing the productionization of a plethora of models can be hard and expensive in terms of documentation and process.
- Chains of models can introduce latency and throughput issues and bottlenecks (the fleet sails at the pace of the slowest ship).
- It's difficult to understand and maintain complex designs.

When you've developed a model design and the integration strategy is agreed on and communicated to the team, the next step is for the team to realize it.

7.4 Making models with ML

Model process support ticket: S2.3

- Agree on the modelling process and set it up.
- Commission and use an experiment tracker.
- Commission and use a model repository.
- Identify and reject obviously poor models.

The actual creation of ML models can be as complicated as architecting a complex deep learning network with specialist layers and feedback circuits, or it can be as simple as pressing the Go button on a user interface. When model creation is complex and involved, the expertise required to create the model is obvious, and the need to use an expert team to do the work is driven by the fact that non-experts will fail to create a model that supports the application. If you use a low-code or tool-driven approach to generating models, it can sometimes seem that expertise is not required because a valuable result looks to be on the table even though no experts are involved.

The reality is that even if the model is created with one click, insight and discipline are required. Everything that gets the model maker to the point of pushing the button and everything that happens to the model after the button is pushed creates value, or it creates damage. Because of this, it's important to define and manage the process that you use for modeling.

7.4.1   Modeling process

The actual process of developing a model is curiosity driven and experimental; it's both an art and a science. Building understanding about the data and the domain and creating deliberate designs for the model is necessary but insufficient for success. To get good models, the team needs to experiment, introspect, and investigate their way to something that works.

This sounds like an ad hoc and unstructured activity, and in a way, it is. Although a scientist may have flashes of inspiration and try something crazy, it's all done in a managed framework. For a scientist, experimental details are written out, upfront in the lab book.

Data scientists need to use the same management framework to achieve similar objectives of rigor and reproducibility. It's easy to mess up and lose some detail of model design, which means the model can't be rebuilt or has elements that are undocumented. Additionally, the investigation needs to be organized and records kept so that effort isn't replicated, redoing work that should have been put to bed the first time round. Not only does repeated reworking of poorly done or poorly documented work waste time and money, it also wastes valuable resources. The actual process to use prevents wasted time, and it's also designed to prevent the team from fooling themselves about the quality of the models they are building.

A big issue in modelling activity is often called *data leakage*, which is the corruption of the model evaluation process by accidentally allowing test information to escape into the training process. Essentially, data leakage means that the algorithm takes a peek at the test data before it's supposed to. A typical data leakage scenario plays out like this: because some model just happens to do well on the validation data, the modelling team tends to focus on similar models and figures out more performance optimizations for the validation problem. Sadly, this fails to translate into real-world performance, and the model is a big disappointment. This can be because the team's actions caused an unconscious optimization over the quirks and artefacts in the validation data.

As an aside, another common mistake is choice of the training and validation data. This happens especially in time series prediction problems, where cases from the future provide a signal that the model latches onto and then replicates that in the test data. For example, we use the data from a hot summer in the validation set for our smart building. Because the test data set is also drawn from the same hot summer, the model cheats on its test performance in a way that will not be replicated in production.

These issues prevent the models from being properly explored. Further, the time that could be spent checking other promising design options gets spent chasing the ghost of a promising one-off performance. What to do?

1 Plan how the available time is to be spent implementing and exploring the performance of the model design.

2 For each part of the design, identify a set of experiments to create and verify the behavior of that component. Each experiment is an episode of modelling and testing. Write down what's expected from this process.

3 Do the modelling and testing as planned and document the results.

4 To understand the results, inspect the results with the appropriate tools.

5 After each episode, review and decide on what changes to make to the plan and whether new features or changes to the data pipelines are required.

6 Select another episode from the backlog and do to same for that one.

The point of doing this is that by putting discipline around the process and documenting and reviewing what is done, you can identify and stop any process of over optimization (with a potential information leak). If things go wrong, then at least you can identify that you need to get more validation data and to check that the models are working good enough to warrant further development. Failing to do this leads to the data scientists stumbling around in the dark trying out things to see if they really work. By interrogating the results, and understanding them, and then reviewing what was learned on each iteration, the development process gains direction and momentum. Of course, this is in theory; just as lab experiments are a hard road to tread, so data science experiments are difficult to do as well.

There is another set of drivers that you and the team should consider when deciding to work in a planned and systematic way during model development. In traditional science, carefully maintained lab books allow experiments to be reproduced and practices checked for safety and professionalism. In the same way, keeping careful records of ML processes allow promising models to be reproduced and audited. This is going to be increasingly important as ML systems become more commonly used and more frequently questioned in our society. Working professionally with good record-keeping makes your models auditable and inspectable, and this makes them more useful and valuable. Next, we'll discuss how to document modelling activity and how to manage and track the results.

7.4.2   *Experiment tracking and model repositories*

The model repository that you selected and implemented as part of the project infrastructure stores instances of models built by the team. Some metadata about the models should be stored there as well. For example, it should contain the version of the algorithm used to create the model, the hyperparameters used for the algorithm, and the links to the training set or training pipeline versions that fed the data to the algorithm.

Table 7.3 shows a small sample of some statistics recorded over several runs. In this figure, we used a simple linear model to make predictions. The variation in performance is due to the different sizes of the test set, and performance is estimated for the experiment using the AUC (area under the curve metric). Notice that the `testSize` parameter was added at 10:38am when the data scientist noticed that there were some differences in performance and that the size of the test set was not being recorded to explain them. Also notice the change in the penalty function selected by the ML package (Elastic_net) when a large test is tried.

Table 7.3   Example of statistics that might be recorded by an experiment tracking system

Start time	Duration	l1_ratio	Penalty	testSize	auc_test
15/02/2022 10:43	1.9 s	0.5	Elastic net	0.5	0.93916314
15/02/2022 10:42	2.1 s	0.5	l2	0.1	0.94286043
15/02/2022 10:38	2.1 s	0.5	l2	0.1	0.94286043
15/02/2022 10:34	2.4 s	0.5	l2		0.94286043
15/02/2022 10:00	2.0 s	0.1	l2		0.94286043
15/02/2022 09:59	1.9 s	0.5	Elastic net		0.93916314
15/02/2022 09:58	2.3 s	0.1	l2		0.94505654

Recording this information is tedious and error-prone, but despite that, we recorded the data in the table using a package (tool) called MLflow (but there are many other similar tools that you can adopt). We ran this tool from the same Python runtime as the ML algorithm (in this case, a simple regression). MLflow has an API that we used to record the details of the experiment. We entered the statistics and parameters into the MLflow database in calls from the modelling code. Each time we ran the experiment, the data about the parameters and performance was pushed, and we can retrieve it either from a GUI or from a simple command-line call.

Not shown in Table 7.2 are the unique identifiers of the models that tie the binaries, assets (such as transfer models, test, training, and validation data sets), and formulas used to construct them to the outcomes and results that we saw during their development. This tie in is where the model repository enters.

Models discovered by ML algorithms are stored as binary files, encoding all the discovered parameter settings and weights that specify the particular model that was extracted from the data. These are saved in the filesystem or in a database. In the case of MLflow, we can store the files in the filesystem using the API that was invoked to store the experiment details.

Figure 7.8 shows the model stored for the run that created the entries in Table 7.2. You can see that the artifacts include the Conda code for all the Python packages we used to create the model and the pickle (.pkl) file that encodes the actual model. These artifacts should be enough to reconstitute and run the model on demand because all the dependencies and requirements to make it work are stored in the repository. The other directories contain the metadata that defines a model and how it performed in the experiment.

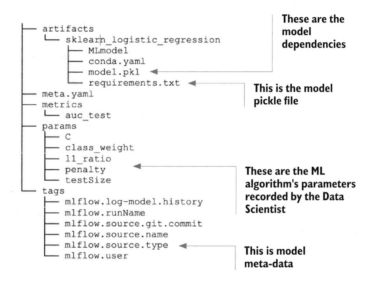

Figure 7.8   The files stored in a model repository that we can use to understand which model is stored, how it was made, how it relates to the experiment tracking information, and to get it up and running again.

The data pipelines developed in sprint 1 and the features engineered at the start of this sprint are supportive of the data scientists' work as well. That's why the pipelines and features were developed! Additionally, this work is framed in the context of the team's understanding of the data, the business problem, and the project's ethical challenges. We can go one step further in making the ML part of the project even easier. You and the team can save yourself a lot of heartache by outsourcing the design of your models and the process of creating them to a machine.

7.4.3   *AutoML and model search*

A popular modern practice is to use an automated search system to iteratively create models. The search works by choosing variations of algorithm parameters and creating and testing models with different structures and biases. This practice evolved because the space of potential models that a deep-learning system can express is vast, and it's not possible to check all the structures that can be constructed by hand. Although, arguably this kind of process arose due to the development of deep learning systems, but since then, the practice is commonly applied to tuning the performance of statistically inspired ML algorithms as well. Because of its heritage, this technique is also known as neural architecture search (NAS) and sometimes as meta-learning.

The great thing about AutoML is that you can replicate the work of a diligent data scientist with a single line of code or the touch of a button. It would be implausible and foolish to deny that there are gains to be made in terms of rapidly improving model performance by using AutoML. Some robust state-of-the-art results have been obtained by using these processes [3], and this approach automates work that can be tedious and error prone. However, there are problems to be aware of.

Model search systems are optimization systems and, therefore, can produce brittle models that work extremely well on hold-out data but fail on test data (or in production). It's just a matter of time until a model search finds some model that happens to perform well on a particular test, just by luck something will fit. We discuss the issue of maintaining the integrity of the testing system that's used to evaluate models in chapter 8, but at this point, it's sufficient to flag that this can be a problem.

It's also hard to justify or explain the architecture or parameter settings discovered by a model search system. This is especially true if the optimal (in validation terms) architecture is discarded (possibly because of brittleness) and an alternative is chosen for some other reason. The process to get to this is now compromised with a gap. Where did the second best come from? Why was this route or tree chosen? The team decided to use an automated search and then ignored it; it's reasonable, but it can look odd to someone outside the process.

Another significant problem is that AutoML can be expensive in terms of compute resources. Although it can be a worthwhile investment, it is important to balance the cost of the learning process with the gains that are made in terms of model refinement, especially if the model is quickly discovered using a deliberate human-driven process.

What is a fraction of a percentage improvement for this application worth in terms of all the money and resources that producing it requires? A more hard-nosed calculation is to balance the costs between the hours spent by expensive data scientists driving the process and the costs in money and energy consumption of an AutoML process.

AutoML is useful in some contexts though. Using an AutoML or model search process at the beginning of modelling to determine what kind of performance may be wrung out of a data set can be a useful way of generating a benchmark for a more systematic and purposeful modeling process. If a systematically derived model gets close to the final performance of the AutoML model, then you can know to stop; it's as good as it's going to get.

Conversely, if AutoML fails, then this is a good indicator that no good model can be derived from the data. More data or better feature engineering might be required. In this case, you have a useful discussion point with the customer. It's not necessarily that the team lacks the skills to do the ML required for the project or that you are being unlucky. It may be that the failure of AutoML indicates that the project simply isn't going to be amenable to ML technology as it stands.

Another use of AutoML is to try an optimization of a model that has been developed to gauge how much further opportunity there may be to improve it. Also, observe where the optimized model is performing better than the developed model that is at hand.

7.5 *Stinky, dirty, no good, smelly models*

Model smell—this is like the "bad smells" that software engineers talk about with source code. In chapter 6, we discussed the other half of the modelling process in detail. Before we get to the hard-nosed stats and straight-laced explanations of why you should select one model over another, it's good to talk about model smell.

Models that perform suspiciously well or suspiciously badly become an unexpectedly large or implausibly small smell. They stink and are dirty, and the right thing to do is dig into it and find out why. Then, having figured it out, you'll need to drag the model outside and beat it with a stick until it stops twitching. Then get rid of it (often throwing it in a local pond is a good move, but you didn't hear that here).

The problem is that a stinky model can have nice performance stats associated with it, which is why being on the alert for such things is important. What is it for a model to smell?

- During evaluation on the validation data, models that smell perform erratically and inconsistently. Small changes to their parameters create large changes in their performance. This is just not the nice behavior that we would like to see, and it flags that there is something badly wrong.
- Models smell because they work better than you expected or because they work even though you know that there is something wrong with them.
- Models smell when they stand out from all the other models that are like them, when a small tweak in some hyperparameter makes a huge difference in performance.

Sometimes, generating a suspect model with some of the properties in the previous list points to some unexpected regularity in the domain. This can be the spur for a new line of systematic modelling investigation. That's fine; it sticks with the principle of documenting the experiments up front and then recording the results, and if it turns out that the model was aberrant after all, it can be safely discarded. It is more likely that the model smell is caused by a bug in a pipeline that trashes the data, because the implementation in the library or toolkit has an issue, or because you have made a configuration mistake.

Most commonly, all the evaluation that you are doing with the validation data from the training set is just not what you think it is. There's a data leak, or time travels in the training or validation set. Alternatively, the model has over-fitted and is simply memorized data. As soon as the model is used on an unseen set, it'll fail because there is no generalization.

This is why it's so important to be on the alert for model smell. Because this kind of model appears to work well, its appearance can seem to rescue you and the team from the black hole of an ML project that simply fails. It's incredibly easy to grab hold of the fabulous results that the stinky model produces and move on to productionization. This completely understandable behavior is disastrous. If you catch a model spell early, then you can use it to find the bugs in your pipeline that need fixing. Because of the care and effort that you and the team have put into the project's infrastructure and process, once those issues are fixed, rerunning your experiments and investigations should be straightforward and fast. There is a good chance that after a few iterations, your models will start to be robust. The stink will go away!

In this chapter, we explained the setup for the modelling activity and outlined the forces and processes of model design. Then we introduced the actual process for the modelling activity and the infrastructure needed to do that. In chapter 8, the other half of the modelling story is covered: the evaluation and selection of the model that we think will do the job for us. You'll also find out how the team in The Bike Shop got on with their modelling challenges.

Summary

- Create informative features for consumption by the ML algorithms in the modelling phase.
- Create additional training data with data augmentation to support more robust models.
- Develop an understanding of the design forces on a model.
- Make purposeful and effective choices about the components of models that you want to develop.
- Understand and use inductive bias to inform your approach to modelling. Consider using hierarchical, grid-based, recurrent, graph-based, or attention-based structures.
- Determine when to use composite models and how to structure them effectively to solve the problem at hand.
- Structure and manage a controlled and purposeful modelling process.
- Track and manage the evolution of models using automated tools.
- Detect and determine models that should be immediately rejected based on their behavior or structure.

Testing and selection 8

This chapter covers

- Structuring testing environments, then migrating code and artifacts to them
- Measuring the properties of models
- Understanding how to test ML-discovered models offline and online
- Understanding how the test results can be used to select models
- Using qualitative evaluation and selection and quantitative measures
- Avoiding deceptive traps when evaluating your models

So far in sprint 2, the team designed the model to be developed using their understanding of the data, the client's challenges and context, and the application that they expect to build. They've used a structured process to develop the model and tracked their progress using an experiment tracker and a model repository. They've also applied their common sense and experience to find and reject models that are suspicious or problematic. It's important now to make sense of the model's outcome and to properly evaluate competitor models to make good choices about the models that they take into production and application development.

Testing is a systematic and discrete process of model evaluation. This process provides comprehensible data and the evidence that the team can use to make a better choice about what model to use in the next step, selection. *Selection* is the process of consuming the data and the evidence and using it to make a deliberate and clear decision about their model (or models) that can be justified to end users, explained to stakeholders, and audited by regulators. You need to understand the appropriate processes for testing and selection, and why the team needs to use them. With this knowledge, you can make some good choices with the team about what should be done in this phase of the project. Let's dive in!

8.1   *Why test and select?*

You might be asking why a separate test and selection process, given that the data scientists in the development team have already determined which models they think are the best candidates for implementation? What is the purpose of carrying out the processes laid out in this chapter?

A rigorous evaluation is essential for creating confidence in the performance of the models to be deployed, but it's time-consuming and expensive to really evaluate a model and compare it to others meaningfully. This means that it's often not productive to embed an evaluation into the data scientists' workflow when, perhaps, 30 generations of models might be conceived and developed in the time it takes to do one full evaluation. Coming up with good candidate models is often economical in terms of the time and effort required, but to evaluate models properly is slow and costly.

A good evaluation requires fresh, unseen data, or in some cases, the evaluation must take place using a live part of the model's application. Sometimes, you might run out of this kind of data. Other times, you might be experimenting on humans in ways that could harm them or cost a company money in lost or upset customers. There's not much that's more expensive than that! The point being, if you're running a live test, it's not defensible to run it over the first model that the team produces or even over all the subsequent generations of models. You've got a limited tolerance for failure, so evaluations must be run selectively and wisely.

Bear in mind that a release to a test environment (which has appropriate security and access controls) may be required to do an evaluation on the wider data set. Managing this release process is slow and expensive, even with the fastest DevOps teams. Typically, a high-performing DevOps project runs one or two releases a day, and a data scientist with a fast algorithm and even faster machine might iterate over four or five models in an hour. This equation might be different if the models require computationally expensive training. In that case, the team may have had a much more limited scope for experimentation, and there will be fewer models to deal with.

This chapter presents a picture of the effort that is required to deliver a proper evaluation of an ML project. To do that, it's necessary to describe the different testing practices and processes that your team typically needs to apply. It's important to emphasize that you do not need to apply all of these tests in each project. You'll test some projects entirely with offline processes (section 8.2), and others will rely heavily on online testing (section 8.2.3). It may be that the model selection process (section 8.3) is light-weight for some projects. Qualitative selection (8.3.3) and calibration (8.3.4) might not come into play at all in many of the projects that your team has to deliver.

It is important is that you have a picture of what kind of testing might be done and what can work with the people in the team who are focused on it as a technical problem. It's also important that the tests and process are well-documented and that they can be reproduced. This can determine how much effort to deploy and help make the choice about what testing process to select. The first step is to understand the process of testing that's useful for your project, and that's what's covered in the next section.

8.2 Testing processes

This section describes different approaches to testing an ML model. Overall, the point about these approaches is that test automation and a structured process will create confidence and accountability for your models. The evidence that you generate in a systematic way will insulate you and the team if there are downstream issues with the models, and it will enable documentation to be created that will satisfy stakeholders like production engineering teams, operational teams, end users, and regulators.

Let's reacquaint ourselves with the three sprint 2 tasks for testing our models.

Test design ticket: S2.4

- Implement and commission the test environment.
- Determine the process to test the models functionally, including the way that you'll create testing data and how you'll manage to avoid data leaks.

Test design ticket: S2.5

- Develop a set of tests to determine the model's functional performance.
- Determine the measurements to use over the test scenarios.
- Design and build an appropriate test environment to support agile and reproducible testing.

Test design ticket: S2.6

- Test nonfunctional features.

8.2.1 Offline testing

Offline testing takes a model and runs it with the data that's been specially collected and reserved for this process. The available data for the project is divided into a training set and a test set. These splits are dependent on how much data is available to the team and how good it is. For example, you might be able to use 70% of the data for training and 30% for testing. The training data is further divided into a training set proper, which is shown to the algorithm and used to learn the models, and a validation or hold-out set.

So far, the data scientists in the modelling team have estimated performance using hold-out data from the training sets or training stream, which was created for the dev environment. In the testing phase of the project, it's important that you test the models using data that wasn't available to the team during modelling. This avoids information from that data leaking into the modelling process. The decisions the team made during the iterative processes of model development can lead them to optimize the performance of the models from the new data. Because they want to get the finest test performance, they should choose algorithms and processes that work best on that test data. This, however, doesn't rule out deceptive results when the final testing is done, and this means that when the model goes into production, it performs badly. By ensuring that the data in the testing process is completely unseen, you can avoid this problem of unconscious optimization.

Cross-validation is an alternative to a simple test/training split. In this process, the entire data set is divided into several disjoint test/training sets. For a 10-fold cross validation, the data set is split into 10 sets, where nine are used to train and one is used to test. For example, table 8.1 uses a data set that's partitioned into eight sets. Set 1 has the test set P1 and a training set of P2 through P8. Set 2 uses P2 as the test set and the other partitions (including P1 but excluding P2) as the training set.

Table 8.1   Generating a cross-validation set

	P1	P2	P3	P4	P5	P6	P7	P8
Set 1	**Test**	Train	Train	Train	Train	Train	Train	Train
Set 2	Train	**Test**	Train	Train	Train	Train	Train	Train
Set 3	Train	Train	**Test**	Train	Train	Train	Train	Train
Set 4	Train	Train	Train	**Test**	Train	Train	Train	Train
Set 5	Train	Train	Train	Train	**Test**	Train	Train	Train
Set 6	Train	Train	Train	Train	Train	**Test**	Train	Train
Set 7	Train	Train	Train	Train	Train	Train	**Test**	Train
Set 8	Train	Train	Train	Train	Train	Train	Train	**Test**

For each partition, you'll use the training pipelines to create a model with the training set (that means P2, P3, . . . , P8 for Set 1) and tested with the relevant test set (P1 for Set 1, P2 for Set 2, and so on). The performance of each the model generated is aggregated and used to create a cross-validated score.

In the extreme case, the test sets can be one example from the overall set with every other example used to train the model. For a data set with 1,000 examples, you train and evaluate 1,000 models. This is called leave-one-out cross validation or *n*-fold cross validation.

Cross-validation is an appropriate method when working with simple models and small data sets. When training data is sparse, it can estimate the model's performance, created with all the available resources. However, it's expensive computationally when working with complex models and big data sets (or both).

There is also some resistance to using cross-validation from outside the ML community, where it is sometimes perceived as unfounded and unprincipled by hard-core statisticians. This is a fair criticism, but in the same way that quite a chunk of practice in statistics (such as declaring a value p of 0.05 as being significant) is unfounded and unprincipled. If you do use cross-validation to provide an evaluation metric and are clear about what you are doing, then you are simply presenting a transparent fact about a particular result in the selection process. There's nothing wrong with doing that.

Partitioning the data available for testing is just one of the processes required to generate repeatable and reliable test outcomes in an offline environment. Implementing these processes manually, however, becomes tedious and error-prone. Today's ML projects can require that you evaluate a large number of models, and the burden of a poor environment can become unsupportable quickly. If that's the case, it's worth investing in an automated and robust testing system.

8.2.2 *Offline test environments*

In previous chapters, work was done to scope the facilities for the testing environment, to determine the extent of the work required to create it, and to decide on the approach that needs to be used. The nitty gritty is to now ensure that these elements are in service and to use them to move the project forward. The actions required are:

1 Gain access to the test environment; obtain the credentials and permissions needed.
2 Deploy the testing infrastructure to the test environment. This includes:
   - A data pipeline.
   - A test harness/mock application.
   - Selected models and associated artifacts for testing.
   - Data gathering and feedback collection.
3 Ensure all the required components are functional (e.g., calibration/smoke test).
4 Run the pipeline to hydrate the environments with data and other required components (e.g., initialization weights/transfer models).
5 Execute the test and gather the results.

This is quite a complex process, and a lot of things could go wrong when going through these steps. It's easy to make a silly mistake, to fail to run the smoke tests properly, or to run a pipeline element out of sequence. If that happens, then the integrity of the testing is compromised, and doubts will arise. Because of this, it's common nowadays to script or automate the whole process. Let's look at a number of ways to do this.

You could use a straightforward shell script to copy files and to invoke commands on the machine that will run the processes. Because of the complexity of modern testing and production environments, and the challenge of managing complex scripting processes, this means that using a shared engine for scripting is preferable. You can typically share this engine across many different projects with the client, and it will become a single well-known point for the client's architectural teams to manage deployments into testing and production.

The engine you choose could be Airflow or one of the systems used to implement data pipeline DAGs (directed acyclic graphs). Usually, these run the arbitrary scripting commands required to invoke infrastructure as code (IaC) or function execution to copy files and start executables. Because CI/CD (continuous integration/continuous delivery) practices have evolved separately, there are, however, several effective and popular tools that you can use as an alternative. This picture is rapidly evolving, but currently, GitHub Actions and Jenkins are both potential choices. In fact, the client's organization may mandate one of these as the mechanism for promoting a build to test and then on to production.

In most software engineering environments, the test and QA environments are segregated from the development and production environment. This is because the changes to the software builds can be controlled by the QA team to properly record and manage the software elements. In an ML project, it's also important to consider access to the data and models that can be personally confidential or commercially sensitive. The extended team probably doesn't need access to medical records or images to test their code, or at least, they may only need a limited set. In the worst case, the extended team might post the real medical images to social media and land you all in jail. These limitations mean that it can be convenient for you to use the partitioned test environment or that it may be necessary to use that test environment because it's the only place that the sensitive data is available.

Based on this, there are three scenarios for test pipeline implementation. Figure 8.1 illustrates these scenarios. First, in scenario (a), we share the testing pipeline across the entire team and use the latest version of the model as part of standard integration testing (as any component would be in an CI/CD pipeline).

Second, in scenario (b), we maintain a separate testing pipeline to allow the system engineering team to test and release versions of the model to integration testing. This pipeline requires artificial data and a dummy model that mocks and simulates the behavior of the production model. In this scenario, we maintain an integration testing pipeline with confidential data and sensitive models within the appropriate security enclave. UI and other supporting code interact with the model, feeding it parameters and recovering results from its output for presentation to the users.

Third, scenario (c) promotes into the confidential test environment from the non-confidential environment for system and integration tests. This is much better than our second scenario, option (b), because it allows for more integration testing before releasing to production.

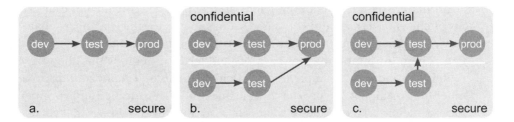

Figure 8.1 Three different flows to production. Option (a) provides a single secure environment, where artifacts are promoted from dev to test and then to prod. With (b), there is a separate confidential flow that is not accessible from some other environments, and components are promoted into prod from both the secured and confidential environments. A more desirable setup is (c), where we do integration testing after the components are promoted into the confidential environment.

8.2.3 Online testing

An online test is a live run of the system on a real-world event. In medicine, this is the gold standard approach for evaluating the performance of a drug or a procedure. In a clinical trial, patients are subjected to a treatment to see if it is useful. In some applications, this type of test is desirable because the application domain can move so fast that an offline testing campaign builds too much latency into the process that an effective model is never collected and deployed. In addition, as for medicine, there are domains that are so not amenable to an offline test, and the community won't accept any result that isn't collected in the wild. Let's look at the three commonly used online testing processes that you and your team may want to consider.

8.2.4 Field trials

The simplest, yet hardest, online test for a model is to be used in a field trial. A *field trial* is a managed deployment of the model for a small group of users. For example, the model could be trialed for use in one office or department, perhaps a small one, or perhaps one that has a friendly and tech-savvy team. Generally, consider the trial for a place where the model has the highest chance of success and also the least chance of causing a disaster.

The team is expected to closely monitor the behavior of the model and its trail. In some cases, they will need to check and verify every example of the model being used to make sure that nothing dangerous happens. Obviously, this version of model will need to be scaled up to a production deployment, but the point of the field trial is twofold:

- To build confidence in the model's behavior
- To gather detailed information about what it's doing and how it performs

It's also important for the team to review the model's behavior with users and to interview the user group to gather feedback on the performance of the model from their perspective. The advantage of a field trial is that it provides information about a model's utility, but there are some drawbacks.

It's hard to design and deliver field trials that produce convincing results. The necessity of choosing a small and contained set of subjects for the trial means that the results may not generalize to the other areas of the application that are needed in production. The most important drawback of field trials, though, is that they are expensive to develop and slow to implement. A field trial can add many months to a project's timeline. For high-value projects, this is fine, and the assurance and confidence that a successful field trial provides is what you need. Luckily though, even if you can't afford the expense and time required to mount a full field trial, there are other online tests that you can use to measure a model's performance.

8.2.5   *A/B testing*

An A/B test puts the model into a more constrained production scenario than we saw for the field trial. A small, controlled proportion of real cases is presented to the model, and the decisions that the model produces are actually used on those cases; this is the A population. The outcomes and progression seen in the A cases is then compared to the B case. The B cases are all those that haven't been processed using this model. This is like the process used to validate clinical trials, where a blind group receives no treatment, or the old treatment, and the outcome of the new treatment is used to assess whether it works or not.

A huge advantage of A/B testing is that it is a real-world experiment. The data is a fresh draw over the domain, and the evaluation criteria is the control. An experiment like this provides strong causal information because performance increases due to coincidence, optimization, or data leakage are ruled out. The result is strongly linked to the real characteristic of the model.

However, A/B testing is problematic in a number of ways. The most obvious problem, which can be difficult to overcome, is that often, there is no infrastructure in the business process that allows the intervention and implementation required to set up and run the tests. Creating the test environment outlined in section 8.2 is technically or commercially impossible. This can be due to technical limitations or to policy restrictions such as security requirements, or it can be due to some physical, legal, or ethical barrier that stops the selection of subjects according to the test protocol.

Even assuming that it is possible to implement A/B testing, it exposes business opportunities or transactions to poor treatment (for example, if the new model is the best, yet the control group is being short-changed, or if the new model is poor, then the exposure group is being short-changed). In the medical domain, this challenge is overcome by the ethical considerations of failing to gather proper knowledge about the treatment's performance for the whole population over a potentially infinite future. Basically, one half of the people in the experiment are sacrificed for the good of everyone else, and without that sacrifice, no progress is made. This may be rational and ethical, but persuading a business owner to allow an AI team to experiment on her customers can be challenging.

Given that A/B tests are plausible, and the business owners are persuaded of its value, this strategy still suffers from the challenge that it can be a slow way to gather information about a model. The model evaluation data created with an A/B test is compelling. It has high statistical integrity, and it's typically easy to communicate A/B test results to stakeholders. However, it's expensive and challenging to set up A/B tests, and it takes time to run the tests over the traffic in the business process. Sometimes, it will be necessary for the A/B test to persist across a business cycle, such as a trading day or an operational quarter, in order for the model to be exposed to a representative set of examples and conditions. Multi-arm bandits are an alternative approach, developed to get over some of these challenges.

8.2.6 *Multi-armed bandits (MABs)*

Multi-arm bandits (MAB) [5] aim to be more efficient and cost-effective than A/B tests. The underpinning idea is to only test a model when it's probable that something useful will be learned from the test. This means that you can use this opportunity to interact with your users to build more efficient models than you might have if you ran an A/B test that doesn't perform as well. A MAB should quicky detect that the model is hopeless and limit its usefulness in the live process.

Imagine a scenario in which you have three processes, and you want to see if they will return a reward. One of them frequently gives the reward, one of them sometimes gives a reward, and one never gives a reward. Figure 8.2 shows three machines and the payouts that they give when you try them.

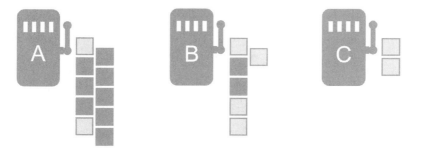

Figure 8.2 **Three one-arm bandits with pay-out records, where each block represents one pull. A light record indicates a zero reward, and a dark one indicates a positive reward. Machine A pays frequently, Machine B pays occasionally, and Machine C never pays.**

Notice that Machine C only has two pay-out records. That's because both A and B produce a reward on the second pull. We know that only one of the machines is a dud, and we know that A and B are paying, so why would we want to put more money into C?

The question after the second pull is which of the machines, A or B, pays the best? In the figure, on the fourth pull, machine B fails to pay, and on the fifth pull, machine A also fails to pay. By the sixth pull, we have 4/6 fails from machine B and 2/6 fails from machine A, so we decide to stop putting money into machine B. Our decision is vindicated because machine A keeps on paying.

It's easy to see that if you are putting money into different one-armed bandits, there comes a point where it stops being sensible to insert money into one machine to see just the payout. This is a problem of balancing exploration versus exploitation: which machine pays and how much can we get out of it?

We can exploit this theory to evaluate an ML model in production or in a controlled test, where real users use the system. There are two ways that information about the performance of the model can be collected: explicitly and implicitly.

An example of explicit feedback is the frequency of purchase of a recommended item by a customer. If the customer selects the items recommended by one model more frequently, that is a good signal that this model is more effective. The explicit aim of the recommender is to create sales, and we can measure the outcome more or less directly.

In contrast, an implicit mechanism (sometimes called a proxy measurement) is something like the amount of time a user spends browsing a website. One reading about spending time on the site is that the user is enjoying consuming the content they are engaging with. Alternatively, it could be the case that the user is frustrated and can't find the content they require. In this case, the available feedback gives an indication of the success of the model but doesn't directly measure it.

Once the mechanism of measuring performance is clear, then you need a method to make use of it. A large and systematic literature provides algorithms that make optimal choices about when to abandon a particular model (or bandit) [3]. The epsilon family of simple approximate approaches is an easy and effective way to implement a bandit-style online evaluation system [4]

The simplest basic epsilon algorithm tracks the performance of all the machines and selects the best one 90% of the time (90% / 0.9 is the epsilon, ε), and then chooses a different one as an exploratory test 10% of the time $(1 - \varepsilon)$. This can be refined by specifying several trials before ε is set to 1 or by specifying a decay factor that adjusts ε at every trial (for example, $\varepsilon' = 0.99 * \varepsilon$). The advantage of this strategy and the more complex epsilon strategies is that they are intuitive, easy to compute, and yield results with low probability of error (choosing the wrong model) at relatively low cost (not many experiments with bad models).

As the model evaluator, there are big differences between what a test with MABs will tell you and what an old-fashioned evaluation on a fresh test set or an A/B test will produce. Setting up a MAB system for testing an ML algorithm gives strong evidence that one of the algorithms being tested is more successful than the others, but it will not provide useful quantification of how much better.

MABs can be seen as ML algorithms in that they learn which machine (or oracle) is best, and they can be formulated in such a way as to select models dynamically as the domain changes. Although MABs won't arm a model selection team with statistics, they do function with a great deal of integrity. A MAB-based test is not susceptible to information leakage, and it's hard for a team to end up kidding themselves about the power of the model in the face of its performance and against defaults or well-tested incumbent solutions. Either the innovative model wins and comes to dominate in the system, or it will be crowded out by the disappointingly traditional but effective alternative.

8.2.7 **Nonfunctional testing**

The nonfunctional properties of the models are obvious test targets, and the results of these tests can heavily influence model selection. Highly functional models (the ones that do well on function tests) that fail the nonfunctional requirements of the client will probably get trashed. Nonfunctionals in ML systems are of interest because ML models typically run millions or tens of millions of times and are often invoked in line with time-critical processes in user interfaces. Expensive ML models can cost you a lot quickly, and slow ML models can annoy all your users.

One example of work looking at this subject highlights some useful nonfunctional properties to test [2]. Testability, data access, flexibility, and integrity are among the requirements uncovered in the paper. Habibullah and Horkoff note [2]:

> . . . *indicate that both engineers and customers lack knowledge and expertise in regards to NFRs for ML. There are a lack of documentation, methods, and benchmarks to define and measure NFRs for ML-enabled software.*

You and the team collected nonfunctional requirements at the pre-project/presales phase. Nonfunctional requirements include:

- *Latency:* How long it takes for an instance of the model to run before returning a result.
- *Throughput:* How many model execution episodes can be run in a certain period on the available hardware. This is different from the latency period for several reasons:
  - It may be that the models have a cold start and are slow on the first execution.
  - It may be that highly parallel hardware is available to run the models on, so even if a single model can only execute one episode per second, ten models running in parallel can have a throughput of nine or so.
- *Memory footprint:* Modern ML models can be large and may require expensive fast memory to run. Determining the size of models is important in determining if they can be feasibly deployed.
- *Cost:* Models that require the use of licensed subcomponents can be expensive.
- *Carbon impact:* Running some models creates a big carbon footprint.

Of the nonfunctionals listed, memory footprint and cost are the easiest to evaluate. There should be no difficulty in creating an inventory of components and their scale. Latency and throughput measures are only accurate in test harnesses that mirror production conditions.

It may be that the relative performance of your model is informative enough to influence your decision making. You and the client must be aware, though, that there is substantial risk with this approach. Models can behave in unexpected ways on new hardware, so beware of relying on parallelism scaling in a linear way. It's common for bottlenecks downstream in the model-serving system, which may cause a scaling system to stall. Even prosaic issues such as power supply limitations or overheating in the server rack supporting the system can choke high performance. For this reason, sustained testing on realistic hardware is the only way to ensure that your system is going to perform as well as you need it to.

The carbon footprint is even harder to test and measure. There are instrumentation mechanisms for code and systems that you can use for this purpose (https://codecarbon.io/). Unfortunately, an ML model in production generally has lots of components like databases, network interfaces, and accelerators, which may not be covered by a particular type of instrumentation. This can lead to pathological situations, where the team optimizes code to be low-carbon intensity by offloading processing to subsystems that are more inefficient but not inside the instrumentation.

The functional measures created and obtained in the offline or online testing of the models and the nonfunctional measurement discussed in this section provide information about which models you should select and use. A decision is still to be made using this information, though, and making that decision is the topic of the next section.

8.3   *Model selection*

Model selection ticket: S2.10

- Use model evaluation data to determine the models to used.
- Use an explicit mechanism to use the model test/evaluation data to choose the models that are to be used in production.
- Account for how the models will be combined in your decision.
- Account for nonfunctional requirements.
- Account for qualitative aspects of the models.

Model selection ticket: S2.11

- Determine and document model selections.

Model selection ticket: S2.12

- Review and obtain customer sign-off on model selection.

Testing and evaluation create information on model performance; however, this information needs to be used to determine which model to employ. In the good old days, it was straightforward to choose a single model, employed in a well understood context; the model that got the highest results won! Now, ML models are often employed in complicated systems and configurations, and selecting which model based on the result of a single test is rarely appropriate. Instead, all the information about the performance of the model must be generated, gathered, and then synthesized into a decision. The stakeholders deploying the system need to understand why you choose these components, so you document why the choices made are appropriate and how the choices were made. Whereas the previous parts of this chapter discussed how testing results can be generated and gathered, this section looks at how the resulting information can be synthesized into a decision.

We now have three types of information. First, we accumulated a set of results from the testing episodes, and second, we have information about the testing mechanism and practice. Finally, we have information on the requirements of our system. With this information, we can determine the qualities of the model according to the testing results, decide on the quality and informativeness of those results, and then rule on the significance of each result. The synthesis of this information into a decision or recommendation about which model to use (or not to use) can be facilitated by a number of different tools. There are two fundamental approaches:

- We can aggregate the information quantitatively to satisfy some notion of which model is optimal.
- We can use an administrative/qualitative process to qualify a model from a pool as appropriate for use.

It is extremely likely that you will need to use both processes. Quantitative data can be employed to produce promising candidates for qualitative selection. What is important is that the information and process used for selection is carefully assembled and recorded—the approach that you and the team decide is the appropriate one for your project must be explicitly documented and used to make your decision. In this way, you will be able to transparently account for the behavior of the model in production because you will have a high integrity answer for the question of why did you put that model there to do that?

8.3.1 *Quantitative selection*

Quantitative selection is the process of combining the measurements from different testing events to create a single, aggregate measure, and then choosing the model to be used based on that measure. In this section, we'll look at three distinct scenarios for making your choice, based on the tests that have been developed to evaluate the models.

8.3.2 *Choosing With Comparable Tests*

When models are evaluated using several comparable tests, you can use straightforward aggregations to combine test results and make a choice. Let's take the case of a model that is to make offers or recommendations to people in many countries. In this scenario, the consumers of interest are young adults, aged 18-25. You can query 40 countries to create a panel of several hundred test cases, building two data sets of 40 data points each. Each data point is the success of a model in a particular country. Each country is equally important to the customer. Here's the dilemma: model A performs well on some of the data points, as does model B. Which should be selected for global use?

If, as in this case, the choice is made over two populations of results, generated by only two models, it can be simple to decide which model to use. Find the mean performances and the standard deviations, then calculate in terms of expectation how distant the performance of the models over the tests is.

If there is low expectation that the models can perform at the same level, then this is a clear indicator that a real performance difference exists, and a good basis for choosing one over the other is established, especially if the expectation goes two ways. If model A's mean performance is several standard deviations of A's results from model B's mean performance and also several standard deviations of B's results distant, then both A and B are producing clearly differentiated outcomes. The model that is functioning best overall is the rational choice. If, on the other hand, model A has a better mean score, but the standard deviation of model B's results includes model A's mean, then it is obviously possible that no real difference between A and B exists.

These decisions can be framed in Bayesian terms as well: see if the samples of model A's performance and model B's performance come from the same distribution. If the expectation that model B's mean performance is rarely achieved by a subset of model A's results, then model B is likely to be superior to model A. Conversely, if there are common permutations of model A's results that achieve the same performance as model B, perhaps the testing is inconclusive.

The level of surprise that you require to be convinced that models A and B really are different is a matter for you to decide. In general, people choose to believe that if 95% of the time the samples drawn from the distribution of model A and model B are different, then that means that we should believe that model A and model B have different distributions, and therefore, the models have different behaviors.

With this use case, however, there are problems. The populations of each country may be different, as well as the economy and the demographic distributions in each country. Sometimes, it's possible to use normalization to handle this. In the case of the multi-country comparison, this would probably be acceptable for something like e-commerce. However, in comparing something like epidemic prevalence or the performance of different vaccines, it might be hard to confidently say that normalization and direct comparison are safe ways to deal with this data and then to make inferences. If so, or if the tests are more obviously different and incomparable, then we need different approaches to combining the information from the tests into a decision.

8.3.3   *Choosing with many tests*

How multiple measurements are aggregated has the potential to influence the selections made. It's both natural (and likely) that the testing program you've come up with yields different measures of performance. For example, if you create a separate test set of hard-but-important examples, then generate a simple aggregate for the performance of the models, performance on run-of-the-mill data would nullify the whole point of doing that in the first place.

This problem has been extensively studied in many domains and is known as *multi-criteria decision making* [6]. There are many approaches that you could use to aggregate diverse and incomparable test results. None of which are definitively the "right" choice, but all of which have different strengths that might make them the best selection in each scenario. One approach is to use a weighted function to prioritize and favor particular members of the test result vector over the others. In plain terms, a decision is made that a certain percentage of the overall score for a model comes from one test, another percentage comes from a second test, and so on, until 100% of the measure is allocated.

In the example of the hard-but-important (hbi) items versus the example of the run-of-the-mill (rotm) data, the choice might be to allocate 50/50. Let's say there are 200 carefully selected hbi's and 200,000 rotm's used in the test set, but we weight each hbi as being 1,000 times more important to the selection of a model than a rotm. There are problems with this approach, however. The weighting selected is arbitrary and hard to explain post hoc. A small change in the hbi performance overwhelms a larger change in rotm, and this is by design. On the other hand, once you go past two or three measures, it becomes hard to discern the source of the model's performance in the comparison.

More sophisticated methods of allocating weight to the different components can help. For example, we can define a function that variously allocates weights on a more rigorous basis by choosing some optimal allocation and working backward or that provides a weighting based on linguistic descriptions of how the balance should work. Sometimes these approaches provide good results or clear explanations, but often they add yet another layer of mysticism into the process.

A popular alternative is to combine rankings of performance rather than the raw outcomes. Returning to a simple hbi and rotm scenario, let's take five models and compare them with this lens. Table 8.2 shows the results of this comparison.

Table 8.2 Comparing five models with aggregate rankings

Model	hbi (raw)	hbi (rank)	rotm (raw)	rotm (rank)	Aggregate	Rank
A	171/200	3	175342/200000	2	5	3
B	167/200	4	172811/200000	4	8	4
C	132/200	5	135241/200000	5	10	5
D	173/200	2	181122/200000	1	3	1
E	190/200	1	175301/200000	3	4	2

Looking at the results, model D is the winner! It ranks second in the hbi test and first in the rotm test, while model E was first for hbi but third for rotm. Using a 50/50 weighting on model E yields 365,301 vs. 354,122 for model D, so with that, we would have selected method E. A ranking aggregate is not intrinsically better, but it yields results that are intuitively understood by stakeholders, and it tends to be more useful the more independent tests that you must combine.

As an alternative to aggregating rankings as in table 8.2, it's sometimes possible to use the idea of Pareto optimality to make decisions about model selection. A Pareto efficient set of models is the set that contains all the models that have the best outcome under one measure. Where there is a draw (several models with the same or broadly similar performance under one test), the model that has the best performance in other dimensions is chosen.

In figure 8.3, we see some results from imaginary models evaluated with respect to the hbi and rotm test sets. The area inside the dotted lines contains the Pareto front for the models. All models in this area have one of the best tradeoffs between hbi and rotm that we have found. Note that model F is in the Pareto set but model G isn't because it's neither as good at hbi or as good at rotm as model F. That double whammy knocks it out of consideration.

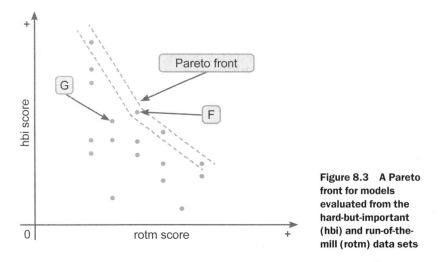

Figure 8.3 A Pareto front for models evaluated from the hard-but-important (hbi) and run-of-the-mill (rotm) data sets

We can use Pareto sets and Pareto fronts to create sets of Pareto optimal candidates versus many different tests, not just two, yet Pareto sets still leave room for more decision making. Creating a Pareto set narrows the candidates, but it still often leaves a choice to be made between set members.

8.3.4   *Qualitative selection measures*

In the introduction to this chapter, some the qualitative metrics from the literature were identified. These included:

- *Model security:* Can the model be tricked or attacked intelligently? Can knowledge of the way that it works be abused? A good example of this is the way that a small change in an image, undetectable by human eyes, can cause a model to confidently mislabel it. This has implications for abuse of road traffic signs to fool self-driving cars or changes in passport photographs to allow an image that matches the carrier for inspectors but also matches another person when fed into a machine.

- *Privacy:* Does the model leak information? Could personal data be extracted from the model if prompts were given to it? For example, let's imagine a language model is trained on medical cases to provide a helpful chatbot (this is a bad idea, but it's also an example, so bear with me). In that case, what happens if I feed a prompt such as medical record for Simon G. Thompson, d.o.b. xxx, . . . ? Would the model complete the prompt by regurgitating some private information? Although this would be boring in my case, it might be hurtful in other cases, possibly causing significant harm. It would also be a serious breach of data protection laws in many places.
- *Fairness:* Does the model contain biases derived from data that are harmful or debunked by common sense or wider domain knowledge? Famously, some language models assume that all doctors are male, whereas nurses are female. This is a stereotype that could do significant harm to job seekers, for example.
- *Interpretability:* Can the model be inspected or explained to humans? Is the explanation true to the actual workings of the model? Can it be used to determine that the model's operation is well-founded and not just due to arbitrary data regularities?

We explicitly mentioned some of these requirements in user stories and in development activities with stakeholders. Some of the requirements, such as security, privacy, and fairness are red lines; if your models don't meet these requirements, then they can't be used. Model interpretability is less cut-and-dried, and different models may be efficient and interpretable in different ways. It may be that the requirements that you assembled during the earlier phases of the project cannot be met all at once. Again, in some cases, that's a hard stop on the project, but a less interpretable model may be available that meets nonfunctional performance requirements. Sometimes a tradeoff of interpretability for nonfunctional performance may be appropriate.

After all the talk of multi-criteria decision making in this chapter, and the agonizing about the appropriate use of ranking methods and weighted data sets and so on, this kind of discussion is maddeningly imprecise. Even fluffier are the reasons to choose between decent models based on purely aesthetic concerns.

Some people might think that this is quite an irrational stance; surely the model that wins quantitatively should be preferred? But, since approximately 1200 AD, western science has used the idea of Occam's razor to prefer simpler models, all things being roughly equal. Beauty and elegance are mathematicians' drivers when seeking good theories. In terms of ML models, this translates to a preference for low size and high compression with respect to the training set, or simply a lower number of parameters optimized for equivalent or near equivalent performance. When in doubt, simple and sweet wins out.

8.4   *Post modelling checklist*

Sprint 2 is almost complete. The final task is to run through the checklist in Table 8.3 and make sure that everyone agrees that everything was completed properly. If that's the case, then you can be confident that you team has created a solid set of models and there's a well-documented set of candidates for application integration.

Table 8.3   Sprint 2 checklist

Ticket #	Item	Notes
S2.1	Feature engineering is implemented.	Features and design information are recorded.
S2.2	Models to be used explicitly are designed.	Model design documented.
S2.3	Modelling process undertaken and models developed.	Model repository used; models identified and captured along with all details required for reproduction.
S2.4	Model performance in dev was properly assessed by the team, and the experimental results are recorded.	Results of experiments are available for inspection.
S2.5	Model issues discovered in dev are recorded.	Defects will often be noticed in development; check that these were documented and that the documentation is available.
S2.6	Test environment was commissioned.	The test environment is set up, and the required data sources for testing are available.
S2.7	Appropriate tests are designed.	The tests that determine if the models are fit for purpose agreed on and documented.
S2.8	Test data has been gathered.	Tests run in the test environment, and results collected and available for evaluation.
S2.9	Model selection is documented.	Model selection methods are documented, and the decisions that were made when using them and the testing data are recorded. Qualitative factors in the decisions should be recorded and agreed on.

It's worth emphasizing again that the testing process may need to be revisited if you discover new problems or constraints in the application integration process. It's possible, or even probable, that the team will need to go back into the activities in sprint

1 to reinvestigate the data. Potentially, they will need to onboard new sources of data, or they need to correct and clean new sources of data errors. The processes and infrastructure used in sprint 1 and sprint 2 provide a good framework for the team to do this. You've made the investment that allows your team to be agile and adapt to problems as they emerge, don't be afraid to exploit it!

The flip side, though, is that it's not a good idea or acceptable practice to skip on documenting what's happening. Iteration and adaptation are inevitable, but make sure that the team is transparent about it and that they are professional about rebuilding pipelines and processes, rerunning tests, and keeping the documentation up to date.

8.5 *The Bike Shop: sprint 2*

The modelling team was presented with two core challenges: build a customer churn prediction system and build a demand prediction system. The work done in sprint 1 shows that these models should have geographic and product type granularities. The models should be built to work in different locales and over the different product types and platforms. In addition, there was a challenge to validate the available data as being adequate for the modelling. The team knows they have to deepen these requirements with nonfunctional information to be able to choose an appropriate modelling technique. The team determines the following:

- In the bike shop application, efficiency and throughput are unlikely to be an issue. There are a small number of users who will expect normal web app latency (2 seconds or so).
- Cost of inference is not likely to be an issue. The Bike Shop application will be used by scores or hundreds of users, not the tens of thousands that would raise concerns. The users will be operating at the speed of business analysis, so two or three updates of models per minute can be expected.
- Security will adhere to normal corporate standards. Because only users authorized to access the raw data (financial and business performance from the sales records) are able to access the models and model output, there is no concern about inferences that can be drawn.
- The models need to provide confidence intervals, and the system needs to parameterize the models so the users can use them counterfactually. This allows the users to try "what if" scenarios and allows the system to show the users a range of prebuilt scenarios to inform their decision-making.
- The system should provide performance monitoring. This allows The Bike Shop to track how well it is doing and lets the users provide feedback on they system's performance. The users can indicate if they think that the model is making egregious predictions. If this becomes a problem, a team of professionals can be brought in to perform maintenance.

Having reviewed the information gathered from the business SMEs that was created by the EDA exercise, the team now feels that they understand what's expected from the modelling. This understanding can now be brought together to create the overall model's designs.

The opportunity to combine open-source news and economic data with The Bike Shop data was identified in the presales process. In addition, the team identified and selected a language model in sprint 1 and secured it as a project asset. Given this, the team made the choice to create models that extracted the current sentiment of the news, the unusualness of it (as a proxy for risk), and the historical pattern of sales, given data on the economy in the relevant sales territory. It was decided to use the same model design for demand forecasting in each region. Combining the data from each region with the news feeds and economic data, to the team creates an individual instantiated model. The team decides that they will use standard techniques to project uncertainty ranges, essentially to multiply uncertainties at each step. Figure 8.4 shows this design.

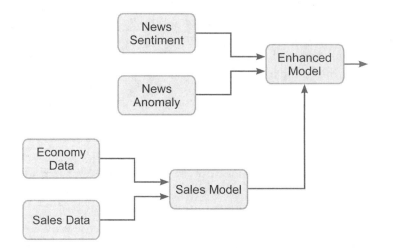

Figure 8.4   Top-level model design for predicting demand at The Bike Shop

Because of the limitations of the News data set, it's decided to create signals that would feed independently into the inferences required for the application. Effectively, the following three component models are required for each regional prediction system. Figure 8.5 illustrates the design for the training model:

- A News Sentiment indicator that extracts the current sentiment from the available news feeds.
- A News Anomaly detector that determines if a startling or very unusual event is being detected in the news feeds.
- A Sales Given Economy model that learns patterns of sales, given the state of the economy.

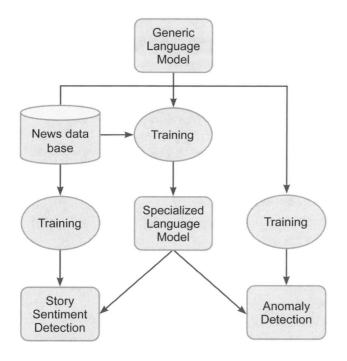

Figure 8.5   Model training design for The Bike Shop's demand prediction system

The team undertakes the prototyping activity to develop the feature set to use in each model (figures 8.4 and 8.5). A representative region, the USA, is identified because it has rich data and is significant for The Bike Shop's business. The team feels that if a good model cannot be created for this region, then it's unlikely that work on other regions will be successful. Conversely, if they create a good model for the USA region, then if other regions cannot be modelled, the system would still have some utility. Table 8.4 shows the list of features developed after prototyping and iterative experimentation using a subset of the available training data with several model types. Sentiment intensity is determined by fine-training a BERT model using a news article sentiment intensity data set [1]. Anomaly detection is done by measuring reconstruction errors for each article versus an autoencoder, learned over the historical news articles for the region.

Table 8.4   Features generated from the sales data

Feature	Description
Aggregation	Aggregate to monthly; group by client and product level 2.
Frequencies	Frequencies of sales.
Month and year	Monthly and yearly feature.
Public data enrichment	"national_income","agriculture_value", "unemployment", "GDP", for example.
Standard devia-tion indicators	How many standard deviations per client, per month, and revenue, volume, and sales frequencies changes?
Look_back	Data from last n number of trades as a feature.
last_trade	Last trade per client.
ema	Exponential moving average.
sma	Simple moving average.
Bollinger Band	Labeling case, which is more than two standard deviation points up or down.
rci	Rate of change indicator.
rsi	Relative strength indicator .
diff	Differences between current value and last n values.

Now that the team has determined the feature set and selected the model type and design, it's possible for them to build a training pipeline to create a model for each region. To do this, they extract data for each region, product platform, and product type from the source_table, calculate the features, and pass the resulting training set to the ML algorithm (figure 8.6).

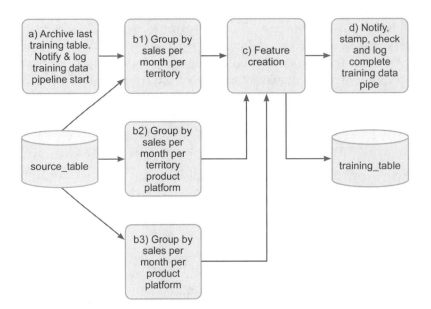

Figure 8.6   Training data pipeline for The Bike Shop.

Figure 8.6 shows the data-preparation pipeline. Note that steps a and d ensure that the relevant team members are notified of a change to the training data and that the new training data version is logged. In this pipeline, the last training set is archived before anything else happens. This supports reproducibility and provides the team with roll-back if something goes wrong in the pipeline or a bug introduces noise into one of the features. Step b produces the group-by aggregations of the data from the sales of individual products in individual countries to all sales in a territory, sales of items in a particular product platform in a territory, and all sales globally in a particular product platform.

In Step c, various processes are run in the data warehouse in Python code to create the features specified in Table 8.4 for the aggregates. In some cases, it's easier to calculate these items for each row before the group-by step. This can also be awkward because the data warehouse may not support the addition of new columns into an old table. The team does extensive work to understand the best division of labor between the data warehouse and the scripting system. The training data is now ready for use by the team for creating models.

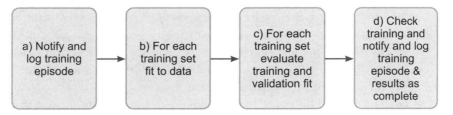

Figure 8.7   The Bike Shop model training pipeline

Figure 8.7 shows the pipeline for model training. As for the other pipelines, a critical feature is that the pipeline isn't run silently; all of the steps are logged on execution. Step c specifies that the training set training and validation fits are executed, and in step d, this data is logged in the management system. The team creates a dashboard showing the training and validation performance of the model sets to understand the overall performance of their approach to the problem. They also create a list of deltas and improvements to the models, and they get to work dealing with these.

Danish takes the lead as the expert data scientist in the team, but Sam is interested in modelling work, so he and Rob team up to cover some of the tickets that the team generates. They chase down the modelling hypothesis and work to get better results. Danish and Jenn work together to deal with a different set of tickets, and Kate works through issues that come up with the training pipelines and monitoring infrastructure. Having organized themselves, the team settles into a steady pattern. There's a lot of frustration at first. The team was optimistic that more sophisticated approaches would rapidly outpace the results that Danish got with some quick and easy benchmarking at the end of sprint 1, but things aren't as smooth as they hoped.

The economy data doesn't seem to be contributing anything to the quality of the time series prediction, nor does the news sentiment or news anomaly flows. The team investigates the models in parts, finding definite signals in the economic data that should provide predicative information. Danish creates some visualizations that show how the economic impact model output is correlated to the changes in sales.

The sentiment and anomaly models show similar behaviors. This puzzle is solved by Kate when she audits the model training and execution pipeline. She finds that the models that the team believed would create the training input for the enhanced model are not generating the features that are being used. Old stub code is still being invoked because someone failed to update the code.

The culprit feels terrible, but the rest of the team also takes responsibility as the code passed their review; they've all been staring at it for three days and did not notice the bug. Everyone is immensely cheered when the code is fixed and a significant uptick in performance is seen as compared to the benchmark model. At this point, the team makes the decision that they should properly evaluate the model portfolio.

The Bike Shop IT team maintains a test environment for evaluating new systems before being released into their production environment. The team requires few of these facilities for testing in this environment, so Rob takes the test environment design that was developed in sprint 1 and works with the IT team to ensure that it's implemented. To ensure that the test is properly executed, Rob writes scripts to deploy the data pipeline to the testing environment. Each of the models that are selected for evaluation have metadata defining the structure and parameterization of the training pipeline that created them. This is used to configure the testing data pipelines. However, there are some important changes.

The team holds a meeting to discuss the performance of the models and, based on previous discussions, they conclude that the sales model doesn't overpredict demand. Karima is clear that having too much inventory is the real killer for the business in the profit-and-loss margins. Overspending on the inventory means that there won't be cash to support other activities, and this means that there's a heavy cost associated with this. Underordering carries penalties as well. The business can't sell what it doesn't have, but if the cash is unspent and available for use, then it can take mitigating action. Danish and Rob work through the data determining what characterizes incidents of overordering. They work with Sam to build some queries that generate a test set that the benchmark classifiers created in the EDA by Danish.

At the same time, Jenn builds a test set of clean data with what she calls representative distributions. You probe further to get to the bottom of what she means by this, and it turns out that she's created a test with data from the three largest countries, Europe, Asia, and the rest of the world (RoW). Her justification for this choice is that these are the important markets. After some discussion, Jenn agrees that it would be sensible to have test sets that cover all territories, including the smallest countries. Overall, that means the models will be tested on:

- *Data set 1:* Sales periods performance of the benchmark model over predicted sales
- *Data set 2:* Performance in large countries
- *Data set 3:* Performance across all countries
- *Data set 4:* Performance in small countries

Kate builds the remaining code required to provide an effective test harness in the test environment, and then Jenn and Kate run the tests over the model designs that the rest of the team have tagged as candidates for selection. The results are interesting. All the models considered to be serviceable by the team perform approximately as well on data set 3. No one is surprised. The relative performance of the models is like their relative performance in dev, although a little reduced.

There is a big difference in performance in data set 4, though. It turns out that the news components are much more predictive in large countries than small ones. After some thought and white box testing, the cause becomes clear: large countries are the focus of well-funded and well-resourced media. More investigation shows that there is a relationship between media freedom and the predictive capabilities of the news sources as well. These insights enable the team to select two separate models, based on appropriateness per country. They build a table of model-to-country mapping and demonstrate how effective it is by retesting it on Jenn's data sets.

At this point, Rob throws a spanner in the works and points out that they have leaked quite a lot of information into the testing process. But there is good news. Jenn can select three new small countries and three new large countries. She builds data set 5 and data set 6, based on this selection, and the new composite model is tested on these. Happily, for everyone, the results on the new, unseen data sets mirror the result on data set 2 and data set 4. This time it's somewhat better, however. Jenn explains that she selected three strong press and three weak press candidates to build data set 2 and data set 4. The team proceeds to sprint 3.

Summary

- Your test environment needs to accommodate the security and privacy requirements of the data that you are handling, allowing access to testing mechanisms for the right people in the team.
- You must deliberately decide what is important to measure about the performance of your models. Just as sometimes the fuel economy of a car is more important than its acceleration, it can be the case that different performance tests need to be evaluated for models in different contexts.
- Model accuracy is a poor way to understand model performance. Consider models in terms of their precision and recall performance or their F1 score. Even better, consider a range of performance measures to get an overall view of what matters about the model's performance on a particular test.

- Nonfunctionals need to be tested and considered as well, so you can rate the results of those against functional performance.

- You can use cross-validation to measure model performance when data is hard to get. Models can be tested on live cases using A/B testing or multi-armed bandits. You must be aware of the costs and trade-offs of testing in terms of the constraints that you face on gathering data or exposing people to the behavior of experimental models.

- Model selection is both quantitative (using the results of your tests) and qualitative (based on wider considerations and model aesthetics).

- Quantitative selection may require you to compare and weigh tests that are done on different bases. Different approaches to doing this are rankings, MCDM (multi-criteria decision making), and Pareto fronts. Which approach you use depends on your project.

- You can test the component parts of your models to reveal how they are failing. You can use causal theories of what the model is doing as part of your decision-making.

- When selecting models and model components, you are often left with a judgement. What's important is that the basis of your decision is transparent, and the decision process is recorded and documented. If the decision comes down to selecting A or B, and there is no clear way for you to establish which, document this and pick the one that seems best to you.

9

Sprint 3: system building and production

This chapter covers

- Embedding your models into the system you are going to build
- Dealing with nonfunctional implications
- Building the data and model-serving infrastructures for production
- Ensuring that the user interface is appropriate
- Ensuring that the logging, monitoring, and alerting elements are properly governed and managed in production

In sprint 2, the team built, tested, and selected models to support the user stories developed in sprint 1. Without more work, the models cannot be used to generate value; essentially, they're just lines of code sitting inanimate in a repository. *To be useful AI, models need to be implemented in the IT architecture that supports the client's business processes and customer delivery.*

There are two characteristics of an ML system, which are a focus of the work in sprint 3, the topic of this chapter. We must implement the data infrastructure supporting the production platform to ensure that the models operate in the data environment that they were trained for. Additionally, we need to retrieve and run the ML models created from sprint 2 for the system to work.

In this chapter, we go over the process of deciding which components are required in the production system and how they will hang together. In later sections, we'll deal with the tradeoffs and decisions that drive the selection and delivery of the data layer, model-serving infrastructure, and interface elements. First, though, you and the team need to work out the type of ML system that you are going to build, and that's what the next section covers.

9.1   Sprint 3 backlog

Table 9.1 provides a summary of the tasks that we'll explore in this chapter. These tasks are the must be completed before your project can move into production and start to deliver value for your users.

Table 9.1   Backlog for Sprint 3

Task #	Item
S3.1	Identify the type of system that will be used to embed the models.
S3.2	Determine the functional and nonfunctional implications of the system you are building.
S3.3	Build the production data flows to enable the models to make inferences.
S3.4	Build the model server and the inference system.
S3.5	Determine the appropriate interface components required by your system.
S3.6	Select a conformant interface development approach, allowing for the delivery of the interface requirements.
S3.7	Build logging, monitoring, and alerting components for the system.
S3.8	Ensure that model governance and hand-over arrangements are agreed on.
S3.9	Produce maintenance and support documentation.
S3.10	Develop a pre-release testing plan.
S3.11	Promote to production.
	Create a post-release test plan.
S3.12	Provide post-release recognition and thanks.

Figure 9.1 shows an ML system from the perspective of what's needed to make it functional in production. At the top, there's a data infrastructure that creates the input to the system. This could include streams of clicks or other interactions from a user interface, but fundamentally, these are the signals that are consumed by the models for inference.

The architecture illustrated in figure 9.1 uses an inference service to invoke the models based on events in the data stream. This service might run in batch mode, processing files of data and producing annotations on each entity in its data set. It might also run responsively, based on an event in an application. The model's output is used by some application code to make the decision about what service should be invoked. That could be as simple as just showing something to the user and using that to make another decision or taking the output and feeding it into the control system of a machine.

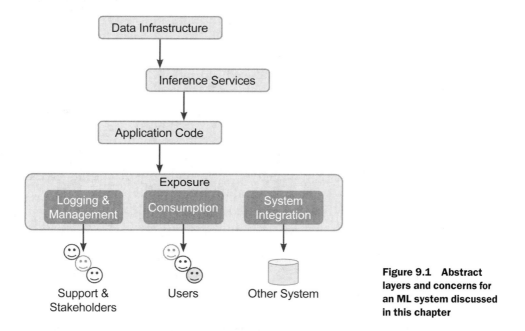

Figure 9.1 Abstract layers and concerns for an ML system discussed in this chapter

At the bottom layer of the stack in figure 9.1 is the exposure interface. As well as interacting with users by publishing model inferences, the system must provide logging and management data (such as alerts in the case of unexpected behavior) and integration information for other systems (such as orchestration signals) in this layer. To implement the functionality of this layer, here are a few recommendations:

- You can use Big Table, Redshift, SQL Server, Oracle, Kafka, or SPARK (and many others) as the data engine that supports different requirements for data infrastructure components.

- You can deploy application code using engines such as Kubeflow, Kubernetes, OpenShift, Flask, Tomcat, or others. Serverless components such as AWS Lambda, Azure Serverless, and GCP's Cloud Functions provide an alternative method of hosting and running models.

- You can use systems such as Splunk and Grafana, as well as user interface development frameworks such as Angular.js for the exposure layers.

9.2   *Types of ML implementations*

> **Production system analysis ticket: S3.1**
>
> - Identify the type of system (assistive, delegative, autonomous) that will be used to embed the models.

> **Production system analysis ticket: S3.2**
>
> - Determine the functional and nonfunctional implications of the system you are building.

For the system to be useful, you need to decide how you'll use the models that you created. Earlier in the development process, this was considered and worked on, but now the models are built and the best selected for use. Broadly, we can identify three types of setting for the models that you develop:

- *Assistive models:* Creates output that's directly consumed by humans. A large data population summarized in a dashboard is an assistive model. For example, if you use a complex set of sensor readings to create a recommendation, that is an assistive model.
- *Delegative models:* Creates a control signal independent of human input but under direct human supervision and management. Disregarding whether they are intelligent, systems that run chemical factories while monitored by human controllers are examples of this type of system, as are fly-by-wire aircraft and autopilots.
- *Autonomous models:* Embedded in systems that do not feature human control or monitoring, either for significant periods of time or through transformative system evolutions. Many robotic systems and drones are autonomous, as are automatic high-frequency trading systems that function outside of human management.

These different types of systems are on a spectrum of autonomy and human control. The more autonomous an ML-powered system, the less opportunity for human control and intervention, but this has consequences. The level of assurance in terms of the reliability of the models created to drive it must be higher, and the system engineering that embeds the models must be more robust and offer a higher level of assurance. Three design forces act more strongly as autonomy is increased.

First, as systems become more autonomous, there is a greater need for them to explain their decisions. The ML component of systems that humans control directly, and in which the humans have agency and accountability for the decisions, do not need to be as transparent as autonomous systems. We may be able to understand the ML component in human-controlled systems, but the human element is always opaque.

Second, the mechanisms that are used to document and record the system's development process must be more robust the more autonomous the system. The organization that deploys the autonomous system must stand behind its decision, and it can only do that if there is a method of accounting for how it was developed.

Third, autonomous systems require better and more robust nonfunctional performance. There is no human to step in and take over if the system stutters to a halt or starts doing something squirrely. Often, the users of an autonomous system are physically unable to intervene or save themselves in the case of a nonfunctional failure.

Having looked at the production system analysis tickets for sprint 3, you should now be able to move onto the next tasks. In the next part of this section, we'll explore more deeply the implications that you and the team must deal with when building assistive, delegative, and autonomous systems using ML.

9.2.1 *Assistive systems: recommenders and dashboards*

Assistive systems are designed to be directly used by humans. Their value is driven by the transparency of human inspection that they provide. Assistive systems provide advice to humans, but they do not control the decisions that are made on the back of that information and guidance.

Assistive systems summarize information, offer predictions, and enable humans to efficiently consume these for decision-making and to create insight. By enabling information that would normally be incomprehensible and used to create value, assistive AI systems have a role in creating economic and scientific value that would otherwise be unavailable.

The Large Hadron Collider, a high-energy particle collider, provides a good example of this type of system. Experiments there utilized ML techniques generated by a challenge competition to find breakthrough physics results in vast data sets [2]. Without this assistance from ML, it's arguable that the physics community would have been unable to take advantage of their most powerful experimental instrument.

A canonical assistive interface is a dashboard. A dashboard is a collection of visualizations that summarize the information that is relevant to a particular business problem, enabling rapid inspection. There is now a wide range of tools, proprietary (such as Looker, Power BI, Qlik, and Tableau) and open source (such as Shiny and Dash), that you can use to create dashboards.

Figure 9.2 shows a standard dashboard on the left that contrasts with an intelligent dashboard on the right, which integrates the output of ML-derived models. In a standard dashboard, data is transformed and displayed using aggregate functions and selection filters. In an intelligent dashboard, additional information is displayed because the model creates filters (e.g., to remove outliers or noise) over the information to make predictions using it. For example, we can deploy a customer churn model that's used to generate output based on user-selected values to determine a competitor's activity and sales investment.

This kind of prediction provides decision-makers with an indication of potential or probable outcomes. If undesirable outcomes appear in the distribution or forecast, then the client can take action to change course by finding the parameter settings that make positive outcomes likely and negative outcomes unlikely. In the customer churn example, the dashboard user might find that increasing the investment in sales creates outcomes with low customer churn, despite any level of competitor activity.

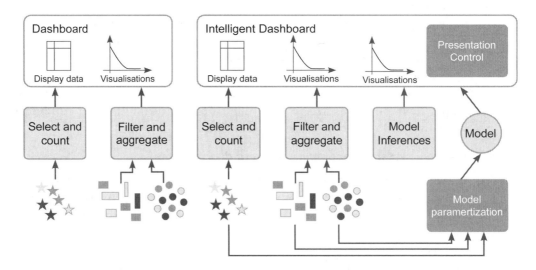

Figure 9.2   A simple dashboard on the left versus an intelligent model-driven dashboard on the right

Although the intelligent dashboard illustrated in figure 9.2 integrates output from ML-derived models, this isn't the only type of assistive system available. Many internet services use assistive intelligence to enhance the user experiences they offer. The diversity and scale of services and available offers are often bewildering to consumers and, sometimes, virtually impossible to navigate without support. We can use ML to provide recommendations and selections, filtering irrelevant results from the user interface and directing the user's attention to selections that are more engaging.

As an example, you could implement a recommendation system using a co-occurrence matrix. You would categorize the items into groups to control the size of the matrix and then increment the value of the co-occurrence when a choice is made by a user. When a user selects a similar item in the future, you can use the co-occurrence with the highest value to generate a recommendation to pique the user's interest.

Let's say that Simon watches *Star Wars* and then the newer *Star Trek* movie. The newer *Star Trek* movie is categorized as Science Fiction Reboots. When someone else watches *Aliens*, for example, you show them a list of Science Fiction Reboots with *Star Trek, Dune, Dawn of the Planet of the Apes, Mad Max Fury Road,* and so on. Table 9.2 shows how this would be represented and what it would look like after one update with lots of design assumptions woven in. The categories are preselected (arbitrarily), and there is no self-similarity allowed. Because the table does not record selections for the same category, the algorithm always recommends a list of something different. Also, there is no mention of what to do if you are dealing with a selection from the Nature category. Do you provide a random list to choose from or no list?

Table 9.2 A co-occurrence table update with preferences for a movie after watching *Star Wars*.

Category	Old science fiction	Nature	...	Science fiction reboots
Old science fiction	X	0	0	1
Nature	0	X	0	0
...	0	0	X	0
Science fiction reboots	1	0	0	X

Now, let's take this system a step further. If we chose an item from the recommendation list at random and then showed it to the user for their next movie, then we could say that the user had delegated the choice to the system. The system becomes delegative, which is discussed in the next section.

9.2.2 *Delegative systems*

We use a delegative system to make decisions on behalf of users when they are unable to exercise direct case-by-case control. This can be because the decisions require the use of an overwhelming amount of data or because the decision must be made faster than a human can make it. Importantly, a delegative system provides mechanisms for the human to review and correct the decisions made or to step in and correct the behavior of the system if the automated decision-maker fails.

The Perseverance Rover [1] is a glamorous example of a delegative AI system. Perseverance is a semi-autonomous robot that landed on Mars at the beginning of 2021. Its mission was to investigate rocks that had formed billions of years ago in a flood area of a large crater. It moved from rock formation to rock formation to discover and sample a range of different rocks, enabling the development of an understanding of the geology of the area. The scientists and geologists on Earth determined the objectives of the rover, manipulated the sampling and testing instruments and tools, and exercised top-level control over its systems and functions. Figure 9.3 illustrates how Perseverance acted independently, using its sensors to construct a proposed path forward across some part of the terrain in front of it. After sending the path to Mission Control for approval, the rover will prepare the command processes to drive the path. Once approval is received, the rover executes the plan by itself.

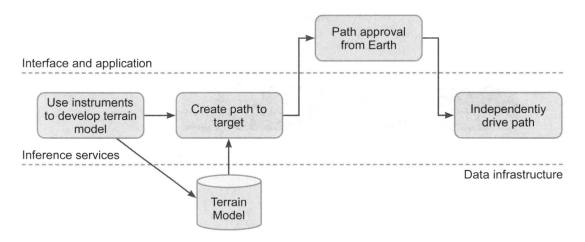

Figure 9.3   The control flow for a delegative remote control rover [1]

The delegative system model was chosen for Perseverance because it balanced the physical constraint imposed by the lag in communications with Mars and the value and risk that the state-of-the-art AI methods created. A manual control system meant that the rover would move too slowly to achieve its scientific goals. This was because each iteration of the drive required at least eight minutes to make (due to the time it takes for the signal to travel to and from Mars). A fully autonomous system would have exposed the billions of dollars invested in the mission to too much risk for NASA to accept. The episodic control described here is one mechanism of many that you can use for managing system autonomy in a delegative AI implementation.

An alternative strategy is to partition the system into independent subsystems, each of which can fail without systemic or unacceptable damage. You can manage each partition individually in the event of failure, provided that the failure of the subsystem can be tolerated for the amount of time or money that resolving it requires.

Mobile phone networks are examples of such systems, where we can use a partitioning strategy to provide delegative control. Each cell of the network works autonomously to provide service to all subscribers within its allocated area. A cell could suffer a failure, for example, because its subscriber database fails or because the antenna steering strategy doesn't allocate sufficient power to enable subscribers to use the service. This localized and limited failure is then reported or detected by the national operating center. They take remedial action according to the service-level agreements that a communications regulator imposes on the operator. If the network is provided for emergency services (police, fire, ambulance, or coast guard, for example), then failover and replication provisions may be in place to provide the required coverage. Alternatively, rapid remediation from a 24/7/365 service and repair team may be designed into the system to sort things out.

This kind of partitioning and rapid recovery strategy is applicable to many applications. Because failure is built into the system, it becomes a liability, and we can't design applications that require constant pervasive availability and service to rely on this mechanism. A life-support system may have a partitioning strategy where some elements continue functioning in the face of other failures, but the system must also include a qualified person (say, a nurse) who can operate the failed elements while they are broken. Overall, the system (machine + nurse) is robust enough to be acceptable.

One error that a team can make in designing a delegative system is to implement fake controls for the human operator. If the system passes control back to the human when it's too late to repair the error, that isn't delegation, it's just plain failure. In the life support example, imagine if the nurse only becomes aware of the machine's failure when the patient suffers a cardiac arrest. That's too late; the damage is already done. In a real-life example, aircraft were placed into a stall by a control system, but only engaging the human pilot after the point at which there was no way to avoid a crash [5]. Tragically, many hundreds of people were killed by this system. Obviously, the real pilot (or nurse) must be brought in with sufficient time and agency to deal with the scenario that's unfolding, and the person must have the agency to make decisions that can avoid disaster.

Fake delegative systems of this type might be constructed due to human and organizational error. They also get constructed as a way to avoid the constraints and challenges of implementing truly autonomous systems. Unfortunately, the evidence of capability that creates sufficient confidence to deploy a truly autonomous system and meet the criteria of "I'll trust my life to this" or "I'll trust my business to this" can be dodged by pretending that there is a failsafe that can step in and prevent the system from killing or bankrupting people. Eventually, this approach ends up killing and bankrupting those who have been fooled into trusting such a system. We'll discuss the extra requirements for autonomy and the strict criteria that are imposed on ethical and functionally successful autonomous system development in the next section.

9.2.3 *Autonomous systems*

Autonomous systems are left to run unsupervised and independently for extended periods without human intervention. We described the Perseverance rover as a delegative system because control episodes are partitioned into elements, which can be reviewed and signed off by humans. If Perseverance drives into a sand trap (like some previous rovers have), then that will not be because the ML and AI planners failed, it's because it was not correctly operated. More accurately, it's because there was a failure, despite the team's best efforts. The ML team built appropriate control measures into the system, appropriate in the sense that the team balanced the limitations and requirements of the system.

A self-driving car, on the other hand, is a completely autonomous system. If you board a self-driving car and ask it to take you to a particular destination, you are not responsible for the accident that the car gets into on the way. The team that developed the car and sold it to you as self-driving is responsible (morally and ethically, if not always legally). A self-driving car (at least for the sake of this discussion) is an operationally autonomous device. The vehicle performs the entire episode of managing a journey from home to destination; the user controls the strategic choice of where to go and, potentially, may exert tactical control by changing some operational instructions (for example, "use the back route" or "slow down, I feel sick").

Delivering a fully autonomous system imposes a far stronger set of requirements on the team than delivering an assistive system. The development of self-driving systems demonstrates this. Self-driving technology has been deployed in urban settings since 2007 as described by Xei et al [12] but 15 years later, has yet to make it into widespread use. This is due to the complexities of the real-world derailed attempts to deploy and operate self-driving vehicles. Conversely, autonomous ML systems are deployed to manage and create the user experience for the most popular social networking and content recommendation systems on the internet.

Large social networks employ algorithms to select posts and stories to be displayed on subscribers' timelines using a recommender system. For the individual user, this may seem like an example of an assistive system; they are able to see a consistent thread of content in an unmanageable ocean of information. The users, however, have no choice about the content that they see or, more importantly, what they don't see. The social network is an autonomous system, intelligently directing the content on its servers to its subscribers.

Self-driving cars reveal one face of an autonomous system; social networks reveal the other. A self-driving application manages the kinetic power of a car. Social networks don't have localized kinetic power, but they do have global and societal scale. An application such as a large social network platform is not possible without AI. Since the development of these systems, they have generated hundreds of billions of dollars of revenue for their creators. Because autonomous systems have such a high value, creating applications that can't be handled by humans and managing systems that are beyond human capability, and yet are obviously dangerous, are they themselves intrinsically dangerous. This is not to say that they shouldn't be built and used!

The power and promise of autonomous systems make them the ideal candidates for solutions to the problems facing us today. Your task is to find the mechanisms that constrain and manage the fundamental dangers and pitfalls that their development and deployment has revealed to date.

Currently, the intent and structure of the system, along with the power and the significance of the application, drive many of the design decisions in this type of project. As the implementation phase is undertaken, the team has to consider all of these decisions in relationship to all the steps and activities that they need to undertake to get the final system delivered.

The first of these is to build a production data infrastructure that hydrates the application with the data it needs to function.

9.3 *Nonfunctional review*

The team has now spent several weeks working with the data, the infrastructure, and the users, and they should have a far more detailed view of what is needed to deliver successfully. Additionally, you have the models generated by ML in your hands, and the patterns of data movement and transformation that are required to create the features and inputs for the models are now well-defined. Putting these things together enables a meaningful set of requirements in terms of the amount of processing time that is available for the different components of the production system and the amount of money and environmental resources that the client has to spend to power each of these elements.

Processing time needs to be considered both in terms of latency (the time to respond to the service request) and throughput (how many service requests can be completed in a given timeframe). Table 9.3 shows a longer list of some of the requirements that you and the team must consider when reviewing the training pipelines for reimplementation and migration.

Table 9.3 Nonfunctional requirements in an ML-powered system

Requirement	Description	Notes
$Cost	How much it costs to execute the system.	Need to consider long life but cheap infrastructure versus short life but more expensive.
Environmental cost	The amount of environmental damage that can be accepted per use of the service.	Thought should be given to environmental impacts including greenhouse gas emissions and the use of noxious chemicals in air conditioning and cooling systems. Be cognizant of the consumption of metals, such as rare earth and gold, which may be involved in fielding your service in some domains.
Latency/wall clock	The amount of elapsed time from a service request to a delivered result.	In some applications, this is considered in terms of a flat requirement such as less than 0.5 s; alternatively, present as an expectation around a distribution or range of outcomes.
Throughput	The number of requests that can be served in a given amount of time.	This defines how many customers utilizing the services can be supported simultaneously by the system.
Queue policy	Preference for serving excess requests.	If there are more requests than can be supported by the system throughput, or a request cannot be served in the required clock time, what should the behavior of the system be? Should strict FIFO/LIFO behavior be enforced? Are there other requirements to prioritize certain requests?
Failure policy	When a request cannot be served without breaching a nonfunctional requirement, what should happen?	Some systems should fail silently, some should provide an exception/failure response and message, and some should serve the request outside of the nonfunctional requirement. In some cases, it's even appropriate to close the system after failure.
Durability	How long the service is to perform without failure.	Some systems become unreliable over time. Determining how long the models must work in service dictates the kind of measures that are required to mitigate this.
Reliability	How many failures (breach of nonfunctional requirements) the system can tolerate.	Consider all sources of failure together as well as looking at them one at a time.

The models and the pipelines, along with the setting for the system, are now in hand. These are the component parts that your team will integrate into the system (however it's going to be constructed). Now you can work out the E2E (end-to-end) performance expectations. You can then determine if you will hit the targets that you're shooting for.

9.4   *Implementing the production system*

This section serves to assist you when implementing your production system. As a reminder, let's look at the sprint 3 tickets associated with this task.

System implementation ticket: S3.3

- Build the production data flows to enable the models to make inferences.

System implementation ticket: S3.4

- Build the model server and the inference system.

System implementation ticket: S3.5

- Determine the appropriate interface components required by your system.

System implementation ticket: S3.6

- Select a conformant interface development approach, allowing for the delivery of the interface requirements.

9.4.1   *Production data infrastructure*

Your models are going into production, where they will be integrated into an application, and they are going to have to function effectively. There are two key components to the production infrastructure: the data pipelines that are going to funnel the application data into the models, including the processes that create the features and the model-serving infrastructure that is going to invoke and execute the models to produce a result. The data is constructed from lots of different sources. For example, if a user clicks a shopping basket, there is data from the click (which button, how long since the last click, etc.), from the basket (the data store that holds previous selections), and from the user data store and the commercial context.

Figure 9.4 shows this implementation pattern at a high level. Data flows in from the stores and the operational activities, such as user interface clicks or sensor data. Processing that data turns it into the features and formats that the model expects. (This step replicates the processes used in the training and testing pipelines.) A mechanism then takes that entity of data and passes it to a running instance of the model.

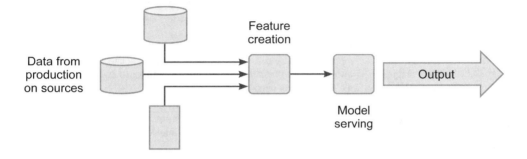

Figure 9.4 An abstract view of the production ML implementation. Data is pulled into and collected in a feature creation process, and then it's submitted to a running instance of the model(s) that are used to generate an inference and an output.

In sprint 1, you created training data pipelines and used those to manage the training data. In sprint 2, you implemented the pipelines for the test environment, replicating the data delivery pipelines in the training environment to the test environment. Now you and the team need to build the production pipelines to feed data into the models selected. The hardware and systems that are available to do this in a production environment are typically different from those that are provided in development.

Table 9.4 describes some of options that you and the team may now face. The data pipelines that you constructed to provide examples to your model from pre-canned resources now have to run on the production infrastructure. Unfortunately (for everyone concerned, but especially for ML engineers), data technology has evolved through many generations. You and the team may be confronted by any one of them. In the worst case, you are going to be confronted by all of them at once. Table 9.4 provides an overview of the types of sources and data engines that you can expect in the production context. Thank your lucky stars that you do not need to pull the data for the pipeline with COBOL.

Table 9.4   Data engines and their use in the production service

Data engine type	Characteristics	Use case/comments
Data lake (HDFS, S3) plus processor (Hadoop, EMR, Dataproc, Databricks)	Storage using a flexible filesystem and large-scale processing.	Large offline and cheap data transforms required; typically coupled with a faster store to support the inference service.
Data warehouse (BigQuery, Redshift, Oracle Exadata, etc.)	Managed data store for training data (typically, the default).	Flexible analytic data infrastructure that provides a general-purpose engine for serving models.
RDBMS transaction server (Oracle, MySQL, Postgres, Spanner)	Good application performance if properly designed and optimized. Can struggle at the limit or become expensive.	Provides a direct reimplementation layer to accelerate a pipeline with minimal technical change.
Document store/NSQL (Mongo, CouchDB, Cassandra, Big Table)	High speed; good at serving large objects.	Need to retrieve large unstructured objects and serve to the inference service.
Memory store (Redis, Memcached)	Extremely high speed, but not persistent or data safe. Can be expensive.	High speed/low latency inference results required with relatively straightforward data transformation and manipulation.

A modern approach is to abstract the data sources in production behind an access layer. In this scenario, the team cannot access or query the actual databases from which they will get the data. Instead, they will be provided with an API address that invokes the query automatically. There are lots of advantages to this pattern. The main advantage is that by introducing an abstraction layer, the system is decoupled from the implementation details of the sources that it depends on.

If this isn't the approach in the production architecture that you use, it may be a good idea to implement it yourselves so you can deal with future architectural evolution. It's much easier to cope with a database upgrade if all the calls and interactions in the system are managed through a well-controlled and well-documented API.

Regardless of the infrastructure used, the key challenge is to replicate the data pipeline developed in sprint 2, which supports the construction of the examples that are presented to the model. You will be able to reuse much of the code that was developed, but this shift often requires that you will need to make changes. This could create a situation where, although the model used in prod is the model developed and tested by the team (with all the artefacts created and used carefully preserved), it behaves differently because the data pipeline is throwing new biases into the mix. The way to control this is to fall back on the data testing systems that you developed in sprint 1 to ensure that the right data was produced for model building.

Testing and verifying the actual and expected behavior of the data pipeline is a key guarantee for model fidelity. The next section looks at another. The second aspect of the production system that needs to be considered is the model-serving mechanism.

9.4.2   *The model server and the inference service*

An *inference service* is a mechanism that provides optimized and efficient compute and storage for executing your models. It is an execution mechanism that meets this project's requirements for latency, scale (number of requests), and cost (overall, given the number of requests expected). Inference services are design and implementation patterns and packages that you use to cope with the challenges of running large and complex models in production.

A large-scale or pervasive ML-powered system might invoke the models that power it billions of times in its lifetime. If an optimization of just 1% is made, then that is equivalent to tens of millions of model invocations. A system such as Google Translate or the Facebook recommender supports a revenue stream that is large and sustained, so a specialist team implements and supports the production services for the ML-compute components. This team can hone and optimize the execution framework to support the required scale and performance of such systems.

In many other scenarios, though, a dedicated team (or bunch of teams) may not be organizationally feasible, even if a business case can be made that they would be a cost-effective investment. Organizations often struggle with cash flow or have strategic imperatives that pull investment from cost-effective activities to mitigate existential risks of competition or regulation. Although some places have well-oiled ML machines purring in production, the rest of the world must muddle through as best we can.

There are two approaches beyond the expensive (and risky) use of a bespoke implementation. The first is to use a mainstream execution engine and to minimally customize it to support your ML function. Table 9.5 flags various execution engines.

Table 9.5   Using generic execution engines for ML models

Engine	Comments
In a database: BigQuery ML, Redshift ML, Oracle OCI, Vertica PMML	Execution in database functions means accepting constraints on how the application runs, but this is a modular and decoupled approach.
Application servers: NGINX, Apache Tomcat, Flask, Appserver	For generic low-scale and permissive latency/cost use cases. Consider because of the low barrier in terms of skills and setup requirements.
SPARK-like solutions: Apache SPARK, Databricks, Dataproc	Good support for bulk and stream processing with permissive cost and latency requirements.
Kubernetes, Kubeflow	Flexible and scalable support for interactive applications with permissive cost requirements.
Serverless: Lambda, Cloud Functions, Azure Functions, Cloud Run.	A flexible, modular, and decoupled approach that's cost effective and performative in some applications but can become expensive in unpredictable ways.

All these options have tradeoffs and benefits. In many applications, it's sensible to run the ML in the database, but doing this impacts the behavior of the database, and it can be expensive. Also, database execution is necessarily inflexible; database engines are updated and maintained with respect to their performance as database engines, not with regards to their prowess as ML engines. The latest ML technology will not be in the database you use, at least not until it's available in an engine less strongly coupled to another core concern of the software stack.

We use application servers to invoke execution from web pages and apps. The frontend on a phone or a browser calls the application server for some off-device, server-side processing, and the application server provides the response. These systems are often massively parallel and scalable and offer state-of-the-art load balancing and error management. They are, after all, the systems that field the requests from billions of users to many of the internet services that we use every day.

SPARK-like solutions provide a variety of ways to manage parallelism in memory with support for accessing a filesystem that contains the data needed to run a model. SPARK is a mainstream programming approach, so many developers have this skill. SPARK interacts with Python and R implementations of models well, so its cost is typically low. SPARK tends to be expensive for on demand applications and isn't good for extremely low latency applications.

Kubernetes (K8s) provides a scalable, persistent processing system. It is especially attractive in a cloud environment, where you can use it as a managed service. Kubernetes can be expensive for bursty workloads, however.

Finally, serverless systems excel at providing extremely scalable on demand processing for bursty workloads, but they have a relatively high startup latency compared to persistent, always on approaches like K8s. It's important to be careful about pricing models underpinning serverless approaches. If cloud providers decide that it's commercially appropriate for them to change the pricing approach of a serverless engine, then this can be disruptive for any ML system using it. Ensure that you have an offramp.

The second approach is to use an engine designed to support ML invocation from the ground up. Interest in this approach, however, waxes and wanes in the ML community. In the ancient history of AI, specialist compute platforms such as Lisp machines described by Withington [11] were developed but were out competed by mainstream processors like the Intel 8086, Dec Alpha, Sun Spark, and Motorola 68000. Perhaps this will happen with ML server engines, but again, perhaps not. Engines like OpenVINO [7] and TensorFlow Serving [4] (Google 2021) are optimized to manage the execution of models that are, in fact, millions or billions of regularized activations created by operations over floating-point numbers. Additionally, a prebuilt engine offers the advantage of optimizations aimed at processor instruction sets such as the Google TPU or Intel processor instructions.

Determining the production implementation for your data flow, the processing required to hydrate your models, and the processing surface that executes them is hugely important. However, if the users can't see what is happening, or if they have insufficient controls to manipulate it in the ways that they need to, then it's all for nothing. Given the importance of good UX, we'll address that in the next section.

9.4.3   *User interface design*

Many would argue that the starting point for any system should be the impact that it has on the people it supports. Advocates of "Design Thinking" might champion the need for structured processes that surface the constraints and requirements of usability. A good example from Liedtka's HBR article [6] was an inappropriate hospital booking system. Its users were old and not computer savvy, as well as ill and disorientated by the maladies that led them to use the system. From this perspective, building a clever automated booking system before understanding how it would be used is a waste of money and time.

Another example of failure caused by an inappropriate interface is the Boeing 737 MAX aircraft and its MCAS system. This system was designed to make flying easy for pilots, providing controls that supported a pilot in the case of a stall. Theoretically, this would avoid a dangerous event that could cause the aircraft to crash. The activation light for this system was an expensive optional extra in the cockpit configuration, and so some airlines chose not to include it in the systems they purchased. Unfortunately, this meant that pilots were unaware when the system was activated, which might have been OK if it only turned on when there was a stall condition. However, in some cases, damaged sensors meant that the system activated when the aircraft was in normal flight, causing it to dive towards the ground and to behave in ways that its pilots didn't understand, let alone know how to deal with [8]. Concealing the workings of the model apparently contributed to the deaths of 100's of people, and consequently, billions of dollars of commercial loss as the 737 MAX was withdrawn from use and retrofitted.

Saleema Amershi [3] published a set of guidelines for developing AI systems in 2019, summarized in table 9.6. Although Amershi talks about AI, it's clear that these guidelines (numbered as G1 to G18) are focused on systems that contain ML models, and so are relevant to your project. You'll note that Table 9.6 is annotated with some asterisks. These signify guidelines that are especially important for UI designers in ML projects. Although all the guidelines presented in this chapter are significant for system value and success, the guidelines G1, G2, G4, G5, G6, G8, G10, G14, G15, G17, and G18 are especially important in that these can prevent catastrophic failure. These guidelines focus on preventing ML systems from committing *sins of commission*, where a system that acts badly is worse than one that leaves its users to decide for themselves.

Table 9.6   AI design guidelines (adapted from Amershi [3])

When to use	Number	Design guideline
Initially	G1*	Make clear what the system can and can't do.
	G2*	As well as describing the system's capabilities, clarify how well the system works.
During interaction	G3	Time proactive interactions with regard to the user's current task and environment.
	G4*	Show information relevant to the user's current context.
	G5*	Provide information in a way that the user can reflect on its social and cultural context.
	G6	Make sure that information and instructions don't reflect unfair social, gender, or racial biases.
When wrong	G7	Support efficient invocation to make it easy for the system work.
	G8*	Make it easy to turn the system off, even after failing.
	G9	Support efficient correction by making it easy to correct and edit the systems output and actions.
	G10*	Scope services when in doubt. If the system isn't sure, then get more information from the user or gracefully degrade the service when unclear about the users' goals.
	G11	Give users access to explanations about the system's behavior.
Over time	G12	Remember recent interactions and maintain those in memory to make it easy for the user to use that memory to get service.
	G13	Learn from user behavior; personalize the system to the user.
	G14*	Adapt cautiously. Limit disruptive and unexpected changes to the system's behavior, especially where the user has needs based on their expectations.
	G15*	Encourage granular feedback. Enable users to provide meaningful information on performance and ensure that there is a mechanism to do that.
	G16	Let users know when their input changes the behavior of the system.
	G17*	Allow the users to monitor and control how the system behaves.
	G18*	Notify users about changes. Inform the users when the AI's capabilities are updated or enhanced so that they can modify their expectations.

These guidelines can help to create a list of instruments and controls that are required for a particular system. The smart building example that was discussed earlier in the book can serve as an example as we delve into more detail about the guidelines:

- *G1:* Everyone in the building should be aware that the environment is managed by an AI system. We could create signage to let people know, and the building's web page could have a note about the system on it.

- *G2:* Information about the performance during field testing and validation should be shared, and the results explained. Draw attention to the carbon savings, explaining that this might mean that some parts of the building are cooler than normal outside of business hours, for example.

- *G3:* Ensure that the system doesn't make radical adjustments to temperature and lighting during core business hours.

- *G4:* Ensure that the environmental and power consumption information for a particular building area is available.

- *G5:* When presenting the information on environment and power, consider the relevance of the raw numbers to the users. Present the information relative to previous data and explain the difference. Relate benefits to items that the users can understand and empathize with; for example, for carbon savings, "numbers of trees felled" or "hectares of forest required to offset."

- *G6:* Consider factors such as biology in the performance of the system. For example, women are often said to feel the cold more than men. Ensure that this is considered in the behavior of the system. Also, make sure that any user testing panels have an even representation of women and men, and ask each what they think of the system's performance.

- *G7:* Provide a complaint and management process. Who should the building's users contact, and how?

- *G8:* Consider that the system might fail and might need to be turned off. Ensure that the building managers know how to do this and that the users know how to contact the building managers.

- *G9:* Provide controls that allow the building managers to control the system in meaningful ways. If the users complain that the building is too hot or too cold, provide ways to modify the system's behavior so that it remains in use, even if not optimally.

- *G10:* Ensure that there is a fail-safe option for the building that returns it to a steady temperature in case the sensor network and controller produce inputs that don't get a strong response from the model.

- *G11:* Record what the system is doing and provide access to that log in a friendly way so that users can inspect the decision making to moderate or increase energy use over a long period.

Over time, an interface developed with G1-G11 guidelines provides a mechanism for users to leave feedback and ensures a process where the company's managers get the feedback. For that reason, provide a feedback page where you can keep a record of the actions taken by the managers and then publish that so the users can see what was done with their feedback. The affordance made for G11 avoids a difficult point: providing an explanation of what the models are doing can be challenging. Rudin details this as a barrier to the adoption and use of AI systems in important applications [10].

The requirement for transparency in the intended application should have been considered in selecting the model. This is a strong system requirement and was part of the decision-making in chapter 8. However, sometimes the best model, selected with respect to all the needs and challenges in the project, may be undesirably opaque. For example, the AI underpinning the protein structure prediction, AlphaFold 2, is a complex set of extremely large and arcane deep networks. These are not interpretable, but it would be great if they were so that biologists would know how and why AlphaFold 2 does what it does. AlphaFold provides some compromise capability by rendering the structures that it creates, showing how they differ from previous hypothesized structures, and how they then function. This allows scientists to evaluate and intuit the effectiveness and value of the black-box predictions that AlphaFold makes.

The best thing for the users and your team may be to use post hoc explanation mechanisms. One popular approach for providing explanations of the inferences made by deep networks such as AlphaFold 2 is to provide activation maps, showing which parts of the processed images cause the highest level of activity in the network. A popular package that supports this style of explanation is LIME [9].

The art of providing a post hoc explanation is improving all the time, but there are strong criticisms of it in Rudin [10]. The judgement you must make is whether the harm that is potentially caused by providing a misleading explanation about a system's actions outweighs the harm caused by disregarding the value that an opaque system could provide to the users. Being clear that the explanation is indicative and may be inaccurate mitigates this potential harm a little, but the users are essentially in your hands. It's your responsibility; exercise care.

9.5   *Logging, monitoring, management, feedback, and documentation*

Support and management component: S3.7

- Build logging, monitoring, and alerting components for the system.

Support and management component: S3.8

- Ensure that model governance and hand-over arrangements are agreed on.

Support and management component: S3.9

- Produce maintenance and support documentation.

If you are delivering a system into production, then it's necessary to implement a set of administrative and managerial interfaces that allow technical support groups to operate it. ML systems are no exception. The system needs to produce informative logging information so you can understand that it is performing as expected and trace what happens if something goes wrong. It also needs to generate alarms in the case of failure, preferably before it fails.

For normal software systems, performance monitoring is nonfunctional. In functional terms, we can expect the software to work, apart from bugs. ML systems can suffer a functional failure in production as well, because the world changes, and the patterns and behaviors that were extracted with the ML algorithms in sprint 2 are no longer relevant. This can happen because the entities that generate the demands and actions for the ML predictions change. Perhaps some of them got old and died; perhaps other pressures such as economic change or the introduction of new technology have radically shifted the dynamics of the domain. For example, a model that provided good predictions for music sales based on data prior to streaming becoming widespread would likely fail today. It follows that this means we must log and alarm functional system behavior as well as nonfunctional behavior to decode if, where, and when this kind of functional failure can happen.

We need to record and capture in the system's logs all the events relevant to its operation, such as database connections, user logins, data updates, and model decisions. The frequency and density of logging is dictated by the application, as is the retention period for the logs themselves. Obviously, there is a cost in terms of the load that calculating performance metrics imposes on the system, and there is a cost for storing the logging data too. This is balanced by the requirements of the application that you established when developing the system.

The density of the logs is driven by requirements and performance considerations. The performance of an alert system is constrained by how humans can interact with it effectively. Support groups often complain about alarm storms that turn every light on their boards red and send messages to all devices every 10 minutes. These alerts are routinely ignored and may as well not exist. The unfortunate side effect of this kind of alarm behavior is that the meaningful alerts are lost in the blizzard of junk and are ignored as well.

Along with logging and alerting, the system must have effectors that you can use to control and manage it. Management functionality can be as simple as the ability to request a reboot to clear problems like filled queues or failed memory allocation. Although it is hoped that the delivered system is bug-free and flawless, it's unwise to plan on that assumption. Providing a restart button can prove to be a cheap and effective solution for unexpected problems. It may also be sufficient to keep a valuable system in the field for years longer than would otherwise be the case.

A powerful method of making a system supportable in production is to enable the users to provide feedback. This is especially useful in the early days of a deployment when the development group is still available to implement any required fixes. Providing a feedback mechanism is table stakes; you've got to do it. What's more important, however, is to get the users to use it. A good method is to directly ask them what their opinion of the system is.

As an example, consider the implementation of a system to support monitoring customer complaints on the internet (for example, on Twitter or Facebook). The system's users can be thought of as call center operatives who are disempowered in the client organization and are not able for social and cultural reasons to speak against the company's systems. Suppose when they are provided with a mechanism for feedback about the system's performance in confidence, they post many complaints. One complaint is that the system takes so long to respond, they sometimes get timed out of their account logins. At first, this seems ridiculous, but when investigating query time on the backend database, the team finds that some queries are running for several minutes. This makes the system both slow and demoralizing to use, and it also destroys any benefits that the ML system was designed to create.

In our example, the problem with the system in production appears because the production database was not configured and indexed in the way that it was supposed to be. The team didn't know this because none of the tests showed that. The problem is resolved with one phone call to the database team. The point of this anecdote is that despite testing, logging, and monitoring, the development team can be blind to problems in production. Asking the users rarely hurts and can (as in this case) be extremely valuable.

One particular feature of ML systems is that, over time, the value of input to the system can change as the world evolves and moves forward. Monitoring system input for these changes is one way that logging and monitoring support the governance of an ML system. This is discussed in more depth next.

9.5.1   *Model governance*

In some applications, the models implemented into the system on day one of operation are used successfully, right up until some change in the state of the art or requirements for the application make them obsolete, then they get withdrawn from service. In other applications, changes in the domain, perhaps caused by swings of fashion, inflation, social structures, or demographics, mean that models become outdated, and their performance starts to degrade. Organizations using ML can deploy hundreds or thousands of models and systems, but unless these are delivered within a systematic management and governance framework, chaos will reign.

A basic governance structure mandates that the systems and models that underpin them are registered with a responsible person within the client organization. The model must be owned by someone. We must also provide the materials and information required to properly access and understand the models so that the owners can deal with it as it evolves. The governance system should at the very least allow the system owner (who is responsible for and empowered to make decisions about the system) to be identified and to link all the artifacts that enable the system to be audited, managed, maintained, and supported for easy discovery and access. In addition, the governance system calls for the history of the production system to be recorded and read:

- When was the system implemented, changed, and reviewed?
- When were problems with the system detected and recorded, and what was done to deal with them?
- If the system was removed from service, when was it withdrawn, and when will it and the associated records of its commission and operation be deleted?

A core requirement that disappears in the bureaucratic chaff is that the model owners must be able to tell when the model has gone wrong and must be able to turn it off, fix it, or put something else in its place. A critical step is knowing that the model has gone wrong. Some simple checks in production can reveal this; for example, counting the types of classifications that the model makes and raising an alert if too many of one type are noticed. However, a more sophisticated approach is to build assertions into the model server and to log and alert if any of these are violated (Kang, et al. 2020).

You must also provide for contingencies. This is like any business continuity plan; it's fundamental that a business won't go bankrupt if the head office is shut for a week or a month due to an earthquake, a bad storm, or other unforeseen catastrophe. Every business should have contingency plans to deal with that kind of eventuality. The same is true for models! If the models stop working, for whatever strange reason, the business using them should not be left to sink. For example:

- Can aggregate behavior or majority class prediction (with appropriate warnings) provide a lower value substitute for the model?
- Can you provide older models that work less well but may be more robust?
- Can you turn off the model, allowing the users to manage for some period without it? How long is that time? Is it realistic that the model can be debugged, retested, and fixed in that time?

In the next chapter, these issues will loom large because they will impact your future work. By getting realistic post-release arrangements in place before the shift to production, you can avoid a lot of heartache and trouble.

9.5.2   *Documentation*

During the project, you should have produced and filed a great deal of documentation. All of this is incredibly useful and valuable, but to deliver a maintainable system, the team needs to prepare some additional documents that support the system in life. These documents are:

- A production team organization chart
- A run book
- A technical overview
- A troubleshooting guide

You can use the production team organization chart to answer who looks after the system, how to contact them, and what credentials, knowledge, and training do they need to do their job? Also, make sure that the set up and structure of the production team considers holidays, sickness, and succession. It's fine for people to be aggressive in saying that folks had better cover things that they are paged to deal with, no matter what. But what if someone quits, or worse, they die? Then, you are bust, and all the posturing and bluster is just a meme.

A run book allows first- and second-line support to troubleshoot the system when it produces errors because of faults or problems in other systems or in its supporting hardware. Other support groups may fix the root cause of these errors, but the relevant "fix this please" ticket needs to get raised, and you will need to tell the users what's happened and what is being done about it. The run book should provide information for every error state that the logging and monitoring system might produce. Some of these will simply say something like "data error: escalate to technical team," but many will also provide simple fixes such as "restart application server using app_server_restart.exe script."

A technical overview provides a briefing for new engineers so they can quickly understand the core components and concepts. This overview typically links to the documentation archive that the team produced, so it should be seen as a high-level map of the system and not a detailed deep dive. Essentially, the team should imagine that they are presented with the code base and the development documentation. What is it that they need to get started quickly? At a minimum, the document should include a diagram showing the major components of the system and the allocation of processing on each, and it should also show a view of the data flows in the system: where the data is coming from and where it is accessed, staged, and processed.

To set up a troubleshooting guide, ask the team to apply their imaginations. What is it that is likely to be wrong with the system? What would they do to fix it?

Ensure that the team pays particular attention to the documentation of the ML component and models in the system. The development documents cover the technical architecture and approach of the modeling, but the documentation must detail:

- How to invoke the model in isolation (what files to run, how data can be passed into it, etc.).
- How to retain the model (again, what to run, how to run it, and environment prerequisites).
- How to evaluate the model's behavior (reference the project documentation but explicitly state what is important about how the model delivers value to the users).

The effort required to develop these documents is considerable and obviously scales with the complexity of the system that you are developing. The payoff from doing this is enormous; a set of good production documents when coupled to a well-stocked development archive provides a fantastic source for the onward development and maintenance of your system.

9.6   *Pre-release testing*

> **Testing ticket: S3.10**
>
> ■ Develop a pre-release testing plan.

The team probably thinks they did enough testing in sprint 2, but the hard reality is, there's more to be done to deploy the production system. Most organizations have testing standards (sometimes called VV&T, meaning verification, validation, and testing). You and the team will be required to develop and complete a testing plan, which is then signed off as complete by the client's IT. Typically, a testing plan requires that you conduct unit, system, integration, and acceptance tests:

■ *Unit tests:* Localized tests that developers use to prove their code works.

■ *System tests:* Show that the code performs as expected; for example, testing the model is a system test as is testing the nonfunctional elements.

■ *Integration tests:* Demonstrate that the different system models work together as expected; for example, the production database works with the code that performs feature extraction.

■ *Acceptance tests:* Demonstrate that the system meets the criteria that makes it useful for its business purpose or the purposes of its users.

During system development, the team did a lot of unit testing (for instance, the data testing described in sprint 1) and system testing (such as the extensive work at the end of sprint 2). Acceptance tests should be facilitated by the work on UX, which was started in sprint 2 as well. However, there are aspects of unit and system testing that need to be created now, and the data infrastructure, UX, and model-serving infrastructure needs to be tested with integration tests. Any other application elements that are integrated with the ML system also require integration testing. The work to be done now is to:

■ Gather and catalog the unit and system tests done so far.

■ Formalize and organize the acceptance tests from the UX work.

■ Ensure that the production components have proper unit and system tests.

■ Design and undertake integration tests to ensure that the implemented system works correctly as a whole.

■ Get the test plan accepted as one that is appropriate.

■ Get your preproduction tests into an automated test system and run the tests successfully.

Finally, get the necessary sign off, showing that the team executed the accepted test plan successfully and that the VV&T group agrees that the system can be productionized.

There is a significant difference between the testing required to deliver a useful ML system and that for a more standard bit of software. The core of this is the performance and behavior of the models that are extracted from the data.

At the time of writing, the standards that most organizations demand for the testing their models are well below what we detailed in chapter 8. Hopefully, that will change. Until then, you and the team are the professionals and the experts. Testing standards and quality mandates are backstops and reminders of the need for you to demonstrate why you are paid to do what you do. Your test plan shows that you have done everything that is expected of you in creating a robust and reliable artifact to deliver for your client and your users.

9.7   *Ethics review*

Is it too late to check that everything is on track concerning ethics? Of course not! At this point, the team needs to make sure there are no emerging issues that they haven't accounted for in the previous exercises, and they need to assemble the documentation they prepared for all the ethical evaluations. Work on this was done pre-project, post EDA, and during the decision-making process for model selection.

Now that the whole system is understood, you and the team need to review the ethical consequences of its deployment. As previously discussed, there are many ongoing efforts to understand the ethical implications and licensing of an ML system; the context of the system determines which, if any, the team will adopt. Also, it's expected that this province will rapidly evolve, and it is the responsibility of you and the team to employ best practices to ensure that the system that you built is ethical. To do so, check the following:

- Is the way that the system will be managed clearly understood by the people accountable for it?
- Is there an appropriate governance process in place that will manage the system's behavior and impact over time, even when the people who are doing it now move on?
- Is the system's performance understood and measured by the way it impacts its users and others in its operating context? Can the team demonstrate this?
- Does the system's interface provide enough information to allow the users to understand what it is doing?
  - Are the available controls that manage the behavior of the system effective and appropriate?
  - Can the users make use of the controls effectively so that they can be reasonably held to account for the system's behavior?
- Have you consulted with the users of the system and the people impacted by its use?
  - Has the team evaluated the impact of the system on those people?
  - Does your team fully understand any harm the system may cause and is this clearly outweighed by the utility of the system?

Regarding the last point, in the case of harm, ensure that there's a responsible person or somebody with the authority and competence to make a judgement about the system's utility available.

9.8 Promotion to production

> **Ticket to put your system into production: S3.11**
> - Promote to production.
> - Create a post-release test plan.

The great day arrives! Everything is signed off, the system isn't dangerous or malfeasant, it works, and it is valuable. Everyone loves it, so what happens next? You schedule a release time/date. In a DevOps environment, this might be the day that the system hits the criteria to make its first release. In a more ossified enterprise environment, there may be a weekly release day or (more likely) a quarterly release day and do expect there to be freezes around milestone dates like Christmas, New Year, and financial-reporting season. Some enterprises have protracted release freezes around periods that are vital for trading or safety as well.

Once everyone agrees on a day and time, then in a modern project, you run a batch file (possibly by clicking a button or by issuing a command-line instruction) that shifts all the artifacts required for the system into production and makes them available for invocation. Typically, we run post-release tests to demonstrate that the system has been transferred completely and properly and that it really is running. This means that the team has four jobs to do:

1 Develop the CI/CD process that promotes all files to the production environment. Hopefully, this is done with standard development pipeline tools (for example, Jenkins). Sometimes, especially in a cutting-edge project, there will be some corner cases for deployment that require another workaround. The important thing is not to end up with a bunch of Post-It notes, or even worse, folklore-style verbal instructions that define the deployment process. Insist on as much automation (and simple-to-use automation) as possible. Why? Because pushing to production is both exciting and stressful, and it often goes wrong. You may have to rejig and redo the system. Automation is your friend.

2 Create a post-release test plan. Again, automate this (as for all your testing) and ensure that you know how it will run and how it will be deployed in production. This is usually a part of the general promotion event.

3 Do the promotion/release tasks, including the testing.

4 Run the post-release testing and verify the results.

As mentioned, it's not unusual for something to go wrong with the production deployment. What's important is that you are prepared for this contingency. Ensure that you have key people available to intervene and that they are empowered with credentials and permissions to do what's needed to sort out any last-minute hitches.

9.9   *You aren't done yet*

> **Task to do when you think you've finished: S3.12**
>
> - Provide post-release recognition and thanks.

It's there, in production and running. This is the point at which to celebrate. Take the team out for lunch, hold a party, get a drink. At the very least, send them all a note of thanks in a team call or via email. The team has come through and delivered, they deserve some recognition. As for you, pat yourself on the back; you were brilliant. Then, look after your own interests, sit back, and think through what happened. The experience that you've gone through is valuable, and you need to recognize and retain it.

It's at this point that it'll dawn on you that there's a life beyond the project. Sometimes you can take a break and switch to something new when you come back, but the reality is that this was your project, and you and everyone associated with it will likely be called in to follow up on whatever opportunities and developments arise. In the next chapter, we'll review post project work. There is a lot to do to support and maintain a system in production, and there's a lot to do to learn from what's happened and to improve your practice for the next project and the ones after that.

9.10   *The Bike Shop sprint 3*

The end of sprint 2 coincided with your vacation, and you took full advantage of the holiday. You were confident that Rob would deliver while you were out, and the first thing you do when you're back at work is to review his sprint report, and you feel vindicated. When Karima calls on your first morning back, you're in a great mood. This doesn't last, though.

Karima feels that there's been a great deal of activity in the project to date, but she's not seeing anything tangible. She uses the phrase "all smoke and no light." This is not good. Karima has clearly had a change of mind about the progress and value of the project; the question is why? You can guess, someone asked her where were the fruits of the investment? With the instinct for survival that all senior business stakeholders have, Karima undoubtedly responded by outlining why her doubts about this project haven't been considered. She then explained how she's made the best of a bad job so far but shouldn't be blamed for what happens. It's not hard to imagine who Karima thinks should get blamed if indeed the project doesn't prove out.

You think fast. Perhaps, you offer, the right thing to do is to have a review session, where the progress and outcome so far can be presented to Karima and anyone else she would like to bring in to talk about the direction of the project, but you have a good backup plan here. While the modelling team has been doing their high-profile work, Clara has been plugging away in the background looking at the frontend of the system. She's building UX components and testing them with the users. You had a quick chat with her late last week, and you're confident that given the time it takes to get people into a review, the team will be able to pull together a concept demo that will convince whoever is rattling Karima's cage that all is well.

You lean back in your chair and mentally kick yourself. You should have seen this coming, but you focused more on the target application earlier in the project. You know, though, that if you had switched the focus onto demonstrating how much value the application could have, rather than making sure it would work, then you could have been in trouble for wasting the client's money on a system that was just fantasy. Back-loading the project is too risky. After reading Rob's report, however, you are confident that the project will work, but the danger lies in it getting scrapped before you can prove it. You look at your coffee and wonder if it's OK to get a stronger drink and shake your head wearily. The weekend feels a long way in the past, and it's only 10:30 a.m.

Still, there's no time like the present to deal with issues of this sort. The first thing you do is to set up a team meeting for first thing tomorrow morning. The next thing you do is message Clara and Rob. Thank goodness they are both in and working today, so you arrange a three-way chat after lunch. You use the time before lunch to review the materials generated in sprint 1 and 2.

In the chat, you let Rob and Clara know that it's time the team outlined how the model's likely application will best meet the customer's needs. Happily, the three of you share the view that the best implementation of the models is to sit them behind intelligent dashboards. This was the initial concept that was discussed with the client. You consider where the project went off track. If, in sprint 2, Clara had flagged that the model would not work from a UX point of view, or if the modelling team had found something that would have derailed the implementation, then you would have been able to talk Karima and Niresh through a change of direction. Ironically, that might have given them a stronger perception of team's engagement with the customer's requirement. Still, the good news is that the project is well on track to deliver what the clients want and what Clara believes the users need. Rob agrees to take the lead in putting the presentation together.

Niresh then messages you to say that there is a slot for a project checkpoint in three days, but he doesn't give any further details. Three days is quite a while in a project like this and looking at the situation that Clara and Rob talked through with you, you feel a lot better for the leeway. Rob's view is reassuring too. He thinks that by the time the checkpoint comes along, the team will have some quite impressive plans to show.

In the morning, you and Rob walk the team through the situation, and you lay out some goals for the next three days. The first goal is to deal with the analysis tickets 3.1

and 3.2. (See section 9.1 if you need a reminder about the purpose of these tickets.) Because of where the team is now and the maturity of the project, you decide that 3.1 can be dealt with in the team meeting. The team agrees. It's obvious that the appropriate approach is to develop intelligent dashboards as an assistive application. Figuring out the nonfunctional impact of this is a bit more complex, but Danish and Kate are happy to take ticket 3.2 and will come back with a review tomorrow morning.

Rob suggests that the best thing to do is to throw some light onto tickets 3.3 and 3.4 and put together a dev environment prototype of the app. To get this done in three days is an ambitious target, but the team seems surprisingly confident. Their previous investigations and Rob's work in sprint 1 uncovered a dashboard tool that Clara and Miguel are familiar with. The required data flows can be easily sketched from the new prod databases, and the external data sources in the cloud environment can deploy the transformations and feature creation steps to a serverless processor. Clara and Miguel start work on implementing the UI, Kate and Rob focus on an implementation design for the model server, and Jenn and Sam look at the data pipeline. All agree to present at the review meeting tomorrow morning.

In the days afterward, you are kept busy fielding architectural questions from the team about the available components. Some of them you can respond to yourself, but you find yourself frequently chatting with Niresh to get additional answers. When the checkpoint meeting comes round that Thursday, Karima shows up with a person that introduces himself as Alan, the finance guy. You recognize him as Alan Williams, who is The Bike Shop CFO. Clearly, he's curious about where his money is being spent. Karima seems quite distracted and unsure of herself, and Niresh is as quiet as a mouse. Alan has a formidable reputation at The Bike Shop—he doesn't suffer fools gladly or at all.

You've briefed the team carefully on the plan. You'll present the project and the value of the work upfront and then Rob will show the prototype. He segues to Clara, who will talk about the UX work and the responses from the users she's in touch with. Miguel will then walk through the UI's features, focusing on making the ML system work for the users. With the remaining time, Jenn and Kate will go over the prod design.

This arrangement proves to be a great choice. Alan listens to your outline of the benefits and looks straight at Karima. He says, "This is exactly what I was talking about." Karima blanches, and you feel a cold chill run down your spin, but then he says, "This isn't all vapor though, is it? What have you got to show me?"

Rob kicks off the demo and immediately Karima relaxes. After 30 seconds, Niresh grins at you (out of Alan's eyeline, of course). Alan is nodding as Clara talks about the user responses, and when Jenn describes the data design, he turns to Niresh and asks, "What do you think?" Niresh says, "I talked it over with the users. We can take this to the conformance board tomorrow and look to go live with it soon thereafter."

Alan stands up, ignoring you, he turns to Karima and says, "Go for it. I'll speak to Pete." Alan turns to the team and says, "Great to meet you all" and walks out. You feel a bit ignored, but then, you are a suit from a consultancy. Karima makes it clear that she's pleased with the presentation and the demo. She asks the team if they are confident that they can have the implementation ready for testing in the timelines that you outlined.

Before tasks S3.3 and S3.4 are completed, however, there are quite a few review-and-response subtasks in the backlog. It looks like it will take a couple of days more to run those. The team carries on picking up and dealing with the tickets in the sprint backlog; standups are short and to the point. The team all knows what they are doing, and they are driving to get it done. Clara is already looking at S3.5 and will start on 3.6 before the end of the week.

Kate knows that the logging environment at The Bike Shop is Splunk, and she quicky provides an appropriate logging and monitoring set up, interfacing into the logs generated by the model server and the data subsystem. Rob and you are entirely taken up with working with the support groups at The Bike Shop to arrange for them to pick up the system. Karima gets walked through a governance process. Sam and Jenn take on the testing. The plan is signed, a test harness is built, and soon everything is green across the board.

Miguel builds the release logic to promote the system to production, a time and date is agreed on and before you know it, you are staring at a dashboard that's available on The Bike Shop intranet. Karima hugs you. Niresh grins happily. The next day you draft an email thanking the team. Just as you are about to send it, an alert pops up. It's your boss. You and the team have been retained by The Bike Shop. They want more, and they're willing to pay!

Summary

- Make a deliberate choice about the type of ML system that you and the team are building. Is it assistive, delegative, or autonomous?
- Own the implications of that choice! The nonfunctional and functional requirements of the various types of ML-driven systems are different.
- You need to build production data flows and a suitable model-serving infrastructure to support the requirements that you've identified.
- User interface requirements for ML systems are different from normal systems. You will need to ensure that the system is appropriately instrumented and that the relevant controls are available to the users.
- Make sure to provide the right logging, monitoring, and alerting infrastructure, or the production support groups won't be able to accept it into service.
- Get your system tested and signed off as fit for production.
- Budget time and effort for pre-release user and integration testing.
- Ethical review is essential when developing a release candidate for the system. This is often the point at which stakeholders realize what it is that has been implemented and its implications. It can be painful, but catching problems at this last hurdle is far preferable to releasing problems into the wild.
- Be ready for the ongoing work that comes with delivering a system into production. Your job isn't over when the users get their hands on your work. In fact, it's probably just beginning.

Post project (sprint Ω)

This chapter covers

- Looking after an ML system after it's gone into production
- Dealing with production failures
- Learning from the project and improving practice

The models are integrated in an application, and the application is delivered to production. Now someone must look after it! In addition to dealing with old ML systems and looking after new ones, this chapter addresses what happens to the team after you complete the project. How can you and your team learn from it, and what should be done to make the next project better?

10.1 Sprint Ω backlog

The backlog in table 10.1 lays out the work that the team needs to cover once you've delivered a system into production.

Table 10.1 Sprint Ω backlog

Task #	Item
SΩ.1	Identify ML-specific sources of technical debt. • Verify model performance as appropriate • Monitor model drift • Check model obsolescence
SΩ.2	Identify and deal with technical debt in general.
SΩ.3	Run a post-project review to determine what the team can learn from your project.
SΩ.4	Seek ways to develop new practices for developing ML systems.
SΩ.5	Identify new technologies that the team can use to be more successful.
SΩ.6	Write a case study about the project to record and share your experience.

10.2 Off your hands and into production?

In chapter 9, we discussed the process of getting the ML model into a system and into production. Major activities in this process included building a monitoring, logging, and alerting system and getting agreement on the governance processes for the system. This setup should provide you with the framework to support the system if you are called on to do so.

Currently, there is an increasing trend for ML teams to manage their projects in production. This is called *shift left* because in a process flow, development teams are seen on the left-hand side passing products to support groups on the right-hand side. The idea is that the development groups should do more of the support group's traditional work. This is because smaller companies are now supporting software development because there is less capital available to spend on production teams. Also, the move to the cloud means that a lot of the concerns of in-house support teams have disappeared. There are no server farms to tend and water, which makes it possible for huge savings simply by shutting them down.

Of course, there are counter arguments. Why get ML teams to look after their systems in production when they could be building other ML systems? One answer is that sometimes the ML systems require specialist skills to sustain production. Another perspective is that there are valuable lessons to be learned from working with a system in the wild. Teams with exposure to maintaining production projects often have a different outlook on what's important in future development processes. It's also worth considering that the team supporting the project will naturally change as time progresses, and junior staff can gain experience as the first line of support for older deployments.

Regardless of these arguments, providing support for a project when it is in production is often a prerequisite of ML projects. When presented with a project proposal, canny CIOs look down the road and see an orphaned project in the making. Given this and the fact that your organization may simply see this as your day job, this chapter will address the challenges that supporting an ML system in the wild can bring.

10.2.1 Getting a grip

Often teams gradually accumulate responsibilities for models in production over time, and frequently no one is quite sure who is responsible for what. It's easy for a team to take the view that, although they helped fix and deploy a bunch of things, those things are really the responsibility of someone else. This means that they can spend their time doing all sorts of other fun things and, well, life will be sweet. Unfortunately, when this kind of nebulous view is tested by a full-on system failure, it turns out that everyone else thinks you are responsible for that. When this happens, life promptly stops being sweet.

If you take the time and resources to manage the ML systems your team has accepted responsibility for, you will find that failures are rare and, if they happen, much easier to deal with. Most importantly, when you explain what happened and how it was dealt with, you will find that you don't look incompetent, disorganized, and generally clueless. Step one is therefore to control the systems that your team looks after.

What systems are you ultimately responsible for? If there is any doubt, make a list with four columns (like the one in table 10.2) and put all the systems that your team have touched or think that they may have any responsibility for into it. In Table 10.2, there is a column for Owner, that's the person who is the business owner of the system, and the one who asserts that it's valuable enough to stay in production. In the case of failure, that person will be the one on the phone to you. There is a column for Who Manages as well. The purpose of this table is to get the Owner to agree that the person named in Who Manages is the person who is responsible for the project.

Table 10.2 Create and maintain a list of your responsibilities, ensure that your manager or supervisor has access to it, and go over it with them to make sure they agree that it's accurate.

System name	Owner	Who manages	Notes
Inventory manager	Karima	You	Reviewed and good 03/22
Demand prediction	Karima	You	Reviewed and good 03/33
Building manager	Alan	David	David isn't sure about this
Auto reply	Alan	You	No governance
Inspection	Josep	David	David agreed
Entity matcher	Alan	You	No governance
Auto review	Alan	You	Last reviewed 01/20

Your starting assumption may be that you are responsible for these systems but strive to find other people to take them on if you can. Discuss this process with your manager. They may prove to be keen to fill the Who Manages column with alternates.

At the end of this process, you will have a definitive view of the responsibilities for you and the team. Daunting as that may be, it's a much stronger position than you were in when you started. Now that you have a clear mandate for managing these systems, you need to organize reviews for each of them:

- Is there governance in place? If not, fix this first and ensure that it's agreed on appropriately.
- Is the support organization still up to date and relevant? Are all the people still working in the post prod team or under contract to provide support?
- Is the documentation still available? This is easy to check. It's also relatively easy to determine that the documentation is meaningful and useful but that can take some focused time.
- Are the relevant tools still available? In particular, are any licensed tools or specialist hardware platforms required either to wrangle the system's data (perhaps because of proprietary formats) or to train the models?
- Has the system been reviewed for end-of-life issues? If not, then do the review.
- Are there any upcoming changes (such as re-platforming) to the system's infrastructure that should be planned for? If so, then develop a plan.
- Is there a clear view of what will happen if the system fails? What will the approach be to getting it fixed?

Reviews need to be repeated periodically, so it's good practice to establish a standard time in the organization if there isn't one already in place. A good starting point is yearly. Note that one issue that's not on the previous list, which affects all software systems, is the accumulation of technical debt. ML systems are particularly prone to this issue, which is discussed in detail next.

10.2.2 *ML technical debt and model drift*

Technical debt describes the gap between the best possible performance of a system and its real performance. This gap is the debt that the system has accumulated, which costs in terms of extra work for the users or other systems.

Technical debt was coined to describe the compromises that are required to get early agile projects into production by Cunningham [1]. Since Cunningham introduced this idea, it has also come to describe the accumulation of problems and issues that tend to grow around computer systems in production over time. Software is static; it doesn't change over time, and yet, the world changes around it. Typically, issues arise when we change the interfaces, leading to incomplete or failed interactions and data flows. Scully and co-authors point out that ML systems are particularly prone to technical debt [2], and there are several specific forms of technical debt that we need to address here.

The lack of a useful logging and monitoring system is a common form of technical debt in a legacy ML system. Our priorities need to include checking that logs that record the activity of the system exist, that there is a mechanism for understanding the performance of the system, and that there is a system of alerts to a support group if the system fails. Chapter 9 contains some advice for setting this up. This should be a priority because logs underpin any troubleshooting exercise, and getting an early warning of system failure can seriously reduce the stress involved in fixing it.

At the time of writing (2022), ML research is creating considerable innovations in algorithm design. This is something that happens slowly in the rest of computer science and software engineering. In fact, the fast pace of research and development in the ML community creates technical debt as old approaches are out-modelled by the latest techniques. When taking on the maintenance of an ML system, it's worth benchmarking its performance against newer techniques. In a few years, more robust and performative techniques will become available. Identifying opportunities to move from brittle and temperamental old models to robust and reliable new ones saves you and the team a lot of heartache. The latest and greatest, however, may be a matter of fashion, and the old models running in production can prove to be there for solid reasons. Using robust evaluation and model selection approaches as we discussed in chapter 8 can help to substantiate this, one way or another. As per the observations of Sculley et al [2], context around ML systems change, and it's the ML itself that changes them.

Often, model drift is the discovery that the model wasn't as good as previously thought. Poor testing and selection practices can lead to inadequate models. If you take on the responsibility for an ML system, it's a good idea to review how it was tested. Hopefully, you'll find some great testing documentation that reflects the processes described in chapter 7 and chapter 8. In the best case, nothing extra might suggest itself to you. However, if you find no evidence or inadequate evidence of proper testing, then redoing this allows you to identify weaknesses in the models and put in place a repair and retrofit program.

As the world around the models evolves and changes, the models extracted in the past may become less and less applicable, even if the models contain solid causal relationships. When those relationships fail, the models fail. This is often called *concept drift*.

For example, if customers buy smart trousers and shirts at the same time and then a global pandemic means that they work from home, their need for smart trousers disappears overnight! Recommending jeans or jogging trousers might be more effective, but the model may not have had the ability to adapt without intervention, and so its performance was compromised. A more common malady than a sudden causal change occurs when the noise levels and types of noise in the data flow to the model change. This can cause the model to make more errors of types that were previously unimportant.

As well as changes generated from the domain, often model performance drifts as the technical interfaces and infrastructure that it depends on are updated. A new API can appear to be functionally identical to the old, but subtle changes in what and how it's fed into the model can gradually change its behavior. Sometimes this behavior is called *feature drift*. By monitoring the model and establishing assertions about its behavior, it's possible to detect this kind of drift.

Conversely, it's common for models to drift badly without anyone noticing, until events suddenly force everyone to recognize what's happened. This kind of chance discovery is not good because it makes everyone associated with the model look bad, it undermines wider trust in the model, and it creates a panic and flap that eats into time and disrupts work programs more widely. Retesting the model and monitoring the features being fed to it to determine if there is change or drift is a good idea.

10.2.3 Retraining

If a model fails or if you detect drift before it fails, you will want to do something about that. This is where retraining comes in. Retraining is the process of training a new model that resolves the issues of the current model in production. There are four components required to do this:

- *The new (or old) modeling approach:* Often, this is the approach developed by the modelling team to create the production model that's gone wrong. However, because it's gone wrong may indicate that a different approach or algorithm is required.
- *A new training set:* This accounts for the parts of the concept or feature set that have drifted and adequately captures the rest of the domain.
- *Testing data or a testing regime (perhaps online):* This captures the behavior for the model—what's changed and what hasn't.
- *Buy-in from the model's owners or stakeholders:* Obviously, a new model has to be built, tested, and deployed.

A key thing to emphasize is the difficulty of getting adequate training and testing sets. It's possible that the team can see a significant shift in the model's input, in advance of having enough data to either properly characterize that shift or to train a new model to capture it. Because of this, early detection of model drift is essential, allowing the team to take action as soon as possible to develop appropriate tests and gather the data required for training and testing.

The last bullet in the list is also key. Rebuilding and retraining the model is a substantial risk. The timing of the move could be important for the business that depends on the model, so it's essential to ensure that everyone understands what is happening, the impact of the change, and when the model is going to be implemented. Again, early detection of the issue is important to give you and the team time to get enough evidence to approach stakeholders. This also lets you manage the inevitable sequence of meetings, emails, and conference calls, which are required to agree on and initiate the work to retrain a model to get everything working properly again.

10.2.4 *In an emergency*

Having lots of reviews and a structured process for managing your models is all very well and reassuring, but what should you do if you get a call at 7 a.m.? On the call, you hear that the fourth line support can't fix the system, they've rebooted it four times, and it just doesn't work. Additionally, the business can't trade because of this. None of your monitoring solutions has picked up change, and you don't have the time to rebuild a training set or to retrain a new model to sort things out.

If the documentation you prepared from chapter 9 is adequate, and the support team concurred on the model governance agreements, then all should be well. Empowered and capable people who know how to work in a systematic way will be available to deal with arising issues effectively. However, that's not always the case.

Occasionally, you may be on a morning call with a panicking CIO because that's not what's available. If you find yourself in this fix, then the best that you can do is to improvise:

- Who can help? (Convene a working group.)
- What process can you create to move this forward? (Set up monitoring calls and create a reporting cadence.)
- What's the first thing that can be done to fix this?
- How do we get that done? (Make sure that you act immediately to determine and eliminate any problems.)
- What's the list of other options to deal with this situation?

Track down people who can help, engage them (although, this may cost), and sort things out. Look for backup plans in case the first, best line to dealing with the issue fails. Document and report on activity regularly (possibly hourly). The typical way to do this is to create a spreadsheet, recording all the suggested ways of dealing with the emergency, all the issues that arise because of it, any mitigations outside of a fix, and actions that have been taken. Don't get into the position of delivering a sequence of failures. Instead, create a set of workarounds and fixes and send progress reports as these are executed and eliminated.

Finally, don't stop your disaster management activity because the system appears to be fixed. Sure, the pressure is immediately eased when some sort of resolution allows business processes to get moving again, but all too often, another sudden failure is around the corner. Move the working group you have assembled from a focus on resolving the current issue to understanding what went wrong and what needs to be done to prevent it from happening again.

Having answers in place, which provide assurance that you're not going to be on another 7 am call in a week's time, is crucial for your health and happiness. It will also help you navigate the problems in review process that's likely to come next.

10.2.5 *Problems in review*

On the other side of a code red, a priority one (P1), a fire drill, or whatever designation your organization gives a full-on, business-stopping failure in production should lie a PIR (problems in review) process. This is a formal activity that investigates what happened and why.

The subtext is also sometimes about blame, but that will probably have been allocated in the five or six seconds after things came to the CIO/CEO's attention. If you are blamed, my suggestion is to martial your arguments, focusing on the process and professionalism that you have brought to bear on building and looking after the ML system:

- Don't turn it into a confrontation: Be studiously professional. Avoid setting the agenda and framing the meeting. This is not a court of law, but if you turn it into one, you might not like the result.
- Steer the meeting back to a fact-finding mission: Advert any he said/she said backbiting and blame allocation.
- Prepare carefully: Ensure that you have a clear timeline of events, and you know exactly what went wrong.
- Be clear about the actions taken to resolve the issue: Provide evidence that the issue was resolved.
- Reflect on any learnings from the incident: If you can, put these learnings to use by implementing changes to how ML systems are managed before the meeting.

To summarize, if you are responsible for a system after you have developed it, or if you are made responsible for other systems in your organization, then the smart thing to do is to work to prevent them from failing. There are lots of tactics you can employ to do this, but it's important to understand how well your systems are functioning and to get an early warning of any emerging problems before things go seriously wrong.

Sometimes failure is unavoidable, accidents do happen. If you are the victim of an accident, then be systematic in your response and get as much support as you can from the rest of the organization. When you're in the middle of a situation like this, things are tough. It's hard to remember that you will come out the other side; you will, and everything will be OK if you look ahead and are systematic in a professional approach to the managing the allocation blame and resolution of the issue.

10.3   *Team post-project review*

Possibly the simplest and most important step to take after the project is delivered and the customers have signed off on it is a team post-project review. Before the review, it is necessary to gather feedback from each team member and share it with the rest of the team. The culture of the team determines whether this should be done anonymously or openly. In teams where there are a few senior contributors and more junior ones, it is often desirable to have an anonymous process, allowing the junior people to speak out. But as a rule, the team lead or manager is in the best position to judge what the right method for getting open, respectful, and constructive feedback is.

A structured approach to getting feedback is to use a post-project review template that addresses several aspects of the project's management and evolution. An example is shown in Table 10.3. Each member of the team should fill out the form.

In a well-functioning and high-performing team, there should be no problem in getting useful and comprehensive feedback. In some cases, it's possible that team members will self-censor and won't come forward with their opinions because of difficult team dynamics. If you think this is happening, then address this individually in private with each team member by asking them to give feedback directly to you. It isn't a good idea to do the process anonymously and directly though because this can provide platforms for destructive and corrosive contributions. Although, this approach gives voice to people who feel marginalized, which is a good thing.

Table 10.3   An example post-project review form for feedback from the team. Rate from 1-5, where 1 equals they strongly disagree and 5 equals they strongly agree.

Questions	Rating (1-5)	Notes
The purpose and direction of the project was clear to me when I started work on it.		
The resources were sufficient.		
The timeline was realistic.		
We worked together well as a team.		
We worked well with the client.		
The result of the project was excellent.		
What was the best technical element in the project?		
What didn't work?		
What could we do better?		
What is the one change that you would make?		

Having collected feedback from the team, you should review and assemble it into a presentation that you can use to give to the team. Alternatively, getting a junior team member to assemble (with your support) and present the feedback can be a powerful development opportunity for them. Many times, if a junior presents the feedback, senior engineers feel more licensed to engage with and discuss solutions to the challenges in the project. One good way of exposing the value of the process and encouraging more openness and introspection by the team is to start the feedback presentation with a list of the issues identified in the last project review, and the steps that were taken to address them in this project cycle.

It is important to enable the team to react to the feedback and discuss it with one another to gauge the significance and validity of what is being reported. A single comment may incite a challenging and important discussion that exposes key issues. On the other hand, the team's discussion may reveal that what appears significant in the feedback is the only thing that anyone could think of to say, and it's not that important to them. The value of this process is in the shared identification and ownership of issues, the process of realizing that they are there and acknowledging that something should be done, and the action that the team takes to resolve the issues.

Once the teams' feedback is obtained and discussed, you can construct a final report on the project. Even if this ends up being a very brief document, it's something that's well worth doing. If there is a follow-up regarding the project, this project report can be extremely valuable in establishing context. To do this, the tasks required are:

1　Gather feedback using the method most appropriate to the team. It's recommended to use a structured form such as the one in Table 10.3.

2　Review the outcome of the sad-mad-glad process for all the sprint reviews, and review the feedback received in this process.

3　Review issues and actions from previous project reviews that were incorporated into your practice for this project.

4　Create a presentation that covers the items in steps 1-3.

5　Convene a meeting with the team, providing a copy of the presentation and agenda in advance. Include a discussion session in the agenda and a next-steps item, where you can agree on the issues identified for action by the team and the steps that will be taken to address them.

10.4　*Improving practice*

The team's reviews and the actions arising from that will evolve your practice, enabling a more consistent application of the approaches to solving client issues. In addition to reviewing what has just happened in a project, it's also important that the team maintains an open outlook to pull in knowledge from the rest of the world. AI and information systems development are both fast moving fields with experience cycles of technical and professional practice, change, and innovation. For example, we have in the

- *1960s:* Mainframes and COBOL, FORTRAN, and LISP.
- *1970s:* RDBMS or SQL, minicomputers (PDP-11, VAX), and Prolog.
- *1980s:* Workstations, personal computers, microcomputers, RISC, the waterfall model, and the first generation of neural nets.
- *1990s:* LAN, WAN, OOD (object-oriented design), and statistical ML.
- *2000s:* Web services, WWW (World Wide Web), social networking, search, agile, and multi-agent systems.
- *2010s:* Big data, mobile computing (iPhone, Android), DevOps, and deep learning/ second generation neural nets.

To meet customer challenges and to create the value that pays the bills, it's vital that the team cultivates a culture of continual learning. As a team manager, it is important that you take steps to encourage and to enable the team to do this. The temptation is to churn people from project to project and to maintain 100% of the people when you are developing a project. The consequence of doing this is that you will have strong revenue figures until the resources that you are driving so hard leave. Replacing a skilled technical resource can take as long as three to six months or as short as a couple of weeks (or sometimes, immediately). In reality, skilled and valued resources often leave a team quickly. As a team leader and manager, it's in your interest to stop this from happening.

One core tactic that you can employ is to ensure that your team has access to professional development opportunities and training. The intervals between engagements or when there are lulls and delays in internal projects due to factors beyond your control are ideal times for this. Not only does training help prevent your team from leaving, when you ensure that your team is trained and given other development activities, it is a way to make them more attractive to clients. The use of novel technical approaches, the rapid adoption of improved working practices, and detailed awareness and engagement with the client's business domain are all commercially valuable to the people who pay for your engagement. This is an important point to mention if you see an opportunity to provide some training for your team when they are engaged in a project. Just like vacation time, it's completely legitimate for training time to occur during an engagement if it's required. To support training and development, you should use the post project period to ensure that:

- All members of the team have a development plan.
- All members have personal objectives that are larger in scope than project delivery.

Offer support, encouraging the team to participate in external groups and activities (meetups, roundtables, special interest groups, etc.). Note that the contacts from external groups may attempt to recruit your team members. If your team is well run and you are doing your job, they will probably fail! Conversely, the contacts that your team (and you) make in these forums may provide future recruits for you. Identify training needs and gaps that team members have and work with them and other managers, if required, to ensure that appropriate training activities are identified and if possible scheduled.

10.5 New technology adoption

If new technology is required by the team to deliver client projects, you must onboard it into your working practice, but beware. Technologies that are introduced by an individual team member can become significant problems. They may represent a single point of failure and managing them in a long project when the most innovative team member may leave is challenging. In addition, it's hard for you as a team manager to work your way into a position where you can justify and explain these choices to clients. A formal process can help to mitigate this.

This process seeks to articulate why a new approach is required, to specify why this specific approach was selected, to demonstrate and develop competence with the approach (beyond the seed implementation), and to share and disseminate the knowledge into the team (and to the team manager at some level at least). To go about this:

1 Identify the project problem. Agree that innovation is required.
2 Document a gap analysis. What is the technology trying to deliver?
3 Analyze the competitors. What other approaches exist and can be used? Why is this one preferrable?
4 Furnish a proof of concept or demonstration. You might be tempted to use a direct application to the client's problem, but valuable lessons can be quickly learned by implementing and documenting a toy version first.
5 Review the technology with peers. Present and explain the solution to the team.

This process typically occurs in flight during a project, but sometimes the issue comes to light during post-project review. If the budget is available to undertake a proof-of-concept study at that point, then do it. Adoption of a novel technology is a good sign that the project has added value above the consultancy charge that paid for its execution, and this makes a good case for further work.

10.6 Case study

Successful and innovative projects can create added value because the team can harvest reusable artifacts from their execution (provided the proper intellectual property agreements are in place). This enables subsequent similar engagements to be done more quickly, with better quality, and lower costs or higher margins.

In some cases, a project can serve as the inspiration for an archetypal case study. Hopefully, the client is open to the idea of being used as a reference in a case study, and often contracts provide for this potential. But if that was not agreed, then you must strip the project's identifying details and, possibly, change the demonstration scenario from the client's business domain to a different context with a shared intrinsic challenge.

In either case, work is required to shift the focus of the project away from the detailed features of the actual implementation to the wider significance of how the problems were solved. This change of focus from solution to case study enables potential customers to see how value was created in the implementation as opposed to determining what value was delivered, which tends to be quite specific to the implementation context and detail.

10.7   *Goodbye and good luck*

Kendo is the Japanese version of sword fencing, where wooden sticks and padded armor are used to safely simulate sword fights. One tenet of some Kendo schools (normally the most brutal and difficult ones) is that you can only teach a new technique or change how a technique is taught if you have returned from a real battle. Because of this, the practice of some schools of Kendo faithfully preserve the learning of people who fought for real. Nothing in it changes, Kendōkas simply try to learn from each other as best they can. There is no innovation. Not many people want a real sword fight, and few of the people who do want a real sword fight are either capable of, or motivated to, teach the next generation the technique.

ML is different, though. It's all innovation, but at this point, you and your team have fought a real battle. You have completed a project, and whether it was a success or a failure, you have learned lessons from what you did that this book can't teach you. You can teach others, though. Don't be afraid of doing that; it's one of the best things you can do. Especially, don't be shy of teaching me things. Reach out and let me know your thoughts and your innovations. I need to hear them as much as anyone.

Summary

- It's likely that the team will get called on to support the system they developed. Over time, this demand will likely taper off, and other folks will take on the remaining tasks. Sometimes these people will be junior members in your team.
- Work to get clarity about what systems you are responsible for supporting. Remember, the resources required to look after them are allocated somewhere in the organization, and by all rights, they should go where the responsibility lies.
- Get a grip on the systems that you have responsibility for. Ensure that proper governance and support arrangements are in place and that there is a plan to deal with them if they go wrong. Review all systems regularly.
- Identify and deal with technical debt. Especially ensure that all systems are properly instrumented so that you know how they are behaving and that there is information available to troubleshoot if there is a failure.
- If a system fails, then get organized. Convene a group to support you and act as quickly as you can to get it fixed.
- Run project reviews to learn from what happened and to support development in your team.

- Ensure that your team has access to learning and development opportunities in the light of what's happening in the project.
- Develop your own point of view on the issues that this book has covered, then share them with me and other people who will need your insight if they are to succeed in the future.

references

Chapter 1

[1] LeCun, Yann, Yoshua Bengio, and Geoffrey Hinton. "Deep learning." Nature 521, no. 7553 (2015): 436-444.

[2] Carpenter, Bob, Andrew Gelman, Matthew D. Hoffman, Daniel Lee, Ben Goodrich, Michael Betancourt, Marcus Brubaker, Jiqiang Guo, Peter Li, and Allen Riddell. "Stan: A probabilistic programming language." Journal of statistical software 76, no. 1 (2017).

[3] Gartner (2018). https://www.gartner.com/en/newsroom/press-releases/2018-02-13-gartner-says-nearly-half-of-cios-are-planning-to-deploy-artificial-intelligence.

[4] Paleyes, Andrei, Raoul-Gabriel Urma, and Neil D. Lawrence. "Challenges in deploying machine learning: a survey of case studies." ACM Computing Surveys (CSUR) (2020).

[5] Bender, Emily, Timnit Gebru, Angelina McMillan-Major, and Mitchell Margaret (2021). "On the Dangers of Stochastic Parrots: Can Language Models Be Too Big?" FAccT'21, ACM Conference on Fairness, Accountability and Transparency. Virtual Event, Canada: ACM Conferences. 610-623. https://dl.acm.org/doi/pdf/10.1145/3442188.3445922.

[6] Brown, T.B. 2020. "Language Models are Few-Shot Learners." ArXiv. May. Accessed January 29, 2021. https://arxiv.org/pdf/2005.14165.pdf.

[7] Jumper, J. Evans, R. et al. 2020. "Alphafold 2 Presentation." Prediction Centre. 12. Accessed January 29, 2021. https://predictioncenter.org/casp14/doc/presentations/2020_12_01_TS_predictor_AlphaFold2.pdf.

[8] Schrittwieser, J., Antonoglou, I., Hubert, T., et al. 2020. "Mastering Atari, Go, Chess and Shogi by Planning with a Learned Model." ArXiv. Feb. Accessed January 29, 2021. https://arxiv.org/pdf/1911.08265.pdf.

[9] DALL-E (2022) https://huggingface.co/spaces/dalle-mini/dalle-mini.

[10] Marcus, Gary. "Deep learning: A critical appraisal." ArXiv preprint ArXiv:1801.00631 (2018).

[11] Kearns, M., and A. Roth (2019). The ethical algorithm: The science of socially aware algorithm design. Oxford: Oxford University Press.

[12] Wynants, Laure, Ben Van Calster, et al (2020). "Prediction models for diagnosis and prognosis of covid-19: systematic review and critical appraisal." BMJ 369:m1328.

[13] Hawkins, Andrew J. (2021). "Elon Musk just now realizing that self-driving cars are a hard problem." The Verge. 5 July. https://www.theverge.com/2021/7/5/22563751/tesla-elon-musk-full-self-driving-admission-autopilot-crash.

[14] Wixom, B., Someh, I., and Gregory, R. (2020). "AI Alignment: A new management paradigm." MIT Centre for Information Systems Research Briefings. November. Accessed January 28, 2021. https://cisr.mit.edu/publication/2020_1101_AI-Alignment_WixomSomehGregory.

[15] Lu, Shen. "China's New AI Laws." Protocol. March 2022. https://www.protocol.com/bulletins/china-algorithm-rules-effective.

[16] Gaumond, Eve. Artificial Intelligence Act: What Is the European Approach for AI? Lawfare, June 2021.

[17] Sutherland, J. Scrum: The Art of Doing Twice the Work in Half the Time. Penguin Books (2015).

[18] Huyen, C. (2020). Machine Learning System Design. Accessed October 1, 2020. https://github.com/chiphuyen/machine-learning-systems-design.

[19] Burkov, Andriy. 2020. Machine Learning Engineering. http://www.mlebook.com/wiki/doku.php: self-published.

[20] Claxton, Robert, Janki Vora, Franco Luka, H. Varvello, Humanshu Sharma, S.G. Thompson, and Emmanuel Otchere (2019). "IG1184 Service Management Sta dards for AI R18. 1." Accessed August 24, 2020. https://www.researchgate.net/publication/336364834_IG1184_Service_Management_Standards_for_AI_R18.

Chapter 2

[1] Ada Lovelace Insitute. "Examining the Black Box." *Ada Lovelace Institute*. April 2020. (accessed October 2021).

[2] *AI Incident database* (2020). https://incidentdatabase.ai/discover/index.html?s= (accessed January 27, 2021).

[3] Association of Computing Machinary (ACM). *AAAI/ACM conference on Artificial Intelligence, Ethics and Society*. May 2021. https://www.aies-conference.com/2021/ (conference publicity accessed January 28, 2021).

[4] Bender, Emily, Timnit Gebru, Angelina McMillan-Major, and Mitchell Margaret. "On the Dangers of Stochastic Parrots: Can Language Models Be Too Big?" *FAccT'21, ACM Conference on Fairness, Accountability and Transparency*. Virtual Event, Canada: ACM Conferences (2021). 610-623. https://dl.acm.org/doi/pdf/10.1145/3442188.3445922.

[5] Government of Canada. *Algorithmic Impact Assessment Tool* (2020). https://www.canada.ca/en/government/system/digital-government/digital-government-innovations/responsible-use-ai/algorithmic-impact-assessment.html.

[6] Guus Schreiber, Hans Akkermans, Ango Anjewierden, Robert de Hoog, Nigel Shadbolt, Walter Van de Velde, and Bob Wielinga. *Knowledge Engineering and Management. The CommonKADS Methodology*. Cambridge, Massachusetts: MIT Press (A Bradford Book) (2000).

[7] Hendrycks, Dan, Nicholas Carlini, John Schulman, and Jacob Steinhardt. *Unsolved Problems in ML Safety*. September 2021. https://arxiv.org/pdf/2109.13916.pdf.

[8] ICO UK. *Guidance on The AI Auditing Framework. Draft guidance for consultation*. https://ico.org.uk/media/about-the-ico/consultations/2617219/guidance-on-the-ai-auditing-framework-draft-for-consultation.pdf: Information Commissioners Office, UK (2020).

[9] Kearns, M. and A. Roth. *The ethical algorithm: The science of socially aware algorithm design*. Oxford: Oxford University Press (2019).

[10] Sale, L. "America's New Luddites." *Web Archive*. February 1997. https://web.archive.org/web/20020630215254/http://mondediplo.com/1997/02/20luddites (accessed January 28, 2021).

[11] Springer Verlag. *Journal of AI Ethics*. December 2020. https://www.springer.com/journal/43681 (accessed January 28, 2021).

[12] Verheyen, Gunther. "Fixed price bids. (2012). https://guntherverheyen.com/2012/10/07/fixed-price-bids-an-open-invitation-to-bribe-cajole-lie-and-cheat/ (accessed 08 04, 2020).

[13] "What Really Happened When Google Ousted Timnit Gebru." *Wired*. June 2021. https://www.wired.com/story/google-timnit-gebru-ai-what-really-happened/ (accessed July 14,2021).

Chapter 3

[1] ICO 2016 Data Protection Impact Assessment. https://ico.org.uk/for-organisations/guide-to-data-protection/guide-to-the-general-data-protection-regulation-gdpr/accountability-and-governance/data-protection-impact-assessments/

Chapter 4

[1] Apache Project (2021). "Apache Airflow." Apache.org. Accessed January 11, 2021. https://airflow.apache.org/.

[2] Bareinboim, Elias, and Judea Pearl (2016). "Causal inference and the data-fusion problem." PNAS - Colloquium Paper 7345–7352.

[3] Beauchemin, M. (2017). "The Rise of the Data Engineer ." Medium.com. 20 Jan. Accessed Jan 11, 2021. https://medium.com/free-code-camp/the-rise-of-the-data-engineer-91be18f1e603.

[4] Beck, Ken et al. (2001). Manifesto for Agile Software Development. Accessed August 17, 2020. https://agilemanifesto.org.

[5] Bender, Emily, Timnit Gebru, Angelina McMillan-Major, and Mitchell Margaret (2021). "On the Dangers of Stochastic Parrots: Can Language Models Be Too Big?" FAccT'21, ACM Conference on Fairness, Accountability and Transparency. Virtual Event, Canada: ACM Conferences. 610-623. https://dl.acm.org/doi/pdf/10.1145/3442188.3445922.

[6] Breck, E. Cai, S. Nielsen, E., Salib, M., Sculley, D. (2016). "The ML Test Score: A Rubric for ML Production Readiness and Technical Debt Reduction." Neurips Workshop.

[7] Brown, A.W., Kaiser, K.A., & Allison, D.B. (2018). "Issues with Data and Analyses." Proceedings of the National Academy of Sciences 115 (11): 2563-2570.

[8] Castro Fernandez, Raul, and Samuel Madden (2019). "Termite: A System for Tunneling through Heterogenous Data." aiDM'19. Amsterdam: ACM.

[9] Farrugia, Ashley, Robert Claxton, and Simon Thompson (2016). "Towards social network analytics for understanding and managing enterprise data lakes." IEEE/ACM International Conference on Advances in Social Networks Analysis and Mining (ASONAM) pp. 121. Davis, California: IEEE.

[10] Hynes, N., Sculley, D., & Terry, M. (2016). "The data linter: Lightweight, automated sanity checking for ml data sets." NIPS MLSys Workshop.

[11] NASA (2020). "NASA Workmanship Standards." March. Accessed September 18, 2020. https://archive.org/details/nasa-workmanship-standards.

[12] Provost, Nancy E. ElHady and Julien (2018). "A Systematic Survey on Sensor Failure Detection and Fault-Tolerance in Ambient Assisted Living." Sensors (US National Library of Medicine (https://www.ncbi.nlm.nih.gov/pmc/articles/PMC6069464/)) 18 (7): 1991 (doi : 10.3390/s18071991).

[13] Robert M. Groves and Lars Lyberg (2010). "Total Survey Error. Past, Present and Future." Public Opinion Quarterly 75 (5): 849-879.

[14] S.C. Misra, V. Kumar, U. Kumar (2009). "Identifying some important success factors in adopting agile software development practices." *Journal of Systems and Software* 11 (82).

[15] Scaled Agile (2021). SAFe 5 for Lean Enterprise. https://www.scaledagileframework.com/.

[16] Subramaniam, Pranav, Yintong Ma, Chi Li, Ipsita Mohanty, and Raul Castro Fernandez (2022). "Comprehensive and Comprehensible Data Catalogs: The What, Who, Where, When, Why, and How of Metadata Management." ArXiv. January. Accessed January 2022. https://arxiv.org/abs/2103.07532.

Chapter 5

[1] Bareinboim, Elias, and Judea Pearl (2016). "Causal inference and the data-fusion problem." *PNAS - Colloquium Paper.* 7345–7352.

[2] IETF (1992). *RFC 1321.* Accessed 2022. https://www.ietf.org/rfc/rfc1321.txt.

[3] McDonald, Kent (2017). "What do user story conversations look like." *Agile Alliance.* https://www.agilealliance.org/user-story-conversations/.

[4] Sculley, D., Holt, G., Golovin, E.D., Phillips, T., Edner,D., Chaudhary, V., Young, M., Crespo, J.F., & Dennison, D. (2015). "Hidden Technical Debt in Machine Learning Systems." *Neurips 2015 Workshops.* https://papers.nips.cc/paper/2015/file/86df7dcfd896fcaf2674f757a2463eba-Paper.pdf.

[5] Shorten, Connor, and Taghi M Khoshgoftaar (2019). "A survey on Image Data Augmentation for Deep Learning." *Journal of Big Data,* 60.

Chapter 6

[1] Ayling, J, and A Chapman. "AI & Ethics." *Putting AI ethics to work: Are the tools fit for purpose* (2021). HYPERLINK "https://doi.org/10.1007/s43681-021-00084-x" https://doi.org/10.1007/s43681-021-00084-x.

[2] Bernhardsson, Erik. "Spotify Annoy Readme.MD." *GitHub.* (2020). https://github.com/spotify/annoy (accessed March 9, 2022).

[3] Cook, D, and D. F. Swayne. *Interactive and Dynamic Graphics for Data Analysis: With R and GGobi.* Springer (2007).

[4] D'Amour, A., Katherine Heller, D. Moldovan, B. Adlam, and B. Alpanahi. "Underspecification presents challenges for credibility in modern machine learning." *ArXiv.* 6 November 2020. https://arxiv.org/pdf/2011.03395.pdf (accessed November 23rd, 2020).

[5] Johnson, Jeff, Douze Matthijs, and Jégou Hervé. "Billion-scale similarity search with gpus." *IEEE Transactions on Big Data* (2019): 535-547.

[6] Lerner, Reuven. *Pandas Workout.* Manning (2021).

[7] Paskhaver, Boris. *Pandas in Action.* Manning , 2021.

[8] Ryu, C. *Cran-R EDA Vignette.* 16 11 2020. https://cran.r-project.org/web/packages/dlookr/vignettes/EDA.html (accessed 12 21, 2020).

[9] Soviany, P., R. T. Ionescu, P. Rota, and N. Sebe. "Cirriculum Learning: A Survey." *ArXiv* (2021). https://arxiv.org/abs/2101.10382 (accessed March 2022).

[10] Tan, Mingxing, and Le Quoc. "Efficientnet: Rethinking model scaling for convolutional neural networks." *International Conference on Machine Learning* (2019): 6105-6114.

[11] Torralba, Antonio, and Alexei Efros. "Unbiased Look at Dataset Bias." *CVPR* (2011). 1521-1528.

[12] Tukey, J.W. *Exploratory Data Analysis.* London: Addison-Wesley (1977).

[13] Wickham, H., Grolemund, G. *R for Data Science.* O'Rielly Media, (2016).

Chapter 7

[1] Chen, Tianqi, and Carlos Guestrin. "Xgboost: A scalable tree boosting system." In Proceedings of the 22nd ACM SIGKDD International Conference on Knowledge Discovery and Data Mining, pp. 785-794, (2016).

[2] Dua, D. and Graff, C. (2019). *UCI Machine Learning Repository,* http://archive.ics.uci.edu/ml. *University of California, School of Information and Computer Science.* Irvine, CA.

[3] Elsken, T., Metzen, J.H., Hutter, F. (2019). "Neural Architecture Search: A Survey." *Journal of Machine Learning Research* 20 (1-21) .

[4] Franco Scarselli, Marco Gori, Ah Chung Tsoi, Markus Hagenbuchner, Gabriele Monfardini. (2009). "The Graph Neural Network Model." *University of Wollongong Research Online.* Accessed March 22, 2021. https://persagen.com/files/misc/scarselli2009graph.pdf.

[5] H. Sepp, J. Schmidhuber. (1997). "Long Short-Term Memory." *Neural Computation 9 (8)* 1735-1780.

[6] Jumper, J. Evans, R. et al. (2020). "Alphafold 2 Presentation." *Prediction Centre.* 12. Accessed January 29, 2021. https://predictioncenter.org/casp14/doc/presentations/2020_12_01_TS_predictor_AlphaFold2.pdf.

[7] Kuhn, M. and Johnson, K. (2019). *Feature Engineering and Selection: A Practical Approach for Predictive Models.* Chapman & Hall.

[8] LeCun, Yann, Leon Bottou, Genevieve Muller, B Orr, and Klaus Robert. (1998). "Efficient Backprop." In *Neural Networks: Tricks of the Trade*, by G. Orr and K. Müller. Springer.

[9] Mallen, J.I. and Bramer, M.A. (1994). "CUPID - An Iterative Knowledge Discovery Framework." *Research and Development in Expert Systems XI.*

[10] Murphy, K.P. (2021). *Probabilistic Machine Learning: An Introduction.* Cambridge, MA.: MIT Press.

[11] Vaswani, A., Shazeer, N., Parmar, N., Uszkoreit, J., Jones, L., Gomez, A.N., Kaiser, L. and Polosukhin, I.,. (2017). "ArXiv." *Attention is all you need ArXiv. preprint ArXiv:1706.03762.* Accessed March 22, 2021. https://arxiv.org/pdf/1706.03762.pdf.

[12] Yan LeCun, Josh Bengio. (1995). "Convolutional Networks for Images, Speech and Time-series." In *The handbook of brain theory and neural networks*, by M.A Arbib, 276-278. Cambridge, MA: MIT Press.

[13] Shorten, Connor, and Taghi M. Khoshgoftaar. "A survey on image data augmentation for deep learning." *Journal of big data* 6, no. 1 (2019): 1-48.

Chapter 8

[1] Aker, A., Grevenkamp, H., Mayer, S.J., Hamacher, M., Smets, A., Nti, A., Erdmann, J., Serong, J., Welpinhus, A., and Marchi, F. "Corpus of news articles annotated with article level sentiment." *Proceedings of theNewsIR'19 Workshop at SIGIR. Aker, A., Albakour, D. Barron-Cedeno, A., Dori-Hacohen, S., Martinez, M., Stray, J., Tipperman, S. (eds).* Paris, France: SIGIR (2019). http://ceur-ws.org/Vol-2411/paper6.pdf.

[2] Habibullah, Mohammad Khan, and Jennifer Horkoff. "Non-functional requirements for machine learning: understanding current use and challenges in industry." *021 IEEE 29^h International Requirements Engineering Conference (RE).* IEEE (2021): 13-21.

[3] Russo, D.J., et al. "A Tutorial on Thompson Sampling." *Foundations and Trends in Machine Learning* (2018): 1-96.

[4] Slivkins, A. "Introduction to Multi-Armed Bandits." *ArXiv.* September 2019. https://arxiv.org/pdf/1904.07272.pdf (accessed May 18th, 2021).

[5] Thompson, W. "On the Likelihood that one unknown probability exceeds another in the view of the evidence from two samples." *Biometrika* (1933): 285-294.

[6] Velasquez, Mark, and Patrick Hester. "An analysis of multi-criteria decision making method." *International Journal of Operational Research* (2013): 56-66.

Chapter 9

[1] Ackerman, Evan. "Everything You Need to Know About NASA's Perseverance Rover Landing on Mars." IEE Spectrum. February 2021. https://spectrum.ieee.org/automaton/aerospace/robotic-exploration/nasa-perseverance-rover-landing-on-mars-overview (accessed March 25th, 2021).

[2] Adam-Bourdario, C., Cowan, G., Germain, C. Guyon, I., Rousseau, D. "The Higgs boson machine learning challenge." JMLR: Workshop and Conference Proceedings HEPML 2014. JMLR, (2014). 42:19-55.

[3] Amershi, Saleema. "Guidelines for Human-AI Interaction." CHI conference on human factors in computing systems. CHI, (2019). 1-13.

[4] Google. Tensorflow Serving. (2021). https://www.tensorflow.org/tfx/guide/serving.

[5] Hawkins, Andrew J. The Verge. Sept 18, 2020. https://www.theverge.com/2020/9/18/21445168/tesla-driver-sleeping-police-charged-canada-autopilot (accessed October 16, 2021).

[6] Liedtka, Jeanne. "Why Design Thinking Works." Harvard Business Review, (2018): September-October.

[7] OpenVINO. OpenVINO documentation. (2022). https://docs.openvino.ai/latest/index.html.

[8] Ostrower, John. The Air Current. March 2019. https://theaircurrent.com/aviation-safety/the-world-pulls-the-andon-cord-on-the-737-max/.

[9] Ribeiro, Marco Tulio Correia. LIME. (2021). https://github.com/marcotcr/lime.

[10] Rudin, Cynthia. Stop Explaining Black Box Machine Learning Models for High Stakes Decisions and Use Interpretable Models Instead. (2018). https://arxiv.org/abs/1811.10154 (accessed October 2021).

[11] Withington, Peter. The Lisp Machine. (1991). http://pt.withy.org/publications/LispM.html.

[12] Xei, M., Chen, H., Zhang, X.F., Guo, X. & Yu, Z.P. "Development of navigation system for autonomous vehicle to meet the DARPA urban grand challenge." IEEE Intelligent Transport Systems. IEEE, (2007). 767-772.

Chapter 10

[1] Cunningham, W. "The WyCash Portfolio Management System," *Proc. OOPSLA*, ACM, 1992; http://c2.com/doc/oopsla92.html.

[2] Sculley, D., et al. "Machine Learning: The High-Interest Credit Card of Technical Debt." Neurips workshop. (2014). https://static.googleusercontent.com/media/research.google.com/en//pubs/archive/43146.pdf.

index